The
South Atlantic
Quarterly

SAQ

M000315866

116:3 · July 2017

After #Ferguson, After #Baltimore:
The Challenge of Black Death and Black Life
for Black Political Thought

Barnor Hesse and Juliet Hooker, Special Issue Editors

AGAINST the DAY

Unrecognizable: On Trans Recognition in 2017
Aren Aizura, Editor

Barnor Hesse and Juliet Hooker

Introduction:
On Black Political Thought
inside Global Black Protest

Recent global trends in the policing deaths and antipolicing protests of black people urge a reconsideration of the orientations and scope of black political thought. One of its central considerations must be *black politics and its anticolonial/antiracial conditions of possibility*. This is because the solidarity logics of blackness implicated in the signifier "black politics" continue to be insurgent in and repressed by Western capitalist, liberal democratic polities. Our understanding of the social, cultural, and existential oppositional activities among dispersed populations of African descent has been largely derived from black antislavery/ anticolonial/antiracial mobilizations spanning the sixteenth to twenty-first centuries. Nevertheless, it remains the case that black politics appears to be one of the least elucidated and most contested concepts in contemporary political discourse. This is partly because whatever has been represented and configured as black politics has also been routinely marginalized, pathologized, repudiated, or attacked in Western political theory and Western polities. Delineating and contributing to a distinctive field of black political thought has always required that we recuperate conceptually the Western-attributed *outlaw status* of black politics. Here the task also

The South Atlantic Quarterly 116:3, July 2017
DOI 10.1215/00382876-3961428   © 2017 Duke University Press

becomes thinking through the *constitutively fugitive* formations of black politics, tracking them as they cut into, interrupt, and expose the modern capitalist, liberal democratic tradition of representing the Western polity outside of its colonial-racial gestations.

Thinking about black politics in this way also requires being attentive to revealing and analyzing the repressions, repudiations, and violations of black politics in the Western colonial-racial order of things and populations. This approach, however, cannot be developed without recognizing that political mobilizations of "blackness" have always had different and dispersed meanings across time and space (e.g., in North America, Latin America, the Caribbean, Africa, and Europe). It entails understanding different political forms of blackness as *territorialization*, where dissenting meanings and oppositional practices are inscribed in solidarities tied to particular events, debates, or situations within historical attachments to particular social boundaries (e.g., nations, cities, and histories).[1] At the same time, we need to think about different political forms of blackness as *deterritorialization*.[2] This involves the creative disembedding of particular meanings of black solidarity from local events and settings, where these meanings become transferable to other places, linking previously disparate black communities in affinity and dialogical networks of discourses and activities. Since 2014 this political dynamic of territorialization and deterritorialization has increasingly become a mainstay in the proliferation of mobilizations against the violence of racial policing across the black diaspora under the political slogan "Black lives matter."

Against Western Normative Thought

How does our approach to black political thought think about the critique registered by various manifestations of black politics? In a revelatory sense, black politics is symptomatic of Western hegemony as white supremacy. Its incidence reveals formations of race and coloniality within Western polities that are regularly disavowed by Western normative thought. This means that black politics is structurally possible only in relation to Western normative regimes whose liberal-democratic-capitalist institutions are embedded in racial/colonial histories and formations belied by Western normative institutions. This has important consequences for how we understand the provenance of black political thought in relation to the Western polity. It means recognizing that, historically, unlike the Renaissance, the Reformation, or the Enlightenment in Western normative thought, antislavery, anticolonialism, and antiracism have yet to be considered significant to theorizing modern Western political categories, identities, and formations. At the same time, we have yet to fully explore how radical interventions and ideas introduced by black politics (e.g., white supremacy, racial capitalism, black bodily integrity, and black fugitivity) have confronted and exposed the conceptual insufficiency of Western normative thought. Schematically, Western normative thought works through categories that presuppose a universal hegemony of Western values (e.g., liberalism's humanist and edifying version of modernity), while treating race as an exception to the episteme of its normative rule. In oppositional distinction, the "black radical tradition" (Robinson 1983) acts as a site of critical thought. It provincializes and problematizes the idea of Western normativity, reinhabiting it with a critical marking and interrogation of modernity's colonial foundations, thereby conceptualizing race as constitutive of the episteme of Western normative rule.

Western critical thought is subversive of the colonial-racial foundations of Western hegemony and white supremacy. The intellectual challenge for the Western critical enterprise of black political thought is analogous to what has been suggested by Edouard Glissant for Caribbean thought in comprehending the dislocating impact of Atlantic slavery on any conventional sense of historical continuity and contemporary presence in social, cultural, and political formations. It becomes imperative to question any intellectual genre of divisions that might fracture the different possibilities of analytical and diasporic coherence in the contextual study of black politics and to develop an openness to "all the perspectives of the human sciences," challenging these divisions and their "inherited categories" where they constitute a potential "obstacle to a daring new methodology" (Glissant 1989: 65). The aim is to generate alternative, critical interventions that inaugurate "a revaluation of the conventions of analytical thought" (65). That revaluation is important because black political thought shares much of the same analytical vocabulary as Western normative thought, as well as breaking with its normativity. Consequently, it becomes necessary to avoid any disabling collusions with political analyses inherited from conventions that have routinely dismissed critiques of their racial and colonial formations. This is what epitomizes the Western critical thinking of Cedric Robinson, Sylvia Wynter, Angela Davis, Stuart Hall, Hortense Spillers, Paul Gilroy, Saidiya Hartman, and Achille Mbembe. Each of these thinkers, in different ways, can be drawn on to explain how the national, classed, gendered, diasporic, black political subject, in its territorialized and deterritorialized incarnations, navigates and contests the violations and oppressions of Western normative ideals and institutions conventionally conceptualized as exterior to each other (e.g., humanism and racism). The Western polity is confronted by black political thought's exposure of it obscuring and denying its imbrication in the liberal and the colonial, democracy and race, universalism and Eurocentrism. Specifying and interrogating the resilient entanglements of race, its colonial disciplinary dynamics and hegemonic discourses of disavowal in Western polities continues to mark resistances to the shared and inherited black diasporic problem of racial subordination and racial violence, racially constrained democratic incorporation, and racially hypervisual exoticization in sports and entertainment (Iton 2008; Carrington 2010). All of this confronts black political thought today as much as it did during the early twentieth century.

Reconstructed Blackness

The principal metaphor of W. E. B. DuBois's *Black Reconstruction in America* ([1935] 1998) remains instructive for our version of black political thought. DuBois's reexamination of the politics of the Reconstruction period of American history (1860–80) is a radical critique of the Western institution of democracy in its racial form and idiom. To demonstrate this, DuBois foregrounds the subordinated black activist experience as the political lens through which to view the events of Reconstruction and its subsequent white historiography. He describes various circumstances in which the political and educational activities undertaken by the black population had been deemed a contaminant of the white institutional legitimation of US democracy, whether the black persons involved were enslaved or free. DuBois also noted that the actual participation of black people in the democratic institutions of Reconstruction, whether through voting, elections, assembly deliberations, or lawmaking, desired to go beyond the kind of freedom made racially available as an unprotected and unguaranteed citizenship by the federal government because it was antagonistic to the racial kind of democracy defined as representative of a modern nation-state. DuBois was aware that black politics ran counter to the white institution of US democracy. That countering emerged because, while slavery had been a constitutive part of democracy in the United States, its abolition now raised the black political question, how does one emancipate democracy from the white jurisdiction of race?

It was in relation to that kind of question that DuBois ([1935] 1998: 721) provides us with his rationale for black political thought, where he writes: "The chief witness in Reconstruction, the emancipated slave himself, has been almost barred from court. His written Reconstruction record has been largely destroyed and nearly always neglected. . . . In other words, every effort has been made to treat the Negro's part in Reconstruction with silence and contempt." Of course, the masculine idiom in which DuBois specified the Negro as the black political subject requires constant interrogation, interruption, and displacement. This should be borne in mind when drawing on DuBois's understanding of two theoretical problems posed for black political thought. First, there was the "racial revolution" of an expanded democracy in the United States following the Civil War, the abolition of slavery, and the short-lived egalitarian possibilities of Reconstruction. This had created and legitimated a white democracy in its practices, if not in its discourses. Second, there was the reemergent white democracy predicated on a disavowal of black politics in its administrative forms and the administrative removal of black populations from deepening their social participation in democracy. This had resulted in the *discrediting* of black politics. For DuBois ([1935] 1998: 715), the disavowal of black politics began with the white political and intellectual erasure of the significance of black people's struggles to resist, escape, and abolish slavery, in an "attempt to enter democracy." For DuBois, the displacement of black politics from US political history and discourse was motivated by the desire to avoid any racial disruption to institutional arrangements that privileged the normativity of *white hegemony*. The politics of the ex-slaves presaged an insistence that democracy be transformed by the eradication of white hegemony and its expansion through black self-representation and participation. It suggested that race was constitutively structural in Western liberal democracy and that black politics existed in a relation of racial antagonism with the Western polity. Through this approach to conceptualizing black politics DuBois was also struggling to explain the Western performative political script of racially governing black populations through the imbricated rule of liberalism-colonialism *and* democracy-whiteness, while formally representing these imbricated aspects of race through governance as if they were constitutionally separate and incommensurable. We can perhaps read the metaphor *black reconstruction* as evoking black politics in a symptomatic reading of the racial political form of the polity and society it confronted, which could not be deduced from the lexicon of US democracy and Western normative thought. Black politics was symptomatic of a white constitutive logic that ensured that Western democracy was underlined by its repression of a black politics that sought to transform or counteract it. In short, for DuBois black politics exposed the normalized white administration of a democratic regime, which became visible when confronted by the black politics that challenged it. As we will see, this metaphor of *black reconstruction* continues to resonate both contemporaneously and globally.

Contemporary Global Black Protest

The *longue durée* of black politics has been grounded in its reactions to the imbrication of the liberal-democratic and the colonial-racial in Western political formations. However, despite our apparent transition to the post-colonial and post–civil rights eras, Western states continue to reproduce and disavow the grounds for black politics. The question of the racial emancipation of democracy, or indeed its decolonization, therefore, recurrently poses irrepressible predicaments for black political thought. A half century after most states in Africa achieved independence and the civil rights movement in the United States succeeded in ending Jim Crow racial segregation, and a quarter century after black South Africans overthrew apartheid, renewed black protest movements around the globe are beginning to question the forms and aims of black politics and the limits of liberal democracy. Globally, black protest movements originating from local concerns are responding in different ways to the inability of liberal democracy to deliver robust racial justice and inviolable equal rights, drawing attention to the unfinished project of decolonization and the unrelenting dehumanization of black lives resulting from the precarity induced by global white supremacy (however much the latter may have morphed). A global wave of black protest is legible from uprisings against police violence in the United States, the United Kingdom, Brazil, France, Canada, and Israel and from student protests in South Africa.[3] A common thread in Western normative critiques of the disruptive tactics deployed by these black protesters is the notion that black rage is counterproductive and that it needs to be disciplined and contained in order to gain the legitimation of representative democracy. However, by focusing on the political experiences of those whom Anthony Bogues (2012) calls its "living corpses," we see that democracy has always been unrepresentative and incomplete because its racial denial of political rights to some—rather than being a contradiction of its core principles—has instead underwritten the white privileged ability of others to claim such rights.

The key insight of the black politics developing in these protests centers on marking Western democracy's white limits. At the same time, it also points to one of the fundamental paradoxes of black politics, namely, the invariable futility of directing activism toward a racially governing regime historically founded on the constitutive exclusion and violation of blackness. Meditating on the meaning of black politics in the postcolonial independence, post–civil rights, postapartheid era, Richard Iton (2008: 30–31) suggests that a "steady rhetorical retreat . . . has characterized black politics since the Cold War," marked by "the celebration of pragmatism, instrumentalism, and compromise . . . and the rhetorical shunning and shaming of protest activities." Iton highlights the poverty of political imagination exhibited by forms of black politics circumscribed by modern/colonial formations whose aim was inclusion within existing state structures and dominant subject formations. For us, this means that the pressing question in black politics is no longer civil separation versus civil integration, if indeed it ever was, but rather the foreclosure of more radical and transformative visions by acceptance of an improved version of the liberal democratic status quo as the limited horizon of political philosophy and political possibility. Faced with such a resilient conjuncture, Iton suggests that we need to move beyond "the predominance of the state as the sole frame for . . . progressive and transformative discourse and mobilization" (17). In his view, this means moving away from exclusive reliance on the formal arena of Western politics and reinvigorating the subversive and anarchic practices of black popular culture to cultivate more emancipatory and transformative political imaginaries. While our aim here is not to suggest that black politics should retreat entirely from the formally political, following Iton we do want to suggest that we need to think *against* and *in excess of* the centrality of the state as the horizon of political intelligibility.

One problem with state-and-rights-centric forms of black political activism is that their discourse becomes fixated on the state's responsibility to resolve its own failures to create and institutionalize racial justice. They promote a bizarre turn to the Western state as the ultimate safeguard of rights it has historically and racially denied. Indeed, to view it as the protector of rights given its long history as the source of violence against black citizens is almost perverse. Moreover, replacing bodies phenotypically marked as white with those phenotypically marked as black in elected office does not magically transform the racial character of the state (Goldberg 2001).

These strategic limitations of formal modes of black politics have been starkly exposed by protest movements in South Africa and the United States. For example, in 2016 the protests of black schoolgirls in South Africa against the failure to decolonize South African education at all levels was captured by the hashtag #StopRacismAtPretoriaGirlsHigh, which quickly went viral. The photographs and videos of young black girls proudly wearing Afros and facing off against adult white school administrators who had deemed natural hairstyles "untidy" or "barbaric" sparked global support far beyond South Africa and eventually led Ministry of Education officials to intervene and suspend the discriminatory hairstyle regulations. Yet the belated state action spurred by the global outcry following the black schoolgirls' protest was that of a South African state that has been dominated by a majority-black political party, the African National Congress (ANC), since the end of apartheid. The handover of political power to a predominantly black party did not radically transform the material conditions of poor, black South Africans, nor did it fundamentally alter the Eurocentric premises of educational institutions. T. O. Molefe (2016: 32) has argued that the ideas articulated by the #Fees-MustFall university student protesters represented "a departure from the nonracial conciliatory 'Rainbow Nation' project of Archbishop Desmond Tutu, [Nelson] Mandela, and the ANC and a new way of grappling with the outcomes of a history of patriarchy, slavery, imperialism, colonialism, white supremacy, and capitalism." South Africa's black student protests emphasized "anti-orthodoxy, solidarity, and revolution" (32), thereby questioning the meaning of state power and envisioning more revolutionary forms of black politics.

Meanwhile, in the United States it could be argued that one of the reasons the Black Lives Matter protests against gratuitous and disproportionate police violence (which is hardly a new phenomenon in nonwhite communities) gained such national visibility was that they occurred during the administration of a black president. That a black man could attain the highest elected political office in the country and yet black men, women, and children continued to be killed with impunity in the streets by the police raised deeply unsettling questions about the strategy of pursuing black restitution through electoral politics, mirroring what had been the dominant form of black politics in the United States in the post–civil rights era. The predictable contradictions of attempts to achieve radical change through formal politics aimed primarily at the state have thus been thrown into stark relief by contemporary black protest movements. We can think of black political thought, informed by these activisms, as attempting to create the conceptual space to articulate more emancipatory and decolonializing forms of black activism in order to begin imagining the process of designing alternatives to the colonial-racial constitutions of our postcolonial Western polities. Contrary to Iton's assessment of black politics in the first decade of the twenty-first century, today we seem to be witnessing the emergence of revitalized black protest movements that articulate powerful ripostes to overly pragmatic, incremental, and state-centric forms of black politics with aspiring to other forms of black political *reconstruction*.

Black Rage / Black Death

How should black political thought understand and engage with the rage and anger in black protests against repeated racial atrocities? We recall an early 1960s interview with James Baldwin where he famously remarked, citing the existential, ethical, and political dilemmas facing black populations in the United States, that "to be a Negro in this country and to be relatively conscious, is to be in a rage almost all the time" (Baldwin et al. 1961: 205). Arguably, today black rage has reached unprecedented public and global visibility, mediated by quotidian police killings of black people, new forms of relentless black activism, and ever-vigilant and vocal black social media. In the United States, the catalyst for the current focus on the politics of black death occurred in 2013 following the killing of the black teenager Trayvon Martin and the acquittal of his civilian killer, George Zimmerman. That was the occasion when the #BlackLivesMatter movement was inaugurated by the activism of three black queer women, Alicia Garza, Patrisse Cullors, and Opal Tometi. Then in August 2014 black rage erupted in relation to the shooting of an unarmed black teenager, Michael Brown, by a white police officer, in Ferguson, Missouri. The subsequent violent response by law enforcement to protests in Ferguson and black social media responses to that event created the spectacle and signifier #Ferguson, which inaugurated a critique of three overlapping racial facts. First, it critiqued the killings of young black people by the police and the racial pathologization of black victims by the police and corporate mass media. Second, it signified the racial terrorism and militarization of the police and the criminalization of black protest. Third, it signified (contrary to claims that the United States had become a color-blind society in the wake of the 1960s and particularly after the election of Barack Obama in 2008) the continued hegemony of white supremacy, which was heightened by the deference to unquestioned police authority expected of citizens and the media post-9/11. Since then, the political visibility and social media dissemination of killings of black people by the police have become virtually quotidian, while the diverse and decentered #BlackLivesMatter movement is viewed as a new civil rights movement for the twenty-first century. It is clear that Black Lives Matter has borrowed tactics from earlier protest movements (e.g., black power, black feminism), particularly the emphasis on publicly disruptive demonstrations and expositional uses of popular culture. It has also pioneered new strategies, such as the use of social media to organize, heighten immediacy, and widen the scope of the public that acts as witness to the disposability of black lives. The Baltimore protests of April 2015, following the police-induced death of Freddie Gray, renewed the sense of crisis in black communities, signifying an evolving and uncertain political conjuncture of repeated acts of police violence against black bodies followed by innovative forms of organized black exposure of such violence that challenge the notion of democratic politics as usual. There is thus a prevailing undecidability in black political forms that needs to be understood if black rage is to lead to more than a tragically predictable impasse: black death, followed by protest, calls to await the work of the legal system, indictment or nonindictment, nonconviction, and repeat, in an endless loop. Black political thought has to grapple with the contemporary crisis of visible and unapologetic white supremacist rule, the pathologization of black rage, and the normalization of spectacles of black pain and suffering.

However, tracing the recent evolution of black protest in the United States should not be taken as license to privilege the United States in our analyses of black politics or in our conceptualization of black political thought. Too often attempts to think about black politics transnationally in the current conjuncture are framed in terms of how the concern with the disposability of black life articulated by the Black Lives Matter movement in the United States has resonated and echoed elsewhere (see, e.g., Hooker 2017). A more conceptually productive approach is to analyze the Black Lives Matter movement as part of a global moment of resurgent black protest, as exemplified in the various South African student movements or in the decades-long movements protesting police violence and brutality against black communities in Brazil led by black women, and in the UK by black defense groups (see Perry 2013; Smith 2016; Bangura 2016). Equally instructive is the question of how black protest strategies become deterritorialized and reterritorialized as they "travel" from place to place.

How does the meaning of the signifier #Ferguson shift, for example, when it becomes part of the French black protest organization called Ferguson in Paris? Founded in September 2014 following the murder of Brown by US police, Ferguson in Paris was created by French activists fighting against

"Negrophobia" and all forms of racism and discrimination. Its goal is "to demonstrate that in France, as in the U.S. and around the world, the same people are oppressed by neo-colonial capitalism, and although the contexts are different in different countries, the oppressive patterns remain the same" (Ferguson in Paris 2016; our translation). Ferguson in Paris thus evokes familiar images: Brown's slain body lying in the street, protesters being tear-gassed and confronted by heavily armed police, and the violent repression of black protest. At the same time, Ferguson *in* Paris dislocates these familiar patterns of racialized oppression by transposing them to the Parisian *banlieues* (suburbs), which have been the site of violent protests against French racism for decades. Ferguson in Paris is thus not a declaration of the sameness of black suburban spaces; it is rather an attempt to shake the certainty of the French about their society's lack of racism by the jarring juxtaposition of a US example of contemporary racial terror and state depredation of black communities with the iconic (and implicitly nonblack) space "Paris." The history of black mobilization in the French *banlieues* predates the Black Lives Matter movement in the United States, but it raises analogous questions about the implications of the spatial politics of race for the preservation of black life. We know that black movements in the United States have dealt with questions of gentrification and disinvestment in urban black communities for decades. The existence of Ferguson in Paris, urban black movements in Brazil fighting displacement and state violence, and black defense organizations in the UK protesting black deaths in police custody makes clear that the links between the construction of urban space, the criminalization of blackness, and the displacement of black bodies and communities are in no way limited to the United States. The displays of black rage in South Africa, Latin America, and Europe are thus not movements sparked in response to Black Lives Matter, nor are they simply echoing US concerns. Each site of activism is implicated in the elaboration of globalized black protest.

Back to Black Life

The individuality and sociality of black people's lives have long been politicized by the violent and governing intrusions of race as a regime of social order. Contributors to this issue of *South Atlantic Quarterly* are thus grappling with and reflecting on the meaning of black life in black politics in the history of the present. We are concerned with how black political thought in its various incarnations can navigate pathways beyond the impasse of this global-racial conjuncture. Echoing earlier black thinkers' refusal to conceptualize the problem of racism as the "Negro problem," we also resist the liberal-democratic problematization of nonformalized black politics as social pathology. We aim to point the way forward for how to *not* conceptualize black politics as a problem. We underline the failures and inhospitality of liberal democratic theory in accepting black anger as a coherent response to racial terror and police violence and suggest that the critique of disruptive forms of black protest as counterproductive (because they preclude white empathy) should be turned on its head by focusing instead on how other forces, such as white grievance, are shaping contemporary forms of state racial violence and subordinating black politics.

In line with our commitment to enlarge dominant understandings of the central questions of black political thought to highlight black queer and black feminist perspectives, we also believe that it is necessary to question the consequences of focusing black politics on black death. There are significant limitations to centering the dead black body in black politics, particularly because the violence experienced by black women is different from that experienced by black men and also because the police are not the only means through which the state acts on black bodies. State violence manifests itself in different ways on different types of black bodies. For black transgender persons, for instance, the violence of the state acts on their bodies in ostensibly nonpublic spaces via bathroom laws or the myriad quotidian dangers of living as a non-cisgender person (Snorton and Haritaworn 2013). A capacious conception of black politics not focused solely on black death may thus be necessary to conceive a politics of black life as an emancipated sociality, by which we mean the emancipation of black comportment and black identity from the white regulations and requirements emanating from the dominant regime of race performativity (see Hesse 2011).

Against that background we believe the following to be some of the major questions about black politics posed by today's global black protest movements: How should we conceptualize contemporary black rage? Have Ferguson and South Africa finally revealed the exhaustion of black politics as conventionally understood in electoral, civil rights, or black power terms? Has this conjuncture demonstrated the deeper impossibility of addressing the problem of white supremacy within the confines of liberal, capitalist democracy? Is the policing of black populations a reconfiguration of the citizen/subject relation initiated during racial slavery? What are the limits or challenges of centering black politics on black death? How can "black" protest include the full lexicon of blackness in national, class, diaspora, gender, transgender, and sexuality terms? Questions such as these suggest that the provenance of black political thought is by no means a provincial one. As Angela Davis (2016: 112) has recently observed about previous eras of black protest, black politics "is a centuries-old struggle to achieve and expand freedom for us all."

Notes

The articles in this collection were originally presented at a panel on black political thought after Ferguson at the 2015 Western Political Science Association annual meeting and subsequently at a Black Politics–History–Theory workshop at Northwestern University in 2016. We thank the audiences at those events, and we especially acknowledge the contributions made by Stephen Marshall and Sherwin Bryant to developing these discussions.

1   For example, the US-based civil rights movement during the late 1950s and the 1960s.
2   For example, the various black power and black consciousness movements in South Africa, the United States, Jamaica, Trinidad, and the United Kingdom during the 1970s.
3   The term is a reference to the successful #RhodesMustFall student protests in 2015 to remove a statue of the British imperialist Cecil J. Rhodes from the University of Cape Town campus and the subsequent #FeesMustFall student protests of 2015 and 2016 driven by opposition to fee increases but also by demands for racially equitable access to universities and decolonization of the curriculum.

References

Baldwin, James, et al. 1961. "The Negro in American Culture." *CrossCurrents* 11, no. 3: 205–24.

Bangura, Siana. 2016. "We Need to Talk about Police Brutality in the UK." *Fader*, no. 108. www.thefader.com/2016/03/29/police-brutality-uk-essay.

Bogues, Anthony. 2012. "And What about the Human? Freedom, Human Emancipation, and the Radical Imagination." *boundary 2* 39, no. 3: 29–46.

Carrington, Ben. 2010. *Race, Sport, and Politics: The Sporting Black Diaspora*. London: Sage.

Davis, Angela. 2016. *Freedom Is a Constant Struggle: Ferguson, Palestine, and the Foundations of a Movement*. Chicago: Haymarket Books. Kindle edition.

DuBois, W. E. B. (1935) 1998. *Black Reconstruction in America, 1860–1880*. New York: Free Press.

Ferguson in Paris. 2016. "Notre Manifeste" ("Our Manifesto"). *Ferguson in Paris* (blog), February 14. fergusoninparis.wordpress.com/2016/02/14/notre-manifeste/.

Glissant, Edouard. 1989. "The Quarrel with History." In *Caribbean Discourse: Selected Essays*, translated by J. Michael Dash, 61–67. Charlottesville: University Press of Virginia.

Goldberg, David Theo. 2001. *The Racial State*. Malden, MA: Blackwell.

Hesse, Barnor. 2011. "Self-Fulfilling Prophecy: The Postracial Horizon." *South Atlantic Quarterly* 110, no. 1: 155–78.

Hooker, Juliet. 2017. "What Black Lives Matter Can Learn from Black Activists in Latin America." *NACLA Report on the Americas* 49, no. 1: 34–35.

Iton, Richard. 2008. *In Search of the Black Fantastic: Politics and Popular Culture in the Post–Civil Rights Era*. New York: Oxford University Press.

Molefe, T. O. 2016. "Oppression Must Fall: South Africa's Revolution in Theory." *World Policy Journal* 33, no. 1: 30–37.

Perry, Keisha-Khan Y. 2013. *Black Women against the Land Grab: The Fight for Racial Justice in Brazil*. Minneapolis: University of Minnesota Press.

Robinson, Cedric. 1983. *Black Marxism: The Making of the Black Radical Tradition*. London: Zed Books.

Smith, Christen. 2016. "Facing the Dragon: Black Mothering, Sequelae, and Gendered Necropolitics in the Americas." *Transforming Anthropology* 24, no. 1: 31–48.

Snorton, C. Riley, and Jin Haritaworn. 2013. "Trans Necropolitics: A Transnational Reflection on Violence, Death, and the Trans of Color Afterlife." In *The Transgender Studies Reader 2*, edited by Susan Stryker and Aren Aizura, 66–76. New York: Routledge.

Debra Thompson

An Exoneration of Black Rage

The contemporary lexicon of black politics contains a litany of emotive reactions to the entrenched racism of American society. After the murder of nine African Americans in a church in Charleston, South Carolina, Claudia Rankine (2015) argued that "the condition of black life is one of mourning." Christopher Lebron (2013) maintains that, as a society, our collective response to pervasive racial inequality ought to be shame. *White fragility*, a term coined by Robin DiAngelo (2011), describes the inability of white people to tolerate uncomfortable conversations about race, which often leads to defensiveness and anger toward people of color. The nonviolent philosophy of Dr. Martin Luther King Jr. (1986) is often invoked as the racial benchmark for love and forgiveness. White guilt, racial threat, racial resentment, white empathy, and even racial terror are all politicized emotions, which include those held individually or collectively and the behaviors born from them, expressed in the political realm.

In one way, it is unsurprising that scholars are beginning to pay more attention to the politics of emotion. In the humanities, cultural studies, and the social sciences, the "affective turn" contends that the centrality of reason and rationality

The South Atlantic Quarterly 116:3, July 2017
DOI 10.1215/00382876-3961439 © 2017 Duke University Press

in explaining political behavior has been overvalued (Clarke, Hoggett, and Thompson 2006; Clough and Halley 2007; Demertzis 2013; Hutchison and Bleiker 2014; Ross 2014; Ahmed 2015; Bericat 2016). Instead, we should take seriously "that we human beings are corporeal creatures imbued with subliminal affective intensities and resonances that so decisively influence or condition our political and other beliefs that we ignore those affective intensities and resonances at our peril" (Leys 2011: 436). Minimizing the importance of affect and emotion will fail to encapsulate both the potential damage that emotional manipulation causes to individuals and societies and the transformative potential that "technologies of the self" may inspire (436). In political sociology, the study of love, anger, shame, fear, hope, and the roles they play in social and political mobilization has been particularly important. Emotions can motivate people to join social movements, are made more potent through social interactions within movement activism, shape activists' rhetoric and discourse, and help to define movement goals (Jasper 2011: 286).

In another way, it is also unsurprising that turns of affect and emotion have often dominated popular debates about contemporary racial politics in the United States.[1] Black Lives Matter (BLM), arguably one of the most important social movements of the twenty-first century (Davis 2016; M. Hill 2016; Taylor 2016), was catalyzed by the collective outrage at the police murders of Michael Brown, Eric Garner, John Crawford, Freddie Gray, Tamir Rice, and far too many other African American men and women throughout the United States and has evoked a range of emotional responses from its supporters and critics. Protesters express grief, anger, fury, rage, terror, and exasperation as incidents of police violence against unarmed or legally armed black people continue month after month, and even those captured on video and circulated online fail to result in indictments of the officers involved. Emotions are etched onto cardboard signs at BLM rallies across the country, reading "Black lives matter," "Hands up, don't shoot," "Am I next?," "No justice, no peace," and "I cannot believe I still have to protest this shit." Heartbroken families are forced to mourn in public as the murder of their kin at the hands of those sworn to protect and serve is replayed over and over on social media. In turn, these public displays of affect by African Americans and their social justice–oriented allies are often met with anger from those who oppose the BLM movement. Most notably, the 2016 presidential campaign was dominated by "anger politics"; political rallies of Republican presidential nominee Donald Trump were characterized by palpable anger, with BLM protesters frequently manhandled, expelled by security guards, and sometimes even attacked by Trump supporters (DelReal 2016). Polls show that Americans are angrier than they used to be over current events (CBS News 2016), and the Pew Research Center (2016) recently found that "partisans' views of the opposing party are now more negative than at any point in nearly a quarter of a century," with approximately 58 percent of both highly engaged Democrats and Republicans reporting that the other party makes them angry.

Though there is a proliferation of American anger at the moment, the BLM movement is neither its cause nor its consequence. On the contrary, the vast majority of BLM protests have been peaceful demonstrations, focused on the disruption of public spaces, everyday errands, and white indifference toward black suffering. Moreover, to simply label the movement as a reinvigoration of racist stereotypes of unnecessarily angry or overly emotional black people misses the nuanced ways that the various components of the decentralized, multiorganizational movement come together to articulate black humanity as well as the pointed critiques of white supremacy and capitalism that form the basis of the Movement for Black Lives' (2016) proposals, as detailed in "A Vision for Black Lives: Policy Demands for Black Freedom, Power, and Justice." Yet both BLM protests and the movement itself have been labeled by white society as irrational, dangerous, and inappropriate, in part because protesters have refused to hide their anger at the systemic racism of the criminal justice system and beyond. By asking hard questions of would-be allies, BLM, in its radicalism, is constructed as an obstacle to the task of gaining white empathy and ineffectual in replicating the moral authority of the civil rights movement. By acknowledging and ignoring stereotypes about overly emotional, irrational black men and women, BLM trades in currencies of white anxiety and fear rather than soothing or alleviating them through quiet tones and sentences that begin with apologies and end with a call for "diversity." By engaging in a politics of anger, rage, and fury, BLM critiques respectability politics as a constitutive element of white supremacy, whereby black people are encouraged to alter their appearances and behaviors to gain access to the rights that should be associated with personhood. Finally, white society often frames black rage as inappropriate because it explicitly challenges the pervasiveness, durability, and applicability of the American Dream, itself premised on the liberal myth of inevitable progress toward a more egalitarian society. In essence, all negative emotions, such as anger, rage, resentment, and exasperation, are usually viewed as counterproductive to democratic politics, but they are viewed as particularly problematic when used to challenge white supremacy.

This is not to say that African Americans are not or do not have the right to be angry. When asked in 1961 of the potential polarity of being black and a writer simultaneously, James Baldwin famously said, "To be a Negro in this country and to be relatively conscious, is to be in a rage almost all the time. So that the first problem is how to control that rage so that it won't destroy you." He continued, "Part of the rage is this: it isn't only what is happening to you, but it's what's happening all around you all of the time, in the face of the most extraordinary and criminal indifference, the indifference and ignorance of most white people in this country" (Baldwin et al. 1961: 205). Black rage, Baldwin suggests, is not rare or sporadic; it is constantly simmering below the surface of black existence, driven by the routinized police brutality toward black people, the latent discrimination of voter identification laws, the quotidian hardships of systemic discrimination, sabotage by white liberals, and the thousand other ways that the experiences of African Americans are different, more difficult, more dangerous, more exhausting, and more infuriating than those of white society. Anger, Audre Lorde (1997: 280) argues in her famous essay, is a legitimate response to racial injustice, a response that is sometimes accused of being useless or disruptive but which, when "focused with precision . . . can become a powerful source of energy serving progress and change."

The purpose of this article is to challenge liberal democratic demands that anger be ejected from political, public, and popular deliberations over racial inequality and social justice and instead to argue that anger and rage are appropriate responses to circumstances of entrenched and pervasive racism. In fact, the very disavowal of black rage and the tacit acceptance of white anger reveal the implicit racial character of American democracy. When expressed by African Americans to combat the injustice of police brutality, both anger and rage are viewed as incompatible, or even dangerous, to the operation of American democracy; meanwhile, the anger expressed by dominant groups (especially heterosexual white men) is easily incorporated into political discourse, normalized as politics as usual. I further contend that the positive aspects of so-called negative emotions, especially when expressed by subjugated populations at the source of their domination, include productive and disruptive dimensions. Anger is *productive* in that it can serve as a unifying discourse that seeks liberation rather than liberal democratic incorporation and is *disruptive* to the hegemony of powerful national narratives such as the belief in the forthcoming postracial era, which is premised on the inevitability of racial progress but which actually hides and enshrines mechanisms of white supremacy. Thus liberal democracy's failure to understand black rage as a legitimate response to white supremacy reveals the limits of the liberal imagination as a means of challenging America's white democracy.

Black Rage in White Democracy

Negative emotions such as anger and rage are rarely considered appropriate expressions in liberal democracies, for a number of reasons. First, emotional expression is situated in binary opposition to rationality, which is a central tenet of liberalism. According to liberal thought, there is a common rational core that endows each individual with the capacity to make decisions through appeals to reason. Modern societies are characterized by varying "rationalization processes" in cultural, political, and economic spheres, which use rational reform to improve social arrangements (Weber [1930] 1992; Kalberg 1980). Emotional displays, speeches, and acts in the public sphere, especially those involving anger, symbolize a loss of control over oneself or a society. In contrast, so-called traditional or primitive societies feature excessive emotionality in place of reason, savagery rather than civilization, and instinct instead of discipline. Postcolonial theory and critical race theory are committed to deconstructing these binaries, which were used to naturalize European colonialism, expand the Atlantic slave trade, and institutionalize differences between Europeans and non-Europeans into the social fabric of modernity, differences that were later and cumulatively codified through the metonym *race* (Hesse 2011). Feminist theorists have also demonstrated the exclusionary function of linking emotionality with femininity and rationality with masculinity; by constructing women as overly emotional, and therefore irrational, patriarchal structures have reinforced male privilege and power. These binaries and other dualisms such as body/mind, individual/social, and civilized/savage are, of course, instruments of white, masculine, heteronormative power and as mnemonic devices tend to obscure more than they reveal. For example, established paradigms in psychology refer to "emotional intelligence," or the capacity to control impulses, be self-motivated, experience empathy for others, and exhibit social competence in social relationships, demonstrating the intractable connection between reason and emotion (Goleman 2005). In acknowledging the important role that emotions play in political realms, we must "recognize that feeling and thinking are parallel, interacting processes of evaluating and interacting with our worlds, composed of similar neurological building blocks" (Jasper 2011: 286).

Second, emotional expressions are believed to be particularly problematic for democratic politics because of their potential to be polarizing and destabilizing forces. In the literature on transnational justice, which explores the transition of postconflict societies to democratic regimes, scholars contend that any practice that encourages divisiveness, such as the retributive processes inherent to criminal law, will not move a country toward reconciliation and healing. Fragile new democracies may be incapable of maintaining stability if political vendettas are permitted to play out and "justice is the price torn societies have to pay in exchange for peace" (Mihai 2016: 29). In essence, expressions of anger, rage, or resentment by or on behalf of the victims of state violence can reinvigorate the potential that the regime will backslide into authoritarianism. The appeal to procedural justice in new and established constitutional democracies is meant to provide an institutional barrier between perpetrators and victims of injustice, working to depoliticize and depersonalize situations that could otherwise be a prelude to further violence. Moreover, the international trend of adopting truth and reconciliation commissions to acknowledge, rather than bury, a violent past is designed to turn negative emotions, such as fury and resentment, into more "positive" and "less divisive" forces such as healing and forgiveness (Minow 1998).

But the United States is not a new or transitioning democracy; it is a white democracy. The contradictions between, on one hand, discourses of equality and freedom and, on the other, the historical and contemporary exclusionary practices of American democracy lead Joel Olson to argue that racial oppression and American democracy are, in fact, mutually constituted. "Racial oppression," he contends, "makes full democracy impossible, but it has also made American democracy possible" (Olson 2004: xv). Here Olson borrows heavily from W. E. B. DuBois, who argued throughout his prolific body of work that American democracy is formed and ruled in the interests of a white citizenry that tacitly or explicitly consents to the various forms of racial domination that have defined the American polity from its conception to its current form. This basic character of American democracy creates a political vision in which white citizens resist any form of politics that does not respect their privileged status. The "wages of whiteness," DuBois argued, are forms of material, public, and psychological compensation available to all white people regardless of class, which unite white people in their collective efforts to oppress African Americans (DuBois [1935] 1998: 700–701; Roediger [1991] 2007). The citizenship rights and protections of white citizens have thus been privileged at the expense of black citizens. The idea of white democracy emerges from the contrast between Western liberal ideas of universalism, such as the principle of equality before the law, and the pragmatic experience of democracy, which is constituted through the ways these universal principles and democratic institutions (e.g., the police) produce and reproduce racial hierarchies.

The privileges associated with whiteness constitute every facet of social and political life, including the determination of which racial groups can express what kinds of emotions in the polis. The very expression of anger in democratic politics is governed by what Arlie Russell Hochschild calls "feeling rules," that is, the social norms that establish the conceptions of entitlement, obligation, or appropriateness that regulate emotional exchanges. These feeling rules, Hochschild (2003: 58) argues, can be privately held, but they are also made known by external reactions to one's feelings (e.g., "You ought to be ashamed of yourself!"; "Aren't you happy about Jack's news?"). Mary Holmes (2004) builds on this original formulation and its application to a politicized sociology of anger by arguing that relations of power are implicated in the determination of feeling rules. Not all people are afforded the right to speak angrily, and, as Peter Lyman (2004: 136) argues, the right to angry speech is in itself a marker of dominance. Anger is therefore used

> in service to the dominant order, but excludes the angry voice of the subordinate from participation in political dialogues. If anger were to become a voice in politics, every kind of subordination—and by extension, domination itself—would become a legitimate political topic. The idea of a dialogue is usually thought to require an equal social relationship, perhaps even friendship, but anger is a form of speech that seems to threaten social peace, thus is not considered a possible ground for dialogue. (139)

More importantly, these "feeling rules" are highly racialized, used in the service of the American racial order to sanction certain emotions as legitimate or brand others as illegitimate, depending on the status of the racial group proclaiming the emotion. The operation of the white democracy demands that oppressed groups suppress their anger in the name of the "greater good" of democratic politics, whether that is defined as consensus, deliberation, or majoritarian rule. However, the operation of liberal democratic rules is neither emotionless nor raceless. In fact, these exclusions reinforce relationships of power, devaluing certain kinds of speech and certain types of speakers—especially those populations that are normatively tied to certain kinds of emotional speech (e.g., women, African Americans)—while valorizing others. Black anger is consequently easily ignored as "irrational," or its expression is more readily punished because of African Americans' subjugated positions on social hierarchies. If acknowledged, black rage is received and relabeled as hostility and aggression because its very existence and expression contravenes social norms. Therefore, it is important to think about the expulsion of anger and rage from democratic deliberations as a political act that normalizes and naturalizes prevailing sets of racial formations and how angry expression can work to challenge racial orders.

While African Americans are angry at relentless police brutality and entrenched racism, the idea of black rage is slightly different, denoting an affective reaction to the white populace's lack of recognition about the reality of this racism and the hollowness of democratic claims of egalitarianism. In August 2014 singer Lauryn Hill released a "sketch" of her song "Black Rage" and dedicated it to the protesters fighting for racial equality in Ferguson, Missouri. Set to the tune of the song "My Favorite Things" from Richard Rodgers and Oscar Hammerstein's *The Sound of Music*, Hill (2014) sings:

> Black rage is founded on two-thirds a person
> Rapings and beatings and suffering that worsens
> Black human packages tied up in strings
> Black rage can come from all these kinds of things.
> Black rage is founded on blatant denial
> Squeezed economics, subsistence survival
> Deafening silence and social control
> Black rage is founded on wounds in the soul.
> When the dogs bite
> When the beatings
> When I'm feeling sad
> I simply remember all these kinds of things
> And then I don't fear so bad . . .
> Black rage is founded on who fed us self-hatred
> Lies and abuse while we waited and waited
> Spiritual treason, this grid and its cages
> Black rage is founded on these kinds of things.
> Black rage is founded on draining and draining
> Threatening your freedom to stop your complaining
> Poisoning your water while they say it's raining
> Then call you mad for complaining, complaining.
> Old-time bureaucracy, drugging the youth
> Black rage is founded on blocking the truth
> Murder and crime, compromise and distortion
> Sacrifice, sacrifice
> Who makes this fortune?
> Greed falsely called progress, such human contortion
> Black rage is founded on these kinds of things.

Hill's interpretation of the contours of black rage is compelling, for a number of reasons. The song was originally performed as spoken word in 2012 during her "Life Is Good / Black Rage" tour with hip-hop artist Nas. The juxtaposition of the two titles, one from Nas's *Life Is Good* album and the other from Hill's new single, is striking: Is black life good, or is it full of rage? The lyrics of Hill's song, discussed further below, indicate that the rage and the good life are more intertwined than dichotomous. The song's aesthetic also invokes a contrast between musicality and lyricism. There is a sense of complexity masquerading as simplicity in Hill's song, amplified by the recording itself: in lo-fi and accompanied only by an acoustic guitar and a backbeat, Hill sings in her living room while her children's voices can be heard in the background. The gravity of the lyrics is punctuated by the levity of youthful play and imagination. In Hill's version, the sound of her children's voices is a haunting echo, while the 1965 movie version of *The Sound of Music* uses the song "My Favorite Things" as an important bonding moment between the main character, Maria, and her new wards, the von Trapp children. During a thunderstorm, Maria tells the children that when she's frightened or sad, she thinks of her favorite things—girls in white dresses, brown paper packages, raindrops on roses, whiskers on kittens, the shift from winter to spring: beauty, anticipation, comfort, rebirth. It is a song about those circumstances that make us fearful and our coping mechanisms for dealing with that fear. But note that Maria's advice is ultimately about deflection—just think of happy thoughts, she suggests, until the fear passes.

These themes of contrast and illusion weave throughout Hill's song. She purposefully crafts a song about black rage that calls out the ways that white supremacy and capitalism exist through and because of their very denial. "Obviously, this is a song about confrontation, right?" Hill told an audience in 2012 (quoted in Grow 2014). The lyrics confer the surreptitious nature of these interlocking systems of oppression that cumulatively constitute black rage through "blatant denial," "blocking [of] the truth," "compromise and distortion," "deafening silence and social control," and "greed falsely called progress, such human contortion." Later in the song, Hill suggests that the confusion that results from racial oppression, which operates through the denial of its existence, is a product of purposeful force. In these ways, white supremacy and capitalism are violent to both bodies and minds ("Victims of violence / Both psyche and body / Life out of context is living ungodly" [Hill 2014]). The "spiritual treason" of white supremacy and capitalism, Hill argues, embeds black rage in "all wounds in the soul." But in stark contrast to Maria's advice to the von Trapp children to use happy thoughts to overwhelm and displace fearful ones, Hill argues that when one remembers the history and contemporary realities of white supremacy—slavery, sexual violence, capitalist exploitation, structural racism, mass incarceration, and the denial that any of these phenomena are relevant to the operation of American democracy—rage can be a viable and powerful defense mechanism. "When I'm feeling sad," Hill confesses, "I simply remember all these kinds of things / And then I don't fear so bad." In effect, fear is mediated by the recognition of the legitimacy of rage, though rage is limited in that it can work only to lessen fear and cannot fully displace or eradicate it.

Hill's song thus reveals a great deal about the nature of black rage. First, the juxtapositions in the song's lyrics and aesthetics suggest that it is impossible to conceptualize black rage as an isolated emotion. Black rage is "founded" in the operation of white supremacy, making it primarily a response to conditions that themselves incite other emotional responses, which then become interwoven with rage. That is, rage is always correlated to that which it was invoked to deflect or displace—heartbreak, fear, terror, sadness, indignation. Rage can also emerge from positive emotions; the powerful contrast between Hill's children playing in the background of the song and the lyrics detailing the conditions that give rise to black rage speaks to the inextricable connection between hope for black futures and the collective fury at black death. Second, the idea that black rage is a response not simply to white supremacy but also to white supremacy's deniability implies that black rage is more than an emotional reaction. The difference between anger and rage, Lyman (2004: 140) argues, is that whereas anger is a reaction to a perceived injustice, rage is a response to the refusal to listen to that appeal for justice. Black rage, therefore, emerges from the circumstances that enable law enforcement to murder black people with impunity and also from the refusal to recognize these murders as part and parcel of, in the words of the Movement for Black Lives (2016), "the war on Black people," which includes police brutality, criminalization, and incarceration. Third, whereas liberal thought positions negative emotions such as anger and rage as obstacles to democratic reconciliation, black rage condemns white supremacy and its constitutive relationship with democracy—that is, the continuing existence of white democracy—as that which makes conciliatory gestures both undesirable and impossible. As Hill puts it: "Black rage is founded on who fed us self-hatred / Lies and abuse while we waited and waited." Speaking at the time about the song's gestation and aesthetic, Hill said: "As artists, we have an opportunity to help the public evolve, raise consciousness and awareness, teach, heal, enlighten, and inspire *in ways the democratic process may not be able to touch.* So we keep it moving" (quoted in Grow 2014; emphasis added). It is white supremacy, the denial of its existence, and the failure of democratic processes, and not black rage, that damage black souls.

Black rage thus emerges from unrelenting circumstances and structures of racial domination in social, political, and economic realms. This anger is not simply an individualized statement of emotion; as Holmes (2004) argues, anger is productive of and produced by social relations. Thus BLM activists are not expressing a decontextualized malcontentment about unconnected, random, or individualized experiences of racial prejudice. They contend quite deliberately: "Black Lives Matter is an ideological and political intervention in a world where Black lives are systematically and intentionally targeted for demise. It is an affirmation of Black folks' contributions to this society, our humanity, and our resilience in the face of deadly oppression" (Garza 2014; see also Taylor 2016). In confronting such destructive violence, activists are furiously unapologetic. "Anger," Lorde (1997: 282) argues, "is an appropriate reaction to racist attitudes, as is fury when the actions arising from those attitudes do not change."

Black rage is perceived as dangerous to and incompatible with white democracy because it challenges national mythologies such as the American Dream, raising questions about the meaning, nature, and operation of American democracy and its constitutive relationship with race. The "creedal story," so deeply embedded in the American democratic ethos, is premised on the idea that America is defined by equality of opportunity and a long-standing commitment to the principle that "all men are created equal." Black outrage at racial injustice challenges the American Dream as a racially coded construct. This is a central theme of Ta-Nehisi Coates's best-selling book *Between the World and Me*. For Coates, the Dream is a dangerous national deception, not unlike the myths and illusions that Hill refers to in "Black Rage." It is "Memorial Day cookouts, block associations, and driveways. The Dream is treehouses and the Cub Scouts. The Dream smells like peppermint but tastes like strawberry shortcake" (Coates 2015: 11). Though he desires access to the Dream, not nearly as much for those Dream-like qualities as for a means of escaping the ways that black bodies are vulnerable and therefore prone to violence, Coates understands that the Dream has never been an option for black folks because "the Dream rests on our backs, the bedding made from our bodies" (11). White Americans, he argues, created that dreamlike narrative, built on a foundation that the Dream is just and that white peoples' possession of the Dream is "the natural result of grit, honor, and good works" (98). Coates writes: "The mettle that it takes to look away from the horror of our prison system, from police forces transformed into armies, from the long war against the black body, is not forged overnight. . . . To acknowledge these horrors means turning away from the brightly rendered version of your country as it has always declared itself and turning toward something murkier and unknown. It is still too difficult for most Americans to do this" (98–99). Black anger, Coates intones, is not dangerous to democratic politics because it expresses emotion in the "rational" public sphere; it is dangerous because it sheds light on the underbelly of democratic politics, makes claims about racial subordination as a legitimate topic for political debate or action, and reveals, as Melvin L. Rogers (2014) points out, that the very institutions primarily responsible for ensuring that democratic life is just and fair by serving and protecting the citizenry are most often at the helm of race-based brutality.

As Coates implies, black rage is also labeled as inappropriate in democratic politics because it is rarely acknowledged, understood, or well received by the white populace. In democratic theory, institutions are presumed to be race-neutral and democratic practices necessitate that some citizens do not see their preferences enacted. In the literature on democratization, for example, the principle of "contingent consent" indicates that the winners of elections must at least informally agree that they will not bar the losers from taking office or exerting influence over policy decisions and in exchange the losers agree to respect the winners' right to make binding decisions for the polity. For their part, citizens must obey the decisions that emerge after free, fair, and regular electoral competitions, even if their preferred candidate or party did not win the election (Schmitter and Karl 1991: 82). In essence, democracies require "good losers," willing to concede their preferences in the interest of democratic stability—what Danielle S. Allen (2004) has termed "democratic sacrifice." But, as Juliet Hooker (2016) argues, democratic sacrifice in the United States is decisively one-sided. The burden of democratic sacrifice has most often fallen on the shoulders of African Americans, who, though among the most democratically vulnerable, are nevertheless expected to exhibit a kind of acquiescent, nonviolent, and emotionless democratic exemplarity not required of other citizens. For their part, when whites have found themselves on the losing side of political debates and decisions, they have largely failed to be "good losers." Hooker's (2016: 455) analysis reveals that "victories in the struggle for racial equality have been followed by eras of deep and sustained backlash in which blacks and other minorities have borne the brunt of racial terror, violence, and xenophobia." It is this asymmetrical democratic relationship, far more than black rage, that prevents the emergence of conditions under which white empathy could act as a potent force in racial politics. That being said, white empathy is both a problematic and an undesirable litmus test for racial justice.

Black rage is subversive of racial and social orders because the expression of anger is most often a resource for dominant groups, sublimated through liberalism into socially useful forms such as force, authority, or moral indignation (Lyman 2004). Force, for example, is a key element of Max Weber's definition of the state as an entity that maintains a monopoly over the legitimate use of force in a given territory. Here force is the domestication of aggression through an authoritative chain of command, which "implies obedience to an order from a legitimate authority as reinforced by the internalization of professional codes of conduct and by mastery of the skills and discipline of military technique" (Lyman 2004: 136). The use of force is only legitimate because it is impersonal and embedded in other rationalization processes, such as those inherent to bureaucracy. In effect, the respective roles of the military and the police are to monopolize domesticated, impersonal anger and aggression in order to maintain power by controlling external threats from outside the nation and internal threats from within. When a society is racially ordered, however, the use of anger as force is easily redirected at those who seek to upset hierarchies. Where black life is concerned, Rogers (2014) writes, white Americans "rationalize the devaluation of Black life and in turn casually endorse the disposability of Black folks. . . . This rationalization will recede so far into the background that it almost becomes indistinguishable from the legitimate and healthy functioning of American democracy."

Thus while black anger is considered dangerous to democratic politics because it contravenes social norms that dictate which groups have the requisite power and position to be angry, challenges the application of the American Dream to subordinate populations, and further alienates white people from the experiences of the black citizenry, making the (problematically necessary) expression of white empathy even more unlikely, *white anger* is built into the essence of American democracy. Carol Anderson (2016) argues that American history is saturated with white anger and resentment at the prospect of black equality. At every moment when African Americans have challenged their subjugation, white people have employed the power of the state, in addition to the extralegal terrorism of the Klan, to protect and defend white supremacy: by establishing black codes after the end of the Civil War; in derailing the Great Migration; in resisting all attempts at school integration after *Brown v. Board of Education*; through the invention of the "Southern strategy" to channel white anger over civil rights into support for the Republican Party; in Ronald Reagan's use of "law and order" and the "war on drugs" to allow the criminal justice system to run amok; and in promoting the otherwise inexplicable vitriolic hatred of President Barack Obama (Anderson 2016; see also Banks 2014). This palatable anger of the dominant group at the potential loss of their privilege and the possible emergence of racial equality is also directed at immigrants; Marisa Abrajano and Zoltan L. Hajnal (2015) demonstrate that white Americans' fears about immigration fundamentally influence their core political identities, policy preferences, and electoral choices and that this white backlash has been an important contributor to the large-scale defection of whites from the Democratic to the Republican Party. Even as the dynamics of American democracy seek to silence the anger of African Americans by condemning it as inappropriate, misplaced, or dangerous, white Americans "appropriate for themselves the right to mobilize anger in defense of the political order" (Lyman 2004: 133–34), as they seek surreptitiously to maintain their privileged positions while simultaneously denying the existence of racial hierarchies.

The Productive, Disruptive Dimensions of Black Rage

In Western political theory the understanding of anger, rage, and resentment as wholly negative owes much to Friedrich Nietzsche's (1989) depiction of the pathological "man of *ressentiment*" as self-poisoning and deceitful, full of vindictiveness, hatred, and contempt. The expression of *ressentiment*, Nietzsche argues, is individually harmful and morally condemnable. *Ressentiment* is not quite the same as resentment: "While resentment is seen as a form of anger directed against a moral wrong, and stems from our legitimate feeling that we are entitled to be treated with respect, *ressentiment* is, by definition, an irrational and base passion" (Dolgert 2016: 361). However, philosopher Martha Nussbaum (2016) has recently argued that resentment is always normatively problematic, whether it is expressed in personal or public spheres. Conceptually, she contends, anger is not just a reaction to a perceived wrongdoing but is also sutured to the idea that the wrongdoer must suffer negative consequences as retribution for the initial injustice. These consequences, whether they take the form of payback or a return of lost social status, cannot undo the original injury, nor can they focus energies beyond the obsessive narrowness of status claims (Nussbaum 2016). The corollary of these condemnations of anger is the perception of more conciliatory emotions, such as forgiveness, love, or generosity, as noble, admirable, and more conducive to the pursuit of justice: "If the unforgiving and unreconciled survivors understood more about the background of the perpetrators, or about what ideals and values really count; if they were more capable of managing their anger; if they thought more rationally about their own good or the good of the nation, then they would try to forgive or let go of their resentment and engage more constructively in the process of reconciliation" (Brudholm 2006: 10–11). Resentment and anger are ultimately moral failings, while reconciliation, forgiveness, and the politics of recognition are the only democratically acceptable alternatives.

But it is the white democracy that continually fails to protect black people. It is the white democracy that exhibits a recalcitrant inability to hold the police accountable for murders of unarmed (or legally armed) black men and women. The institutional failures at the heart of this purposefully designed ineptitude are many. In cases of police-related fatalities, grand juries evaluate evidence presented by the prosecutor's office before determining whether an officer should be indicted and stand trial. This system has come under increased scrutiny as grand juries in Ferguson, Cleveland, and Staten Island, New York, failed to indict the officers responsible for the deaths of Brown, Rice, and Garner. Critics argue that the grand jury system tends to favor the police, in part because prosecutors, who work closely with the police and have incentives to remain in good standing with law enforcement agencies, can decide what evidence the grand jury hears, what witnesses will appear and in what order, and whether an officer's account can be subject to cross-examination by including other eyewitness testimony (McKinley and Baker 2014). Most states also give police officers wide discretion to use "reasonable force" to make an arrest or protect themselves. In shooting cases, for example, "officers often testify that they perceived a deadly threat and acted in self-defense. This stance can inoculate them even if the threat later turns out to be false" (McKinley and Baker 2014). Perceptions of reasonable force in the face of deadly threat, however, are saturated with racial bias. Substantial evidence on racial attitudes indicates that African Americans are perceived as more aggressive, more dangerous, physically stronger, and less prone to feeling than white people (Boykin, Desir, and Rubenfeld 2016).

If grand juries do decide to indict police officers, they are rarely found guilty of the charges against them. Between 2005 and 2014, only forty-seven officers were charged with murder or manslaughter following a fatal on-duty shooting, and approximately ten of those officers were convicted, though police departments voluntarily reported over twenty-six hundred "justifiable homicides" to the Federal Bureau of Investigation during the same period (McKinley and Baker 2014; Stinson 2015).[2] A recent *Washington Post* analysis of the cases in which the police were charged following a shooting found that there was usually a confluence of factors that made the case exceptional: "a victim shot in the back, a video recording of the incident, incriminating testimony from other officers or allegations of a coverup" (Kindy and Kelly 2015). And even with one or more of these factors at play, "jurors are very reluctant to punish police officers, tending to view them as guardians of order, according to prosecutors and defense lawyers" (Kindy and Kelly 2015).

The catch-22 of attempting to place blame on individual police officers via the criminal justice system is that the atomistic individualization of circumstances of police brutality can be used to avoid systemic change, foreclosing any meaningful discussion about the violent nature of the police as an institution. Individualized blame allows public officials to claim that it's just "one bad apple," effectively changing the subject from a discussion about the injustice of race and policing in America to a focus on the apparently isolated actions of a few. As Matt Taibbi of *Rolling Stone* sarcastically states: "Fix that little in-custody death problem, we're told, perhaps with the aid of 'better training' or body cameras (which Baltimore has already promised to install by the end of the year), and we can comfortably go back to ignoring poverty, race, abuse, all that depressing inner-city stuff." But, he continues, "body cameras won't fix it. You can't put body cameras on a system" (Taibbi 2015). High-profile murders are only part of the problem, Taibbi argues. More important is the system of police brutality—a system that is so entrenched in black communities that white people, still overwhelmingly supportive and trustful of the police, are shielded from its operation and effects. It is made possible by "broken windows," "stop and frisk," and "zero tolerance" policing and more exploitative by bureaucratic rabbit holes where various forms of police misconduct are buried in red tape and desperate people are forced to sign legal waivers in exchange for the expungement of (wrongful) arrests. The system is also made more powerful by formidable institutional obstacles, including union contracts, the blue code of silence, and a lack of machinery to discipline "rogue" cops that together prevent systemic police reform (Taibbi 2015). The moral defensibility of black rage is further buttressed by the well-founded fear that these kinds of injustices are not simply in the past but rather will continue to occur into the foreseeable future.

Much as the historic demarcation of the "Negro problem" during legalized white supremacy problematized the wrong part of the equation, the tendency within liberal democratic thought to problematize black rage, I want to suggest, similarly misses the point. Black rage isn't the problem; white supremacy is. Efforts to promote democratic reconciliation, therefore, will always seek to expel black rage from public discourse because the conditions are predetermined by the limits of the white democratic imagination. Andrew Schaap (2004) writes that democratic reconciliation in societies divided by a history of political violence depends on the transformation of relationships among groups from enmity into ones of "civic friendship." Such a transformation is unlikely to occur through the same conciliatory processes that consistently fail to hold the perpetrators of injustice accountable for their actions. Writing on the struggle of indigenous people against the internal colonialism of the Canadian state during the Idle No More uprisings, Glen Coulthard (2014: 109) suggests that what the state understands as *ressentiment*, the incapacitating ability or unwillingness of indigenous people to get over the past, is actually resentment: the legitimate, "politicized expression of Indigenous anger and outrage directed at a structural and symbolic violence that still structures our lives, our relations with others, and our relationships with land." Similarly, I contend that the expression of so-called negative emotions such as anger, resentment, and rage, when used to highlight racial injustice, seek to construct a different kind of democratic politics. Black rage, I argue, has *productive* and *disruptive* elements, both of which are legitimate, appropriate, and perhaps even fundamental to the creation of a different kind of political system that is not constituted by white supremacy.

Black rage is productive as a unifying discourse that seeks liberation rather than the same kinds of liberal democratic incorporation that have failed to eradicate racial injustice. The literature on the use of emotions in social movements demonstrates that even negative emotions can have a strong motivating and binding power (Jasper 2014: 209). Anger can mobilize people to take action against injustice (Thompson 2006: 124), especially when such injustice is an affront to an individual's sense of morality. James M. Jasper (2014) explains that both "moral shocks" and "moral batteries" are important motivators for individuals to participate in a social movement. News of each killing of a black man or woman by the police, though tragically unsurprising, is a moral shock to progressively minded people that results in "a visceral unease in reaction to information and events which signal that the world is not as it seemed, thereby demanding attention and revaluation" (Jasper 2014: 210). Though there may be disagreement about the precise details of the confrontation that led to such police brutality, the fact that many of the victims were often unarmed and arbitrarily targeted is an affront to most people's sense of right and wrong, which, even for those who rarely interact with the police, can mobilize them to take action. BLM also exhibits the tension of a "moral battery," when positive and negative emotions (e.g., anger and hope) combine to motivate action (Jasper 2011: 291), strengthening both the intensity of black rage and the hope that this renewed fight for racial justice will enable social change. Hill makes this clear in the various emotional, aesthetic, and lyrical juxtapositions of "Black Rage." In essence, anger can be productive as a motivating force but is rarely the sole basis for social mobilization.

Anger can create solidarity in the search for social justice and help to create a collective identity based on common aspirations (Collins 2000; Ahmed 2015). As Frantz Fanon (1963) indicated, rage and resentment can initiate a coming to consciousness through which the colonized recognize the precarious position of the colonizers and can break free of their subjugation. Anger translated into collective action is "a liberating and strengthening act of clarification, for it is in the painful process of this translation that we identify who are our allies and with whom we have grave differences, and who are our genuine enemies" (Lorde 1997: 280). Of course, anger is not the only emotion with unifying potential. Making a broader claim for the recognition of black humanity, BLM organizers use loyalty within the black community and anger toward police brutality to catalyze political action. As Ashley Yates, a Ferguson activist and cofounder of Millennial Activists United, stated at a rally in October 2014, "If you can see a dead black boy lie in the street for four and a half hours and that doesn't make you angry, then you lack humanity" (quoted in Harris 2015). By fusing reciprocal emotions (what members of a social movement feel toward one another, including love and loyalty, but also envy and betrayal) and shared emotions (the collective feelings of a movement toward subjects or objects outside the group) (Jasper 2014: 209), BLM intensifies conceptualizations of black "linked fate," the idea that African Americans believe their individual self-interests are linked to the interests of the race as a whole. Linked fate is an acute awareness or recognition that what happens to one African American will also affect other African Americans, even across cross-cutting gender or class lines (Dawson 2000).

Subsequently, this unifying function of black rage is also potentially disruptive to the operation of white supremacy. In this way, the anger of BLM is a form of disruptive or interdependent power. Frances Fox Piven, in her work on poor people's movements, argues that moments when the powerless in society become defiant are exceptional but can also have a defining impact. These are extraordinary moments when ordinary people "rise up in anger and hope, defy the rules that ordinarily govern their daily lives, and, by doing so, disrupt the workings of the institutions in which they are enmeshed" (Piven 2006: 1). It is both the drama of these protests and the disorder that follows them that can propel new issues to the center of political debates, driving forward reforms as panicked political leaders do their best to restore order (Piven 2006).

BLM could be one of these "big bang" moments that Piven writes about, using black rage to disrupt standard narratives about the universality of how American democracy is experienced by its citizenry. BLM demonstrates that white experiences and expectations of democracy are often universalized as "normal" but are in fact very different from the lived experiences of many African Americans. The tactics employed by BLM are exemplary of disruptive power. Activists organize protests and marches, stage die-ins in public spaces, shut down highways and busy intersections, use direct action to target and block access to hubs of transportation and commerce, and provide instructions for white people on how to be good allies. BLM was also vocal during the Democratic primaries in 2015 and early 2016, driving Bernie Sanders from the stage in Seattle and challenging presidential candidate Hillary Clinton at numerous political events. When incendiary Republican candidate Trump planned a campaign rally in Chicago in March 2016, BLM joined University of Illinois at Chicago students, Democrats, labor unionists, and members of other organizations in protest, ultimately forcing Trump to cancel his event. BLM protests are mobilized via social media—especially Twitter—through which organizers not only can direct the actions of hundreds of thousands of people but can also capture, document, and spread word of instances of police brutality during protests in real time. Fredrick Harris (2015) writes that, for this reason, "the spontaneity and the intensity of Black Lives Matter is more akin to other recent movements—Occupy Wall Street and the explosive protests in Egypt and Brazil—than 1960s activism."

The disruptive power of black rage is discursive as well. After the election of President Obama in 2008, many Americans felt that the postracial era was on the immediate horizon. Though postracialism refers to the substantial shifts in attitudes about race between this generation and its predecessors (Bobo et al. 2012), it is, more critically, "a twenty-first century ideology that reflects a belief that due to the significant racial progress that has been made, the state need not engage in race-based decision-making or adopt race-based remedies, and that civil society should eschew race as a central organizing principle of social action" (Cho 2009: 1594). The "post" in postracial implies that race and racism are artifacts of a world history we are now beyond. It signals transcendent and unidirectional racial progress—away from the racist past and the era of civil rights and toward a cosmopolitan, egalitarian future. The discourse of postracialism was easily employed as a liberal, socially palatable alternative that appealed to the "universalism" of racial indifference and negated the enduring persistence of racial inequality (Cho 2009: 1600–1604)—until BLM explicitly, angrily challenged both the morality of racial indifference and the claim that racism no longer exists.

The rhetorical use of "All lives matter" as a postracial rejoinder to BLM (Orbe 2015) in some ways demonstrates the disruptive potential of black rage; if black lives are indeed included in "all lives," then what explains the incredible racial resentment about the mantra "Black lives matter"? The answer is that, as Michael C. Dawson argues, white and black Americans live in different *lifeworlds*, a term that Jürgen Habermas uses to describe "a storehouse of unquestioned cultural givens from which those participating in communication draw agreed-upon patterns of interpretations for use in their interpretive efforts" (quoted in Dawson 2011: 5). Dawson argues that relationships between black and white Americans are characterized by the absence of "agreed-upon patterns of interpretations." The white worldview is premised on the belief that racial justice has been achieved and that there are minor "anomalies" in the functioning of American democracy. Its hegemony in the American imagination is maintained through conscious acts of political amnesia about the reality of racism and the demonization of blacks who seek to challenge this worldview (Dawson 2011: 5–6). Black rage works to disrupt the white lifeworld, sometimes quite literally as demonstrators use protest tactics designed to interrupt the normal operation of daily life in decidedly white spaces. These disruptions are important for their potential to challenge the racial amnesia and aphasia that underpin white lifeworlds and discourses of postracialism.

Conclusion

One of the main criticisms of the expression of anger in public spheres is that it can too easily descend into violence and destruction. Black deaths at the hands of the police are immediately followed by calls for calm and nonviolent protest, echoed by political elites from both parties and all levels of government. In an article published during the height of the Ferguson protests, Brittney Cooper (2014) argued that the inevitable focus on looting and "black-on-black crime," rather than police brutality, misses the larger point: "We are talking about justifiable outrage. Outrage over the unjust taking of the lives of people who look like us. How dare people preach and condescend to these people and tell them not to loot, not to riot? Yes, those are destructive forms of anger, but frankly I would rather these people take their anger out on property and products rather than on other people." Yet anger does not necessarily beget violence; though black rage can be harmful, the ensuing violence is rarely as destructive as what spurred the anger in the first place. Further, if we insist on keeping track of the historical circumstances under which perceived injustice has led to racial violence, it is clear that while black rage tends to make white people uncomfortable, "nothing is more threatening to black people on a systemic level than white anger" (Cooper 2014).

Although, as this article has argued, the expression of rage, anger, and resentment at police brutality, pervasive racism, and white indifference is appropriate and even necessary to challenge white democracy, there is a tacit danger that anger will be displaced by other, more comfortable emotions. For example, in lesbian, gay, bisexual, transgender, and queer (LGBTQ) activism, love is often the mobilizing affect of choice in an effort to prove that homosexual relationships are similar to heterosexual ones: "Love is love," so the slogan goes. However, as Alexa DeGagne (2016) argues, evoking love in this way undercuts critiques of systemic inequalities faced by those who could not, or had no desire to, marry, as well as those whose social justice concerns—overcriminalization, poverty, police and public violence, and discrimination in the acquisition of health or social services—could not be solved by entering into a private relationship. Similarly, black anger is too often considered the enemy of hope; in a review of *Between the World and Me*, Michelle Alexander reluctantly criticizes Coates for failing to offer his audience any kind of hope for the future. "Like Baldwin," she argues, "I tend to think we must not ask whether it is possible for a human being or society to become just or moral; we must believe it is possible" (Alexander 2015). The view that anger cannot lead to hope is misguided. The expression of anger occurs precisely because we hope for a more just and equitable society; in fact, we furiously demand it.

Notes

1   Affect refers to "bodily capacities to affect and be affected or the augmentation or diminution of a body's capacity to act, to engage, and to connect, such that autoaffection is linked to the self-feeling of being alive—that is, aliveness or vitality" (Clough 2007: 2). Emotion is the display, projection, or articulation of feelings and sensations that are categorized and labeled based on previous experiences. This article is concerned mostly with emotions and especially those emotions that have been articulated as "anger."

2   The *Washington Post* reports that between 2005 and April 2015 only fifty-four officers were charged following a fatal police-involved shooting. Approximately three-quarters of these officers were white, while all but two of the forty-nine victims were black (Kindy and Kelly 2015).

References

Abrajano, Marisa, and Zoltan L. Hajnal. 2015. *White Backlash: Immigration, Race, and American Politics.* Princeton, NJ: Princeton University Press.

Ahmed, Sara. 2015. *The Cultural Politics of Emotion.* 2nd ed. New York: Routledge.

Alexander, Michelle. 2015. "Ta-Nehisi Coates's *Between the World and Me.*" *New York Times,* August 17. www.nytimes.com/2015/08/17/books/review/ta-nehisi-coates-between-the -world-and-me.html.

Allen, Danielle S. 2004. *Talking to Strangers: Anxieties of Citizenship since* Brown v. Board of Education. Chicago: University of Chicago Press.

Anderson, Carol. 2016. *White Rage: The Unspoken Truth of Our Racial Divide.* New York: Bloomsbury.

Baldwin, James, et al. 1961. "The Negro in American Culture." *CrossCurrents* 11, no. 3: 205–24.

Banks, Antoine J. 2014. *Anger and Racial Politics: The Emotional Foundation of Racial Attitudes in America.* New York: Cambridge University Press.

Bericat, Eduardo. 2016. "The Sociology of Emotions: Four Decades of Progress." *Current Sociology* 64, no. 3: 491–513.

Bobo, Lawrence D., et al. 2012. "The *Real* Record on Racial Attitudes." In *Social Trends in American Life: Findings from the General Social Survey since 1972,* edited by Peter V. Marsden, 38–83. Princeton, NJ: Princeton University Press.

Boykin, Olevia, Christopher Desir, and Jed Rubenfeld. 2016. "A Better Standard for the Use of Deadly Force." *New York Times,* January 1. www.nytimes.com/2016/01/01/opinion /a-better-standard-for-the-use-of-deadly-force.html.

Brudholm, Thomas. 2006. "Revisiting Resentments: Jean Améry and the Dark Side of Forgiveness and Reconciliation." *Journal of Human Rights* 5, no. 1: 7–26.

CBS News. 2016. "Poll: Anger in America—on Race, Gender, Politics, Police Violence." January 3. www.cbsnews.com/news/poll-anger-in-america-on-race-gender-politics-police-violence.

Cho, Sumi. 2009. "Post-Racialism." *Iowa Law Review* 94, no. 5: 1589–1645.

Clarke, Simon, Paul Hoggett, and Simon Thompson, eds. 2006. *Emotion, Politics, and Society.* New York: Palgrave Macmillan.

Clough, Patricia Ticineto. 2007. Introduction to Clough and Halley, *Affective Turn,* 1–33.

Clough, Patricia Ticineto, and Jean Halley, eds. 2007. *The Affective Turn: Theorizing the Social.* Durham, NC: Duke University Press.

Coates, Ta-Nehisi. 2015. *Between the World and Me.* New York: Spiegel and Grau.

Collins, Patricia Hill. 2000. *Black Feminist Thought: Knowledge, Consciousness, and the Politics of Empowerment.* New York: Routledge.

Cooper, Brittney. 2014. "In Defense of Black Rage: Michael Brown, Police, and the American Dream." *Salon,* August 12. www.salon.com/2014/08/12/in_defense_of_black_rage _michael_brown_police_and_the_american_dream.

Coulthard, Glen. 2014. *Red Skin, White Masks: Rejecting the Colonial Politics of Recognition.* Minneapolis: University of Minnesota Press.

Davis, Angela. 2016. *Freedom Is a Constant Struggle: Ferguson, Palestine, and the Foundations of a Movement.* Chicago: Haymarket Books.

Dawson, Michael C. 2000. *Black Visions: The Roots of Contemporary African-American Political Ideologies.* Chicago: University of Chicago Press.

Dawson, Michael C. 2011. *Not in Our Lifetimes: The Future of Black Politics.* Chicago: University of Chicago Press.

DeGagne, Alexa. 2016. "On Anger and Its Uses for Activism." Paper presented at the annual meeting of the Canadian Political Science Association, University of Calgary, May 31.

DelReal, Jose A. 2016. "'Get 'Em Out!' Racial Tensions Explode at Donald Trump's Rallies." *Washington Post*, March 12. www.washingtonpost.com/politics/get-him-out-racial -tensions-explode-at-donald-trumps-rallies/2016/03/11/b9764884-e6ee-11e5-bc08 -3e03a5b41910_story.html.

Demertzis, Nicolas, ed. 2013. *Emotions in Politics: The Affect Dimension in Political Tension.* New York: Palgrave Macmillan.

DiAngelo, Robin. 2011. "White Fragility." *International Journal of Critical Pedagogy* 3, no. 3: 54–70.

Dolgert, Stefan. 2016. "The Praise of Ressentiment; or, How I Learned to Stop Worrying and Love Donald Trump." *New Political Science* 38, no. 3: 354–70.

DuBois, W. E. B. (1935) 1998. *Black Reconstruction in America, 1860–1880.* New York: Free Press.

Fanon, Frantz. 1963. *The Wretched of the Earth.* Translated by Richard Philcox. New York: Grove.

Garza, Alicia. 2014. "A Herstory of the #BlackLivesMatter Movement." *The Feminist Wire* (blog), October 7. www.thefeministwire.com/2014/10/blacklivesmatter-2.

Goleman, Daniel. 2005. *Emotional Intelligence: Why It Can Matter More than IQ.* New York: Bantam Books.

Grow, Kory. 2014. "Lauryn Hill Dedicates 'Black Rage' Song to Ferguson." *Rolling Stone*, August 21. www.rollingstone.com/music/news/lauryn-hill-black-rage-new-song-ferguson-20140821.

Harris, Fredrick. 2015. "The Next Civil Rights Movement?" *Dissent*, Summer. www.dissent magazine.org/article/black-lives-matter-new-civil-rights-movement-fredrick-harris.

Hesse, Barnor. 2011. "Self-Fulfilling Prophecy: The Postracial Horizon." *South Atlantic Quarterly* 110, no. 1: 155–78.

Hill, Lauryn. 2014. "Black Rage (#BlackLivesMatter Edition)." YouTube video, 4:27. Posted by Nathan Bean, November 26, 2014. www.youtube.com/watch?v=xAhFAgQGf88.

Hill, Marc Lamont. 2016. *Nobody: Casualties of America's War on the Vulnerable, from Ferguson to Flint and Beyond.* New York: Atria Books.

Hochschild, Arlie Russell. 2003. *The Managed Heart: Commercialization of Human Feeling.* Twentieth-anniversary edition. Berkeley: University of California Press.

Holmes, Mary. 2004. "Feeling beyond the Rules: Politicizing the Sociology of Emotion and Anger in Feminist Politics." *European Journal of Social Theory* 7, no. 2: 209–27.

Hooker, Juliet. 2016. "Black Lives Matter and the Paradoxes of U.S. Black Politics: From Democratic Sacrifice to Democratic Repair." *Political Theory* 44, no. 4: 448–69.

Hutchison, Emma, and Roland Bleiker. 2014. "Theorizing Emotions in World Politics." *International Theory* 6, no. 3: 491–514.

Jasper, James M. 2011. "Emotions and Social Movements: Twenty Years of Theory and Research." *Annual Review of Sociology* 37: 285–303.

Jasper, James M. 2014. "Constructing Indignation: Anger Dynamics in Protest Movements." *Emotion Review* 6, no. 3: 208–13.

Kalberg, Stephen. 1980. "Max Weber's Types of Rationality: Cornerstones for the Analysis of Rationalization Processes in History." *American Journal of Sociology* 85, no. 5: 1145–79.

Kindy, Kimberly, and Kimbriell Kelly. 2015. "Thousands Dead, Few Prosecuted." *Washington Post*, April 11. www.washingtonpost.com/sf/investigative/2015/04/11/thousands-dead-few-prosecuted.

King, Martin Luther, Jr. 1986. *A Testament of Hope: The Essential Writings and Speeches of Martin Luther King, Jr.* Edited by James M. Washington. New York: HarperCollins.

Lebron, Christopher. 2013. *The Color of Our Shame: Race and Justice in Our Time.* Oxford: Oxford University Press.

Leys, Ruth. 2011. "The Turn to Affect: A Critique." *Critical Inquiry* 37, no. 3: 434–72.

Lorde, Audre. 1997. "The Uses of Anger." *Women's Studies Quarterly* 25, nos. 1–2: 278–85.

Lyman, Peter. 2004. "The Domestication of Anger: The Use and Abuse of Anger in Politics." *European Journal of Social Theory* 7, no. 2: 133–47.

McKinley, James C., Jr., and Al Baker. 2014. "Grand Jury System, with Exceptions, Favors the Police in Fatalities." *New York Times*, December 7. www.nytimes.com/2014/12/08/nyregion/grand-juries-seldom-charge-police-officers-in-fatal-actions.html.

Mihai, Mihaela. 2016. *Negative Emotions and Transitional Justice.* New York: Columbia University Press.

Minow, Martha. 1998. *Between Vengeance and Forgiveness: Facing History after Genocide and Mass Violence.* Boston: Beacon.

Movement for Black Lives. 2016. "A Vision for Black Lives: Policy Demands for Black Freedom, Power, and Justice." http://policy.m4bl.org/.

Nietzsche, Friedrich. 1989. *On the Genealogy of Morals and Ecce Homo.* Edited by Walter Kaufmann. Translated by Walter Kaufmann and R. J. Hollingdale. New York: Vintage.

Nussbaum, Martha. 2016. *Anger and Forgiveness: Resentment, Generosity, Justice.* New York: Oxford University Press.

Olson, Joel. 2004. *The Abolition of White Democracy.* Minneapolis: University of Minnesota Press.

Orbe, Mark. 2015. "#AllLivesMatter as a Post-Racial Rhetorical Strategy." *Journal of Contemporary Rhetoric* 5, nos. 3–4: 90–98.

Pew Research Center. 2016. *Partisanship and Political Animosity in 2016.* Washington, DC: Pew Research Center. www.people-press.org/2016/06/22/partisanship-and-political-animosity-in-2016.

Piven, Frances Fox. 2006. *Challenging Authority: How Ordinary People Change America.* Lanham, MD: Rowman and Littlefield.

Rankine, Claudia. 2015. "The Condition of Black Life Is One of Mourning." *New York Times*, June 22. www.nytimes.com/2015/06/22/magazine/the-condition-of-black-life-is-one-of-mourning.html.

Roediger, David R. (1991) 2007. *The Wages of Whiteness: Race and the Making of the American Working Class.* New York: Verso.

Rogers, Melvin L. 2014. "Introduction: Disposable Lives." *Theory and Event* 17, no. S3. http://muse.jhu.edu/journals/theory_and_event/v017/17.3S.rogers.html.

Ross, Andrew A. G. 2014. *Mixed Emotions: Beyond Fear and Hatred in International Conflict.* Chicago: University of Chicago Press.

Schaap, Andrew. 2004. "Political Reconciliation through a Struggle for Recognition?" *Social and Legal Studies* 13, no. 4: 523–40.

Schmitter, Philippe C., and Terry Lynn Karl. 1991. "What Democracy Is . . . and Is Not." *Journal of Democracy* 2, no. 3: 75–88.

Stinson, Philip M. 2015. "Police Shootings: A New Problem or Business as Usual?" *Uprooting Criminology* (blog), September 1. http://works.bepress.com/philip_stinson/62.

Taibbi, Matt. 2015. "Why Baltimore Blew Up." *Rolling Stone*, May 26. www.rollingstone.com/politics/news/why-baltimore-blew-up-20150526.

Taylor, Keeanga-Yamahtta. 2016. *From #BlackLivesMatter to Black Liberation.* Chicago: Haymarket Books.

Thompson, Simon. 2006. "Anger and the Struggle for Justice." In Clarke, Hoggett, and Thompson, *Emotion, Politics, and Society,* 123–44.

Weber, Max. (1930) 1992. *The Protestant Ethic and the Spirit of Capitalism.* Translated by Talcott Parsons. New York: Routledge.

Juliet Hooker

Black Protest / White Grievance: On the Problem of White Political Imaginations Not Shaped by Loss

At the end of the nineteenth century, the African American thinker, journalist, and antilynching crusader Ida B. Wells (1970: 70) observed that the cause of the pervasive antiblack violence and racial terror that characterized the post-Reconstruction era was the white Southerner's *"resentment* that the Negro was no longer his plaything, his servant, and his source of income" (emphasis added). Wells's observation more than a hundred years ago illuminates a key political problematic and philosophical dilemma of our racial present. In the early twenty-first century, politics in the United States and many parts of Europe appears to be driven by white inability to cope with (often symbolic) losses and the racial resentment that accompanies it. Simultaneously, the anti–police violence protests that erupted in Ferguson, Missouri, in 2014 and Baltimore in 2015, and the subsequent disproportionate police repression of citizen protesters, marked an important inflection point in US racial politics. The protests signaled a potential moment of black political radicalization, when pragmatic forms of black politics principally aimed at descriptive representation have been overshadowed by a vocal movement seeking to dismantle some of the key pillars of contemporary

The South Atlantic Quarterly 116:3, July 2017
DOI 10.1215/00382876-3961450 © 2017 Duke University Press

white supremacy: mass incarceration, violent policing, a biased criminal justice system, and the pervasive criminalization of black life.[1] These connections are reflected in the Black Lives Matter movement's call to defund the police and invest in black communities instead. The visibility of the Black Lives Matter movement has thus once again foregrounded fundamental questions for black political thought about the forms of black politics and the aims of black protest.[2]

A recurring theme in reactions to the current global wave of black protest, from uprisings against police violence in the United States to the "fallist" university student protests in South Africa, has been a critique of the use of disruptive tactics by protesters and their refusal to abide by the so-called norms of democratic civility.[3] Refusals to contain black rage are said to be counterproductive because they alienate potential white allies. Yet such critiques are based on a number of mistaken assumptions about the history of black activism. This is especially true of the dominant official romantic narrative of the 1960s US civil rights movement, which emphasizes its commitment to nonviolence rather than its more confrontational tactics (see Hooker 2016). What is often left uninterrogated in calls for more "civil" forms of black protest, moreover, are the very conditions of possibility for the production of "white empathy." Indeed, there is a certain irony in the expectation that the aim of black politics should be to elicit white empathy, as there is an important distinction between empathy and political solidarity. To have empathy is to be able to see and identify with the pain or suffering of others. Empathy can thus remain in the realm of feeling without implying action, and it can also depend on seeing the other as like oneself in some fundamental way. In contrast, political solidarity does not depend on prepolitical bonds and requires taking action to redress injustice. The struggle for racial justice thus requires much more than white empathy (see Hooker 2009).

More centrally, however, if, to paraphrase Wells, white resentment erupts when nonwhites are "no longer playthings, servants, or sources of income," then an important question for black political thought (and democratic theory) is how to theorize the kinds of (white) political imaginaries and practices of politics wrought by the absence of political loss. Instead of focusing on how different forms of black politics affect the legibility of black loss, then, this essay interrogates how white grievance, particularly the inability to accept loss (both material and symbolic), continues to be the dominant force shaping contemporary racial politics.

To be sure, not all individual white persons are motivated by a sense of racial grievance.[4] Yet the success of Donald Trump's xenophobic, racist, misogynist campaign, which led to his victory in the 2016 presidential election in the United States, and the successful campaign for "Brexit" in the United Kingdom driven by racial resentment against immigrants (see Emejulu 2016) provide ample evidence that much of contemporary politics in the developed West is being driven by a specific form of racial nostalgia that magnifies symbolic black gains into occasions of white dislocation and displacement.

Drawing on Frederick Douglass, W. E. B. DuBois, Danielle S. Allen, Joel Olson, and Charles W. Mills, I sketch the elements of white commitment to mastery or political rule and trace the political constitution of "white grievance." Theorizing white inability to cope with loss as a political and ideological force that is relatively mainstream and structural shows that it would be a mistake to cordon off this political phenomenon as an anomalous or extremist development. Specifically, I argue that the political imagination of white citizens has been shaped not by the experience of loss but rather by different forms of white supremacy and that this results in a distorted form of racial political math that sees black gains as white losses, and not simply losses but defeats.[5] As a result, in moments when white privilege is in crisis because white dominance is threatened, many white citizens not only are unable or unwilling to recognize black suffering; they mobilize a sense of white victimhood in response.[6] If political solidarity is an elusive and at times unattainable goal, then the problem of racial justice is how to confront the phenomenon of white loss, real or perceived, material or symbolic. The political and philosophical problem driving contemporary racial politics is not uncivil black protest or black rage but instead white citizens' continued investment in forms of political mastery or rule that are not only incompatible with but indeed directly opposed to racial justice and democratic politics.

Whiteness and Political Rule

As Allen has aptly noted, democratic politics requires that citizens be able to cope with loss. She asks: "How are citizens to think about the fact that a regime constructed for the good of all (liberal democracy) must make day-to-day decisions that are better for some or that are directly hurtful for others? . . . All citizens must confront the paradox that they have been promised sovereignty and rarely feel it. Herein lies the single most difficult feature of life in a democracy. Democratic citizens are by definition empowered only in order to be disempowered" (Allen 2004: 41). Yet, historically, democratic loss was hardly evenly distributed. In herrenvolk democracies such as the United States (characterized by political equality among whites and tyranny for nonwhites), what developed instead was "the two-pronged citizenship of domination and acquiescence . . . [which] dealt with the inevitable fact of loss in political life by assigning to one group [whites] all the work of being sovereign, and to another group [blacks] most of the work of accepting the significant losses that kept the polity stable" (41). As I have noted elsewhere (see Hooker 2016), I disagree with Allen's framing of the peaceful acceptance of political loss by racialized minorities who have already suffered losses as a form of civic virtue. What I am interested in thinking about here, however, is how we might understand the consequences of what Allen refers to as "the work of being sovereign" on the civic capacities and political dispositions of members of the dominant group. In other words, if acceptance of loss is necessary for democracy, what happens when a group that is unaccustomed to loss is confronted with it? What kinds of political imagination and practices of politics are wrought by this absence of political loss? Once the reality of racialized citizenship is taken into account, it is clear that it is those citizens who need it most who have been least conditioned to cultivate the necessary democratic capacity of accepting the experience (true for all citizens) of frustrated sovereignty.

.   In effect, the problem is that if politics entails ruling and being ruled in turn, as Aristotle suggested, whites (or members of the dominant group in a herrenvolk democracy) have been accustomed only to ruling, not to being ruled in turn. As Olson has argued, white citizenship has historically been a form of racial standing. "The privileges of white citizenship . . . are public, psychological, and material. . . . Whiteness grants working-class whites a special status—not quite rich but *not quite powerless*—that becomes the focus of white citizens' political energy rather than challenges to elite rule" (Olson 2004: xx–xxi; emphasis added). For the white majority, being good democratic citizens would thus entail accepting the loss of exclusive access to political power and privileged social and economic standing. White dominance has resulted in a narrow political imagination that constrains the way whites understand citizenship, as asymmetrical access to institutional political power vis-a-vis racial "others." It has also resulted in "a shallow definition of freedom limited to economic opportunity, the absence of government interference in private ventures, and the right to elect public officials. . . . [It] presumes that the community is an obstacle to individual freedom rather than its conduit" (61). In such an understanding of democratic politics as a zero-sum game in which gains by other groups are experienced as losses by the dominant group, white losses become magnified while black losses are rendered invisible.

This unspoken racial syllogism—white loss is unacceptable; black gains are illegitimate; black loss is therefore invisible—is in turn made possible by the workings of what Mills has called "the epistemology of ignorance." Mills (2007: 20) defines "white ignorance" as "an ignorance, a nonknowing, that is not contingent, but in which race—white racism and/or white racial domination and their ramifications—plays a crucial causal role." The "racialized causality" of white ignorance encompasses both

> straightforward racist motivation and more impersonal social-structural causation, which may be operative even if the cognizer in question is not racist. . . . Racialized causality can give rise to . . . white ignorance, straightforwardly for a racist cognizer, but also indirectly for a nonracist cognizer who may form mistaken beliefs (e.g., that after the abolition of slavery in the United States, blacks generally had opportunities equal to whites) because of the social suppression of the pertinent knowledge, though without prejudice himself. So white ignorance need not always be based on bad faith. Obviously from the point of view of a social epistemology, especially after the transition from de jure to de facto white supremacy, it is precisely this kind of white ignorance that is most important. (21)

White ignorance is a crucial feature of the politics of white grievance. It allows whites to deny the unearned advantages they have accrued as a result of white supremacy, and it also makes it possible for them to reject the assumption of any responsibility as individuals for its continuation.

In the essay "The White World," DuBois recounted the views of a liberal (for 1940) white friend, who was simultaneously noncognizant of his adherence to whiteness and committed to the white world's domination over the darker world. "Now until my friend had reached the age of thirty he had not known that he was a white man, or at least he had not realized it. . . . But lately . . . he had noticed with some disturbed feeling that Negroes in particular were not nearly as agreeable and happy as they used to be. He had not for years been able to get a good, cheap colored cook and the last black yard man asked quite exorbitant wages" (DuBois 1986: 671). In matters of politics, likewise, "he could not conceive of a world where white people did not rule colored people" (673). The attitudes and opinions of DuBois's liberal white friend illustrate one of the key ways in which white ignorance functions politically. The unconscious level at which affective attachment to white dominance operates for many white persons—including the lack of recognition that they see themselves as "white," that is, that they are just as enmeshed in and committed to "identity politics" as nonwhites—enables a mistaken belief that they are committed to color blindness. Ironically, white citizens are thus simultaneously attached to white dominance and committed to minimizing the impact of historical white supremacy. As a result, gains by nonwhites are experienced as instances of loss, even if these losses are just, that is, even when they redress long-standing racial injustices and inequalities. It is thus important to note that black and white losses are not equivalent in normative terms. If the so-called liberal democracies of the West are to become truly racially egalitarian, white citizens will need to accept the loss of political mastery. They will have to come to accept being ruled in turn.

Ostensibly, this acceptance of the end of white political dominance already occurred in the United States with the end of racial segregation and belated legal enforcement of black electoral participation via the Voting Rights Act of 1965. But these civil rights victories, momentous as they were, did not fundamentally transform the character of the racial state or, as a result, white expectations of political dominance.[7] The result is that whites as a group have been theoretically confronted with the possibility of sharing political rule with nonwhites but in practice have rarely had to experience it. As Olson observed, racial standing allowed working-class whites to avoid feeling "powerless." This feeling of frustrated sovereignty or powerlessness is what Allen argues needs to be managed for democratic politics to endure. She suggests that "democratic citizens have a special need for symbols and the world of fantasy precisely because their real political world does not and cannot give them the autonomy, freedom, and sovereignty it promises" (Allen 2004: 22). Allen's insight is helpful for understanding the wrenching loss that many experienced at the election of the first and only black president in the history of the United States. The president's whiteness had been symbolic reassurance that political power also remained thus. White citizens, who as a group have historically been able to exercise political rule, have thus been conditioned to expect continued white dominance as a key feature of their political identity, which in turn renders white loss unacceptable.

There are two specific features of the conflation between whiteness and political rule that are relevant for a discussion of the philosophical problem posed by white inability to cope with loss. One is the expectation that policy debates should be oriented toward their grievances and material needs, that is, that politics should center the concerns of whites as a group. For instance, the rejoinder that "all lives matter" to "black lives matter" protests perfectly captures the seeming absurdity of how attempts to redress existing injustices (in this case the disproportionate police killings of unarmed black citizens) can generate feelings of exclusion. In other words, if all lives already mattered equally, it would not be necessary to assert that black lives *also* matter. The other feature of the (often unconscious) conflation between whiteness and political rule is the complex distortion of historical narratives about white supremacy. On the one hand, there is a reflexive desire to relegate racism to the distant past in order to deny nonwhite subordination in the present, combined, on the other hand, with a simultaneous nostalgia for unchallenged eras of white dominance. The public remembrance and reverence for symbols of the Confederacy in many states in the US South in the name of supposedly nonracist appeals to "tradition" illustrate this dynamic, as does the slogan "make America great again." The effect of these two aspects of the conflation between whiteness and political rule for contemporary racial politics is that when white vulnerability (real or perceived) is politicized, it results in moments of existential crisis of whiteness with profoundly dangerous consequences.

Racial Politics in the Obama Era

The public euphoria that greeted the election of the country's only black president, an occasion widely seen as evidence that the United States had finally become the vaunted postracial society it had supposedly always aspired to be, quickly gave way, during the two terms of his presidency, to an era of heightened white racial resentment and outright racist backlash. Indeed, Obama's election was not the result of radical transformations in racial attitudes. An empirical analysis by Vincent Hutchings (2009: 917), for example, found "scant evidence of a decline in the racial divide. Blacks and Whites remain as far apart on racial policy matters in 2008 as in 1988. . . . Younger cohorts of Whites are no more racially liberal in 2008 than they were in 1988." There is also substantial evidence of a resurgence in old-fashioned racism during Obama's presidency (Tesler 2013).[8] In many ways this should not have been surprising, as, historically, progress toward racial equality in the United States has been followed by eras of retrenchment and reconsolidation of white supremacy. Emancipation and Reconstruction, for example, were followed by the consolidation of Jim Crow, racial segregation, and official adherence to white supremacy during "the nadir" era of US race relations characterized by racial terror, political disenfranchisement, and. xenophobia. Likewise, the civil rights victories of the 1960s were followed by the retrenchment of the welfare state (which was justified by racially coded appeals) and the concomitant rise of mass incarceration that continued to ensure material racial inequality despite the absence of mandated racial segregation. Historically, then, white citizens have not coped well with loss. They have not shown the kind of peaceful acquiescence to loss that Allen argues is necessary for democratic stability. Yet emancipation and the civil rights victories of the 1960s were wide-scale transformations in the US racial order, whereas the election of a single black officeholder, albeit to the highest political office in the land, did not alter the disproportionate mass incarceration rates of blacks and Latinos, the income and wealth disparities between whites and nonwhites exacerbated by the 2008 financial crisis, the continued deportation and harassment of undocumented immigrants, or the continued confinement of poor nonwhite citizens to "the carceral spaces of the prison and the ghetto" (Browne and Carrington 2012: 117). It is undeniable, however, that the election of a black president, as symbolic a gain as this was for nonwhites, was experienced by some sectors of US whiteness as a moment of existential crisis, when expectations of white privilege were upended and white dominance was threatened. This negative reaction was perhaps best exemplified by the rise of the Tea Party and its calls to "take our country back."

To understand why the election of a black president was experienced by a significant portion of white citizens as a moment of existential crisis—despite the fact that Obama campaigned and governed as a mainstream Democratic politician committed to racial reconciliation and to transcending race—it is instructive to recall the fears of a "black emperor" elicited by the enfranchisement of African Americans following the abolition of slavery almost a century and a half ago. Douglass (1872–73: 4–5), the brilliant black thinker, orator, and ex–fugitive slave, mocked these fears of "black supremacy," which fancifully imagined that were the United States to allow its black inhabitants to cease being mere chattel, "the republic . . . [would] give place to a vast American empire under the sway of a jet black emperor who shall have a snow white empress—a court of all shades and colors—and a code of laws considerately enacted to protect the unfortunate whites from insults offered by the insolent and dominant blacks!" If the mere prospect of the end of enslavement and subsequent black enfranchisement conjured "the phantom of black supremacy" (5) and miscegenation for white observers during the nineteenth century, then it is possible to understand how the election of a black president in the twenty-first century could become a lightning rod for this persistent fear of black rule.

A key factor driving resurgent white nationalism in the United States is thus the compounded losses that some sectors of whiteness see themselves as having suffered since 2008. First there was Obama's presidency (including his initial election and then reelection), coupled with the reemergence of a highly visible and energized black protest movement. Not only has this level of sustained black protest not been seen in the United States since the 1960s; the Black Lives Matter movement emerged in the age of social media, when black suffering and black losses could be amplified and broadcast in a way that made them viscerally accessible via the continuous loop of viral videos showing police killings of unarmed blacks. While it is undoubtedly true that the visual evidence was disputed and the encounters with the police endlessly dissected, Black Lives Matter protesters refused to adopt frames of black respectability to couch their assertion that black life was disposable in the United States, and their critique was leveled directly at representatives of the state: from the police, prosecutors, district attorneys, and the criminal justice system as a whole to elected officials such as mayors and governors. There is thus an important paradox in the racial politics of the Obama era. On the one hand, there has been a palpable rise in feelings of white grievance among some sectors of US whiteness as a result of symbolic black gains. But, on the other hand, these so-called black gains are rather tenuous. Indeed, the difficulty of grappling with current perceptions of white loss is that during the post–civil rights era black politics has been constrained by neoliberalism and political pragmatism; it has been predominantly oriented toward palatable forms of liberal reform. The paradox of contemporary white loss is thus that it is driven by symbolic black gains (such as the Obama presidency) that function to support the status quo of, at best, incremental change toward racial equality, accompanied by the retrenchment or slow erosion of the significant civil rights victories of the 1960s.

The Terrain of White Grievance: Material and Symbolic Loss

If the post–civil rights era has not been a period of rapidly expanding black/nonwhite gains, if it has rather been characterized by, at best, incremental and tenuous advancement, how are we to understand the current sense of white grievance?[9] The emerging explanation for white racial resentment in the Obama era has been that it is driven by working-class whites who feel left behind economically and alienated from the political process. Yet the white working-class voters who appear to be most motivated by a sense of white grievance are in fact still economically better off than most nonwhites (Silver 2016). Of the factors that drove support for Trump's presidential victory in 2016, for example—in a campaign characterized by racist rhetoric that explicitly sought to mobilize a sense of white grievance—economic losses were only part of the answer. Instead, racial resentment appears to have motivated many of his supporters. According to political scientists Jason McDaniel and Sean McElwee (2016a, 2016b), "polling data suggests that racial attitudes, including racial resentment and explicit racial stereotypes, [were] the more important factor" driving support for Trump. Indeed, when the geography of white loss is mapped, it is clear that racial resentment is not confined to the South, that it spans liberal and conservative states, as well as rural and suburban communities (Irwin and Katz 2016). White grievance thus cannot be understood only in economic terms. While material and symbolic loss are neither disconnected nor opposed to each other, accounting for symbolic loss is crucial to understanding why white racial resentment has become a galvanizing political force in an era of rights retrenchment and tenuous (at best) economic advances for nonwhites. I argue that in the Obama era, white racial resentment has been driven in important ways by symbolic loss.

To make sense of white grievance in the context of incremental or largely symbolic black/nonwhite gains, it is necessary to make a conceptual distinction between material and symbolic loss. This is to suggest not that these two dimensions of white loss are discontiguous from each other but rather that it is possible to distinguish between them for analytical purposes. Distinguishing between material and symbolic loss is important because it has normative implications for how we assess different forms of white grievance. For example, white material losses raise issues of fairness in a democratic polity when they are framed as part of a larger problem of rising socioeconomic inequality. They are more normatively suspect, however, if what is being mourned is relative white economic advantage over nonwhites. Symbolic losses tend to be even more problematic, because they flow directly from white citizens' continued investment in forms of political rule that are incompatible with racial egalitarianism. Indeed, racial justice and democratic politics precisely require that whites learn to accept loss, both material and symbolic.

It is undeniable that the white working class has suffered significant material losses in recent decades.[10] The United States in the 2010s is a society defined by growing economic inequality, where the differences between the top 1 percent and the rest are stark. In economic terms, it could be argued that only the 1 percent is winning, that everyone else is losing. Working- and middle-class whites and nonwhites are thus suffering from similar economic trends, yet many of the former have (wrongly) attributed their declining economic prospects to competition from nonwhite workers, especially migrants.

In fact, working-class whites still, on average, have higher incomes than working-class blacks and Latinos. Indeed, the economic structural changes that are now limiting the prospects of middle- and working-class whites began to affect African Americans in the 1970s. Latinos and African Americans also disproportionately suffered the brunt of the economic losses of the 2008 financial crisis and the ensuing recession. According to the Federal Reserve Bank of St. Louis (2013), during the Great Recession "families that were younger, that [were headed by individuals who] had less than a college education and/or [that] were members of a historically disadvantaged minority group (African-Americans or Hispanics of any race) suffered particularly large wealth losses."

Material losses are thus not confined to the white working class. Yet it is middle- and working-class whites who have apparently been politically galvanized by declining economic opportunities and economic insecurity. In fact, the shared losses of the white working class and the black and Latino working and middle classes are obscured by long-standing socioeconomic gaps between blacks/Latinos and whites in the United States. Thus the problem is not that whites are the only group experiencing material loss or that white economic losses are the result of black gains. Rather, the loss that working-class whites are experiencing is of their relative privilege vis-à-vis blacks and Latinos, which is eroding. Where material losses are concerned, then, to the extent that contemporary white racial resentment is being driven by the loss of white economic privilege or advantage, it is normatively suspect. White material losses do represent a legitimate grievance, however, if they are framed as part of a larger problem of rising socioeconomic inequality that is also affecting nonwhites.

It would thus be a mistake to attribute white racial resentment solely to material loss. Trump supporters, for example, some of whom have erupted in outbursts of white rage, have expressed feeling empowered by his unequivocal embrace of white nativism and his populist, xenophobic, and racist appeals targeting Latino immigrants, Muslims, and Black Lives Matter protesters. White grievance is also gendered and sexualized in particular ways, as Trump supporters also express misogynistic and homophobic fears about gains by women and lesbian, gay, bisexual, transgender, and queer (LGBTQ) citizens. These disaffected and aggrieved white voters believe that "minorities commit crimes with impunity, that illegal immigrants get benefits at higher rates than Americans, that gays and Muslims are afforded special status by the government" and "lament that Confederate symbols, and the people whose heritage they represent, are sidelined while diversity is celebrated"

(Ball 2016). Contemporary white grievance thus is not only propelled by economic decline but rather seems to consistently span both material and symbolic losses.

White grievance in the Obama era is driven primarily by material losses. Instead, it is symbolic losses that increasingly seem to propel white rage. There are numerous examples of symbolic white loss, from online outrage that the two main characters in the 2015 *Star Wars: The Force Awakens* film are a female Jedi and a black stormtrooper, to complaints about the measures implemented to ensure greater diversity of Oscar nominations, to the backlash against Beyoncé's performance at the 2016 Country Music Awards because of the expressions of black pride and supposed demonization of the police in her visual album *Lemonade* (Corbett 2016). I briefly analyze three emblematic instances of symbolic loss—the Blue Lives Matter and All Lives Matter campaigns, the controversy over the decision to add a black woman to a US treasury bill for the first time, and the debate over the removal of symbols honoring the Confederacy in the wake of the Charleston, South Carolina, massacre—to show how white grievance is generated by continued expectations of political, economic, and social dominance.

White Symbolic Loss: All Lives Matter, Harriet Tubman, and the Confederate Flag

According to Alicia Garza (2014), one of the three black women who coined the hashtag #BlackLivesMatter, which later became a national organization, it was intended "as a call to action for Black people after 17-year-old Trayvon Martin was posthumously placed on trial for his own murder and the killer, George Zimmerman, was not held accountable for the crime he committed. . . . Black Lives Matter is an ideological and political intervention in a world where Black lives are systematically and intentionally targeted for demise." That the response to a movement created to bring attention to the disproportionate violence faced by black people should be the slogan "All lives matter" reveals how white grievance is in many ways constituted in response to symbolic losses. The symbolic decentering of whiteness implied by saying #BlackLivesMatter could only be taken as a devaluation of white lives by those who believe that politics should always center the concerns of whites as a group. There are profound material consequences to the symbolic loss of authority experienced by the police in the wake of Black Lives Matter protests, however, as illustrated by the emergence of Blue Lives Matter legislation that makes it a hate crime to target police officers. These laws, which have been proposed in Florida, Kentucky, New York, Texas, and Wisconsin and enacted in Louisiana, equate the risks that police officers face (because of their chosen occupation) with discrimination based on race, gender, sexual orientation, and religion. The rationale for Blue Lives Matter laws rests on a conflation of critiques of the use of excessive force by police officers and militarization of law enforcement with "hatred" of the police. This in turn functions to transform the police, who routinely go unpunished for killing unarmed black people, into the real victims. As the poet Claudia Rankine (2014: 135) eloquently phrases it: "Because white men can't police their imagination black people are dying." The Black Lives Matter movement challenged the unquestioned deference to state authority and the hagiography of the police that became de rigueur in the United States after 9/11, and this symbolic loss mobilized fears of anti–police violence embodied in Blue Lives Matter legislation that works to displace and obscure the actual dead black body. The symbolic and the material are thus clearly connected, and indeed inextricably intertwined, in the politics of white grievance. Blue Lives Matter as a response to the symbolic displacement of Black Lives Matter has clear material consequences for the politics of race, policing, and blackness. It erases the dead black body, furthering the continued disposability that Black Lives Matter was meant to highlight and counter.

Compared to the Blue Lives Matter counterprotests, the decision by the US Department of the Treasury to add the fugitive slave, abolitionist, and advocate of women's suffrage Harriet Tubman to the $20 bill as part of a broader redesign of US currency would seem like an improbable instance of white loss. The addition of Tubman, along with Sojourner Truth, Susan B. Anthony, Elizabeth Cady Stanton, Lucrecia Mott, Alice Paul, the opera singer Marian Anderson, and the Reverend Martin Luther King Jr., to the roster of white male founders and presidents on US currency better reflects the country's gender and racial diversity. And even after these additions, white males will still significantly outnumber women and racial minorities on US currency. Why, then, did Tubman's inclusion generate so much controversy? The *American Spectator*, for example, argued that while "Tubman was a remarkable, tough-minded woman . . . she was not the main story of slavery, the Civil War, or abolitionism. . . . She's history as optics and affirmative action. . . . For those who want to re-script the nation's past, American history is too male and too white. To correct that imbalance, heroes, symbols, and legends must conform to strict rubrics of race, class, and gender" (Sewall 2016). For those who viewed this as an instance of white loss, it represented a dislocation of white males from their central role in US history. At the same time, the claim that Tubman's inclusion is "history as optics and affir- mative action" reflects an axiom of the politics of white grievance that women, racial minorities, and LGBTQ citizens are the recipients of special, unearned "gifts" from a state that is now committed to perpetual white loss. The article also echoed the fears of "black supremacy" that stalked Douglass's contempo- raries and raised the specter of black rage: "A regime whose creation stories and legends turn on 'enslavers' and 'invaders,' however, cannot long survive. Ritual shaming is not a nation builder. Sooner or later bold paladins will feel it's their duty to even the score with their oppressors, or failing that, their privileged descendants" (Sewall 2016). In this apocalyptic vision, symbolic white loss is the Trojan horse for violent white subordination.

The controversy over Tubman's inclusion on US currency perfectly captures the contorted racial math of the Obama era, where tenuous or purely symbolic black gains are experienced as magnified white losses. As many black commentators observed, the decision to replace Andrew Jackson with Tubman is exemplary of the kind of token change that has character- ized black politics in the post–civil rights era. It is an example of symbolic representation without institutional transformation. Black observers ques- tioned the meaning of the decision to place Tubman on US currency in 2016, when, almost daily, black citizens were being killed by agents of the same state that sanctioned the institution of slavery that Tubman valiantly fought against. They also noted the irony of a black woman who had been bought and sold as property being placed on US currency, when ex-slaves and their descendants have never been compensated for their unpaid labor. Not surprisingly, then, many black observers viewed the decision to place Tubman's visage on US currency, not as some kind of major gain, but as a ruse of power instead.

An even more pointed instance of the unacceptability of white loss is the shift in the debate about the removal of Confederate symbols that fol- lowed the mass murder of nine innocent black citizens in a church in Charleston by an avowed white supremacist shooter in 2015. The Charleston massacre was undoubtedly an instance in which blacks suffered horrific losses. It took place in a historic black institution, Emanuel African Method- ist Episcopal Church, associated with various black freedom struggles, including the failed slave revolt led by Denmark Vesey in 1822. Its victims, who ranged in age from twenty-six to eighty-seven years old, had gathered together for a prayer service. The Charleston shooting was thus one of the rare instances where the innocence of the black victims could not be ques- tioned and where the racism motivating the shooter was also incontrovertibly established. Following a familiar pattern that has also been replicated in high-profile cases of police killings of black men that have sparked subsequent protests, the relatives of the black dead were asked to express immediate forgiveness to ensure democratic stability. They and the rest of the black community were expected to peacefully accept their deadly losses. At the same time, because the shooter was photographed displaying various symbols of white supremacy, including the Confederate flag, the debate over the meaning of monuments to the Confederacy was immediately reignited. Many who had in the past opposed demands to take down the Confederate flag now joined calls to remove it from the South Carolina statehouse. One commentator in *National Review*, for example, argued that the Confederate flag "represents something more than visceral racial hatred" and bemoaned how "today's 'racial activists' are keen to cast the Civil War as a simple contest of Good-versus-Evil" (Tuttle 2015). He nevertheless also explicitly invoked the idea that white symbolic loss might in this instance be necessary to atone for the immeasurable black losses suffered as a result of the Charleston massacre: "If reducing the visibility of these symbols would offer relief to those genuinely hurt, and would remove an object of contention keeping persons of different races from cooperating to advance *true* racial justice, that is something supporters of Confederate symbols should be able to do."

The about-face on the removal of the Confederate flag in South Carolina following the Charleston massacre is instructive regarding the lack of equivalence between black and white loss. While this was an instance in which, for the most part, a sense of white grievance was not mobilized in response to a symbolic white loss (the removal of the Confederate flag), it also required horrific and undeniable black losses in order to render minor (in comparison) white loss palatable. To put it starkly, nine innocent black citizens—Sharonda Coleman-Singleton, Cynthia Hurd, Susie Jackson, Ethel Lance, DePayne Middleton-Doctor, Clementa Pinckney, Tywanza Sanders, Daniel Simmons, and Myra Thompson, because we must say their names— had to die to engender peaceful white acquiescence to this instance of symbolic loss. Needless to say, this is not a sustainable balance sheet of loss.

Blue Lives Matter legislation, Tubman's addition to the $20 bill, and the removal of the Confederate flag after the Charleston massacre thus raise important questions about when white grievance is mobilized and the costs of peaceful white acquiescence to loss. How does the frame of loss help us to understand white racial resentment and particularly the political mobilization of white grievance? During the Obama era, white grievance, especially in response to symbolic loss, has been politicized in a way that echoes earlier resistance to the civil rights movement's efforts to end racial segregation in the 1960s. Viewed through the lens of white loss, attempts to reshape historical narratives to more accurately depict the perspectives of both dominant and oppressed groups are experienced as a deeply unfair dislocation of whiteness, and white maleness in particular, from its central place in US history. As a result, only additive solutions are viewed as legitimate (in the case of the currency redesign, for example, keeping Jackson but adding Tubman), because they continue to validate expectations of white hegemony. From the Black Lives Matter movement, to the face on the $20 bill, to the flag flying over state capitols throughout the South, important sectors of US whiteness have experienced the Obama era as a period of repeated symbolic losses that signal the end of unquestioned white dominance. The irony, of course, is that fears of "black supremacy" and white oppression are surfacing in response to, at best, tenuous or token black gains, coupled with real and deadly material losses. As whites mourn their lost privileges, blacks mourn their dead.

Racial Justice in an Era of White Grievance

In the wake of Ferguson in 2014 and Trump's election, the central question of contemporary racial politics is not whether there will be black uprisings in response to continued injustice but whether whites can learn to cope with political loss. The problem of contemporary racial politics is not black rage but rather white grievance. Can whites learn to accept that their declining economic status is not the result of a trade-off whereby blacks or nonwhites (especially immigrants) are benefiting at their expense? Racial politics in the United States today seems headed for an intractable impasse. On the one hand, there is a highly visible black protest movement galvanized by ongoing police violence, while, on the other hand, there is a large cross-section of whites mobilized by a deeply felt sense of grievance and racial resentment. This does not bode well for the possibility of strides toward racial justice in the immediate future. The legal scholar Derrick Bell (1995) has argued that, historically, black gains in the United States have been achieved when they converged with white self-interest. In the current economic context of declining opportunities for the 99 percent and rising inequality, it is difficult to see white majorities being able to view black or nonwhite gains as anything other than special rights that detract from whites' own prospects. Interest convergence in an era of white grievance driven by deeply felt symbolic losses and objective material decline seems highly unlikely.

It is therefore instructive to turn to an earlier moment in US history to think about the philosophical problem of white moral and political imaginations not shaped by loss. During the nadir or post-Reconstruction era, white supremacy was unquestioned, but there was nevertheless widespread white violence and racial terror, fueled by the backlash against fleeting Reconstruction-era black gains. Then, as now, the racial math was both simple and complex. Blacks were no longer enslaved, but they were also still unfree. Whites were politically, socially, and economically dominant, yet they were so afraid of racial equality that their dominance had to be symbolically and materially reaffirmed in the ritualized public spectacle of lynchings. The dead black body was, then as it is now, the terrain on which white fears of loss of political rule and economic dominance were contested.[11]

In "Why Is the Negro Lynched?," an essay published in 1894, during the height of post-Reconstruction-era racial terror, Douglass described the US body politic as "disfigured" by the "ghastly horrors" of lynching. US democracy, he argued, was being rendered monstrous by the accumulating bodies of black dead produced by the unchecked racial violence of the nadir era. "There is nothing in the history of savages to surpass the blood-chilling horrors and fiendish excesses perpetrated against the coloured people of this country, by the so-called enlightened and Christian people of the South . . . [who] gloat over and prey upon dead bodies," he wrote (Douglass 1955: 492–93). Douglass further argued that the unchecked racial violence of the post-Reconstruction era was directly connected to slavery, which had warped the civic capacities of whites by accustoming them to economic and political mastery and a thorough disregard for black life. White participants in Southern lynch mobs had been "brought up in the exercise of irresponsible power" (505). White Southerners could engage in such violence because they "care no more for the Negro's rights to live than they care for his rights to liberty, or his right to the ballot or any other right" (506). But Douglass's critique of the way US democracy was disfigured by racism was not confined to the South; he noted that the North was also guilty of engaging in less violent forms of repression. "You kill their bodies, we kill their souls" (508).

It is haunting to read Douglass's words (written more than a century ago) today, when police violence continues to *kill our bodies*, while the tacit (and at times explicit) acquiescence to black death by many white citizens motivated by racialized fears of crime continues to *kill our souls*. To extend Douglass's insight, if white humanity is diminished by indifference to black loss, black citizens are doubly burdened by the seemingly unceasing repetition of the following cycle: dead black body, protest, indictment or (more likely) nonindictment, eventual nonconviction, killer walks free. As black citizens continue to be killed, those who remain are forced to bear witness to the dead, to say their names. This too is a continued assault on their souls.

In an apt lesson for how we should approach the problem of white grievance in the twenty-first century, Douglass concluded that the solution to lynching and racial terror was not to frame it as an issue of black struggle. Instead, what was required was change on the part of white citizens. Douglass forcefully rejected the framing of antiblack violence as a "Negro problem." This formula, he argued, "lays the fault at the door of the Negro and removes it from the door of the white man, shields the guilty and blames the innocent, makes the Negro responsible, when it should so make the nation" (518). Douglass's insight precisely speaks to the argument of this essay that the question of what comes after Ferguson, and after Trump, is whether and if white citizens can learn to cope with loss, whether they can reconcile themselves to no longer being able to rule without being ruled in turn. As Douglass argued in 1894: "Let the white people of the North and South conquer their prejudices. . . . Let them give up the idea that they can be free while making the Negro a slave. Let them give up the idea that to degrade the coloured man is to elevate the white man. . . . They are not required to do much. They are only required to undo the evil they have done" (520). In other words, whites must learn to cope with political loss. The resurgent white nationalism and nostalgia for prior eras of nonwhite subordination of the Trump era are a result, to cite a popular meme on black Twitter, of the inability to handle white tears. The often symbolic white losses being mourned are not the kind of political loss that the formerly enslaved and their descendants have had to bear, but the loss of unearned privilege and unjustified advantage. Needless to say, they cannot expect their nonwhite fellow citizens to mourn these losses with them or to share their nostalgia for prior eras of unquestioned white dominance. To be good democratic citizens they must peacefully acquiesce to political loss without mobilizing white grievance.

Notes

1   The rise of the modern carceral state is instrumental in understanding the contemporary links between race, criminalization, and violent policing (see Alexander 2010; Hinton 2016). As the US Department of Justice report on Ferguson (2015) documented, there is also a clear link between neoliberal economic policies that lead to the use of police and court fees as sources of municipal revenue and the overpolicing of poor black communities.

2   The Black Lives Matter movement is a broad coalition of groups and individuals struggling against police violence; it is not only the Black Lives Matter organization per se.
For the movement's policy platform and demands, see Movement for Black Lives 2016.

3   The term *fallist* derives from the successful #RhodesMustFall student protests in
2015 at the University of Cape Town to remove a statue of the British imperialist Cecil J.
Rhodes from campus and the subsequent #FeesMustFall protests of 2015 and 2016 at
various South African universities against fee increases. The demands of student
protesters were quite broad, however, and encompassed issues such as pay for university staff that had been outsourced and privatized, lack of black demographic representation in institutions of higher education in South Africa, and calls to decolonize
the curriculum.

4   I use the terms *white* and *whiteness* to designate a political category that emerged at a
specific historical point in time, that is, with the development of the modern concept of
race and European colonial projects and that continues to confer certain privileges.
More specifically, "white citizenship is the enjoyment of racial standing in a democratic
polity. It is a position of equality and privilege simultaneously: equal to other white citizens yet privileged over those who are not white. It is both a structural location in the
racial order and a product of human agency. Individual whites may consciously defend
their privileges, reject them, or deny they exist, yet the structure of the racial order
makes it difficult for individual whites to 'jump out' of their whiteness at any given
time. The category does not explain every belief or behavior of every white person but
encompasses the structures and social relations that produce white privilege and the
ideas that defend it" (Olson 2004: xix).

5   I refer to black gains specifically here, but the argument applies to those of nonwhites
in general, as illustrated in the United States by the executive orders issued by the
Trump administration banning travel from seven majority Muslim countries or proposing to build a larger border wall between the United States–and Mexico to prevent
Latino immigration.

6   The concept of white privilege refers to the unearned advantages that have accrued to
individual white persons as a result of white supremacy, such as not having to worry
about being killed by the police when pulled over for a routine traffic violation or having
one's credentials and academic achievements questioned in professional settings. By
white dominance I mean that despite demographic changes and the crisis of the white
working class, it remains the case that whites as a group are still economically, politically, and socially dominant in the United States.

7   While descriptive racial representation is hardly a measure of political equality, the lop-
sided composition of US elected officials, especially at the highest levels, illustrates the
issue of continued white expectations of dominance. As of November 2015, for example, only 9 of the 1,963 total members of the United States Senate had been African
American, and only 1 had been a black woman.

8   On the Obama era, see Bobo and Dawson 2009 and Browne and Carrington 2012.

9   Not only do blacks and Latinos have the lowest median household income in the United
States and higher unemployment rates, but the gap between white and black/Latino
income has increased since the 1960s (Woodruff 2013). Disparities in health and education also persist at all levels. In schools, for example, black children are more harshly

and disproportionately punished in comparison to white children (via suspensions, expulsions, etc.), creating a "school-to-prison pipeline" that disproportionately affects their life chances. During the period 2011–12, according to the Department of Education, across the United States, black boys were suspended three times as often as white boys, and black girls were suspended six times as often as white girls (Crenshaw, Ocen, and Nanda 2015).

10   The impact of global economic trends, such as the loss of manufacturing jobs in the United States, has also been accompanied by social dislocations that have affected family structures and health outcomes. Economic changes that favored women's ability to gain jobs in the new economy have altered traditional gender roles and challenged traditional conceptions of masculinity (Rosin 2010). Less economically advantaged white communities are also being affected by difficult social problems, such as unemployment and surges in drug and alcohol addiction, all of which have contributed to an increase in white mortality rates (Case and Deaton 2015). The alarm produced by these trends has led to warnings about a crisis of white working-class values reminiscent of explanations of black poverty rooted in black pathology (see Murray 2013).

11   It is important to note that during the nadir era, while black men were the iconic victims of lynching, Latinos were also lynched and black women also suffered from gendered forms of racial violence, often in the form of unacknowledged sexual assault (see Delgado 2009; Threadcraft 2016).

References

Alexander, Michelle. 2010. *The New Jim Crow: Mass Incarceration in the Age of Colorblindness.* New York: New Press.

Allen, Danielle S. 2004. *Talking to Strangers: Anxieties of Citizenship since* Brown v. Board of Education. Chicago: University of Chicago Press.

Ball, Molly. 2016. "The Resentment Powering Trump." *Atlantic*, March 15. www.theatlantic .com/politics/archive/2016/03/the-resentment-powering-trump/473775.

Bell, Derrick. 1995. "*Brown v. Board of Education* and the Interest Convergence Dilemma." In *Critical Race Theory: The Key Writings That Formed the Movement*, edited by Kimberlé Crenshaw et al., 20–29. New York: New Press.

Bobo, Lawrence D., and Michael C. Dawson. 2009. "A Change Has Come." *Du Bois Review: Social Science Research on Race* 6, no. 1: 1–14.

Browne, Simone, and Ben Carrington. 2012. "The Obamas and the New Politics of Race." *Qualitative Sociology* 35, no. 2: 113–21.

Case, Anne, and Angus Deaton. 2015. "Rising Morbidity and Mortality in Midlife among White Non-Hispanic Americans in the Twenty-First Century." *Proceedings of the National Academy of Sciences* 112, no. 49: 15078–83.

Corbett, Erin. 2016. "'She Hates Cops, White People': Internet Bigots Have White Hot Meltdown after Beyonce Performs at CMAs." Raw Story, November 2. www.rawstory.com /2016/11/she-hates-cops-white-people-internet-bigots-have-white-hot-meltdown-after -beyonce-performs-at-cmas.

Crenshaw, Kimberlé, Priscilla Ocen, and Jyoti Nanda. 2015. *Black Girls Matter: Pushed Out, Overpoliced, and Underprotected.* New York: African American Policy Forum and Center for Intersectionality and Social Policy Studies.

Delgado, Richard. 2009. "The Law of the Noose: A History of Latino Lynching." *Harvard Civil Rights–Civil Liberties Law Review* 44, no. 2: 297–312.

Douglass, Frederick. 1872–73. "Reminiscences of the Antislavery Conflict as Delivered During the Lecture Season of 72 and 73." Speech, Article, and Book File, Frederick Douglas Papers, Library of Congress. www.loc.gov/item/mfd.22022.

Douglass, Frederick. 1955. "Why Is the Negro Lynched?" In *Reconstruction and After*, vol. 4 of *The Life and Writings of Frederick Douglass*, edited by Philip S. Foner, 491–523. New York: International Publishers.

DuBois, W. E. B. 1986. *Dusk of Dawn: An Essay toward an Autobiography of a Race Concept.* In *Writings*, edited by Nathan I. Huggins, 549–802. New York: Library of America.

Emejulu, Akwugo. 2016. "On the Hideous Whiteness of Brexit: 'Let Us Be Honest about Our Past and Our Present If We Truly Seek to Dismantle White Supremacy.'" Verso Books blog, June 28. www.versobooks.com/blogs/2733/.

Federal Reserve Bank of St. Louis. 2013. "The Financial Crisis and the Impact on Households." In *Annual Report 2012*. St. Louis: Federal Reserve Bank of St. Louis. www.stlouisfed.org/annual-report/2012/essay-2.

Garza, Alicia. 2014. "A Herstory of the #BlackLivesMatter Movement." *The Feminist Wire* (blog), October 7. www.thefeministwire.com/2014/10/blacklivesmatter-2.

Hinton, Elizabeth K. 2016. *From the War on Poverty to the War on Crime: The Making of Mass Incarceration in America.* Cambridge, MA: Harvard University Press.

Hooker, Juliet. 2009. *Race and the Politics of Solidarity.* New York: Oxford University Press.

Hooker, Juliet. 2016. "Black Lives Matter and the Paradoxes of U.S. Black Politics: From Democratic Sacrifice to Democratic Repair." *Political Theory* 44, no. 4: 448–69.

Hutchings, Vincent. 2009. "Change or More of the Same?: Evaluating Racial Attitudes in the Obama Era." Public Opinion Quarterly 73, no. 5: 917–42.

Irwin, Neil, and Josh Katz. 2016. "The Geography of Trumpism." *The Upshot* (blog), *New York Times*, March 12. www.nytimes.com/2016/03/13/upshot/the-geography-of-trumpism.html.

McDaniel, Jason, and Sean McElwee. 2016a. "Racial Resentment and the Rise of Donald Trump." *The New West* (blog), Western Political Science Association, March 27. http://thewpsa.wordpress.com/2016/03/27/.

McDaniel, Jason, and Sean McElwee. 2016b. "Trump Supporters Have Cooler Feelings towards Many Groups, Compared to Supporters of Other Candidates." *The New West* (blog), Western Political Science Association, May 16. http://thewpsa.wordpress.com/2016/05/16/.

Mills, Charles W. 2007. "White Ignorance." In *Race and Epistemologies of Ignorance*, edited by Shannon Sullivan and Nancy Tuana, 13–38. Albany: State University of New York Press.

Movement for Black Lives. 2016. *A Vision for Black Lives: Policy Demands for Black Power, Freedom, and Justice.* policy.m4bl.org/downloads/.

Murray, Charles. 2013. *Coming Apart: The State of White America, 1960–2010.* New York: Crown Forum.

Olson, Joel. 2004. *The Abolition of White Democracy.* Minneapolis: University of Minnesota Press.

Rankine, Claudia. 2014. *Citizen: An American Lyric.* Minneapolis: Graywolf.

Rosin, Hanna. 2010. "The End of Men." *Atlantic*, July–August. www.theatlantic.com/magazine/archive/2010/07/the-end-of-men/308135.

Sewall, Gilbert T. 2016. "The Debasing of Our Civic Currency." *American Spectator,* May 6. http://spectator.org/the-debasing-of-our-civic-currency.

Silver, Nate. 2016. "The Mythology of Trump's 'Working Class' Support." *FiveThirtyEight* (blog), May 3. http://fivethirtyeight.com/features/the-mythology-of-trumps-working-class -support.

Tesler, Michael. 2013. "The Return of Old-Fashioned Racism to White Americans' Partisan Preferences in the Early Obama Era." *Journal of Politics* 75, no. 1: 110–23.

Threadcraft, Shatema. 2016. *Intimate Justice: The Black Female Body and the Body Politic.* New York: Oxford University Press.

Tuttle, Ian. 2015. "The 'Blood-Stained Banner' in Charleston." *The Corner* (blog), *National Review,* June 18. www.nationalreview.com/corner/420003/blood-stained-banner -charleston-ian-tuttle.

United States Department of Justice, Civil Rights Division. 2015. "Investigation of the Ferguson Police Department." *Justice.gov,* March 4. www.justice.gov/sites/default/files/opa /press-releases/attachments/2015/03/04/ferguson_police_department_report.pdf.

Wells, Ida B. 1970. *Crusade for Justice: The Autobiography of Ida B. Wells.* Edited by Alfreda M. Duster. Chicago: University of Chicago Press.

Woodruff, Mandi. 2013. "The Income Gap between Blacks and Whites Has Only Gotten Worse since the 1960s." *Business Insider,* August 29. www.businessinsider.com/the-income -gap-between-blacks-and-whites-2013-8.

John D. Márquez and Junaid Rana

Black Radical Possibility and
the Decolonial International

Can I Get a Witness?

In what was the age of Barack Obama the term *postracial* has come to serve a particular purpose. Although racism and white supremacy are claimed to be relics of the past, current social conditions signal an intensification of those same phenomena without the same public debate. The very notion of a black president of the United States seems to stand in for evidence that a racial democracy or even a white supremacist state contradicts the evidence of social possibility. The mystification of racism and white supremacy is such that throughout much of the Obama presidency the uptick in racial violence seems illegible and unmentionable. For scholars of race who have charted such genealogies, the challenge is to account for shifts in outlook when there is large-scale public denial (Omi and Winant 2015; Roediger 2008). The crimes of white supremacy are certainly so vast that they cannot be wiped out or easily transformed via an election or even through a series of legislative acts, especially when taking as a given that the edifice of liberal modernity is itself racial capitalism (Robinson 1983; Melamed 2015). The divide of social structure and hierarchy in the US

The South Atlantic Quarterly 116:3, July 2017
DOI 10.1215/00382876-3961461 © 2017 Duke University Press

racial democracy is premised on the conditions and principles of liberalism and the incumbent teleology of modernity and the perfection of a system of racial capitalism to engineer the surplus-capital relationship as a flexible and shifting logic.

In this context the unrest and developments sparked in Ferguson, Missouri, with the protests of the police murder of Michael Brown in 2014 were at first surprising and, moreover, represented what might be seen as a break, a moment that abruptly unsettled the popular appeal and persuasion of postracial discourse. The reverberations of those events in Ferguson when compared to a broader challenge to white supremacy, either domestically or on an extranational scale, were not completely unexpected. Those of us who analyze or theorize social movements, for example, have anticipated a rise in antiracist insurgencies for some time now. The Los Angeles rebellion of 1992, the Cincinnati "race riots" of 2001, the London "riots" of 2008, in addition to uprisings in Lisbon and Oakland and others elsewhere, were all sparked by incidents of police brutality and all represent precursors of Ferguson. Similarly, the development of an antiracist response to police terror was not quite a prophetic moment. Rather, the direct actions in Ferguson represented an opening and an imperative that were immediately about a sense of visibility and even further represented an organizing and analytic challenge. The organizing that both led to Ferguson, albeit separate from the spontaneous direct actions that were certainly informed by prior political histories, and came after it represented a turn that at the outset was marked by a confluence of social changes. The visibility of the protests in Ferguson reinforced a growing and more extensive spectacle that was shifting into a national movement that has come to be known as Black Lives Matter (BLM), which in this essay we aim to interrogate for its logic and scope.

We are, to be sure, not exploring a new terrain by focusing on the genealogy or significance of police brutality and its relationship to insurgent political mobilizations. Police brutality has long been on the radar of antiracist movements, just as it has been central to race/ethnic studies scholarship. Such violence also has been tied to deindustrialization and a corollary prison industrial complex (James 1996; Kelley 1996) or has been theorized as part of a more pervasive continuum of racial/colonial violence derived from the foundational and genocidal logics of Western modernity (Rodríguez 2011; Vargas 2010; Maldonado-Torres 2008). What has changed, as a result of the Brown case, is that many elements are informed by a specific analysis that is tied to protest strategies, past and present, and the emergence of approaches tied to what is often loosely referred to as the BLM movement. Such a connection did not appear only as an organic formation but came from the struggles and histories that preceded Ferguson and that, we argue, are tied to radical epistemologies that include histories and intellectual approaches to liberation struggles and social movements.

To this end, our primary aim is to delink BLM activism from what we argue is its neoliberal appropriation, the mainstreaming of it into the US political process. The rage we witnessed at Ferguson and similar sites thereafter is not reducible to an effort to refine or improve a domestic civil rights agenda. We've seen this happen before. The infamous Moynihan report, as Grace Kyungwon Hong (2015) explains, represents the essence of neoliberal adjustments spun in the wake of militant direct actions against racial capitalism across the United States in the late 1960s. Hong, moreover, demonstrates how this appropriation (coupled with the violent subjugation of the US Third World Left's organizations and leaders) represented an attempt by the state to curb a growing critical dissent in US cities and, subsequently, helped set the stage for a new modality of global US hegemony under the auspices of post-Fordist capitalism.

Such shifts, or the mainstreaming of antiracist cultures, we believe, did not and do not constitute a radical change. Including a more diverse array of voices or subject positions in processes of liberal reform is not a rupture from Western modernity's discontents. It does not undo what Anibal Quijano (2000) has famously dubbed the "coloniality of power." Radicalism, we believe, lies more in what José Esteban Muñoz (1999) has described as "disidentification," an intentional rupture from normative protocols through which difference is or has been measured and thus governed in modern social formations. The fires that were set in Ferguson, as a result of the same kinds of direct action that transpired in the 1960s and that led to the neoliberal turn, conveyed that African American youth there were not only angry about being expendable. Those fires conveyed that youth of color were actively disidentifying from conventional political protocols, that they were uninterested in liberal reforms and were willing to participate in a decolonial turn, a rupture. And, more importantly, black youth were willing to destroy symbols of a political order that offers them no refuge (and never has), in the hopes that such destruction would galvanize conversations, if not movement, toward building alternatives to the routine of death with impunity. The potential of radical change is thus not reducible to unprecedented measures of belated inclusion. Radicalism is within the heat of the flame and, optimally, in the intellectual and organizing work that carries forth the impulse of insurgency (not of reform) in and on the ashes.

We emphasize the significance of insurgent acts not only to push back against conservatives who criminalize "riots" as counterproductive. We also push back against liberals. Hip-hop artist Killer Mike, for example, recently commented on the direct actions at Ferguson: "Riots work. . . . Post-riots, they have two new black city council members, they have advocates in the community now, and the police chief retired" (Kreps 2015). We support this response to an extent, valuing its emphasis on incremental change and the grassroots efforts that often make it possible. We also deviate from the liberal telos of Killer Mike's defense. Radical acts are intended to invoke conversations about what truly constitutes radical transformation. Liberal reform is the target of insurgent acts, not their goal. That, we contend, is what differentiates a decolonial approach from a liberal/progressive one.

A decolonial approach is made possible by insurgent acts. It is as much a diagnostic as it is a speculative maneuver. A liberal approach, for example, gestures toward a refuge from racial/colonial violence, one that can be accomplished via the more comprehensive incorporation of racialized subjects into the body politic or the US political economy as equals. This teleological schema identifies incremental structural reforms, as made possible by a combination of (a) juridical adjustments by the state and (b) multicultural understanding or learned tolerance of difference among the body politic, as a method through which black or brown bodies will no longer be interpreted as deserving of extraordinary measures of policing and surveillance. In other words, a (neo)liberal approach suggests that the more the US body politic appreciates a group's history (as a result of ethnic studies curricula in our schools, activism, and media) and the more protections the state offers the group as a result of such increased understanding, the better that group will be able to access the US middle class, a utopic refuge, and thus not be victimized by conditions such as police brutality.

A decolonial approach diagnoses the US nation-state as essentially disqualified from offering refuge from racial/colonial violence because it is fundamentally structured by and through this condition. Its political economy derives from the production of black bodies as either enslaveable or excess, a power-knowledge interface that black studies scholars have effectively shown to be uninterrupted. It also derives from the production of indigenous peoples as irredeemable obstacles to the manifest destiny of this nation-state and thus as deserving of removal (genocide), a foundational logic that also naturalizes US global imperialism.

If we bear in mind this diagnostic reading of the US nation-state, a decolonial approach also requires us to speculate, imagine, and theorize.

The energy and impetus of insurgent acts such as those we witnessed at Ferguson also push, if not require, us to speculate alternatives to not only the interrelated structural forms of oppression that constitute the "coloniality of power" (Quijano 2000). They require us to fundamentally interrogate, if not defy, what decolonial thinkers such as Walter Mignolo (2003), Enrique Dussel (1977), and Sylvia Wynter (2003) have theorized as the ontological confines of modern or Eurocentric thought, that is, the "coloniality of knowledge" and the "coloniality of being," power/knowledge interfaces that are inherent to modern colonial formations such as the United States and that can and so often do limit how we think about self, community, progress, or justice. Modern and colonial thought often coerces us to respond to our expendability counterintuitively. As we plea to colonial authorities for our lives to matter, we also neglect how race itself signifies a process and system through which lives are essentially and existentially devalued, placing a strain on the concept and reality of racial justice. Again, we feel that insurgent acts are fueled by a disavowal of the status quo or this routine of petition, if even for a moment. They, for us, signal an implicit investment in another world that is possible and a willingness to organize for it (Anzaldúa 2015; El Kilombo Intergaláctico 2008). This quality, we believe, recuperates some of the radical synergy of previous movements such as the black radical tradition and the US Third World Left that neoliberal maneuvers have aimed to relegate to the past.

Inasmuch as it identifies the US nation as inherently flawed, a decolonial approach also forces us to imagine the origins of racial-colonial violence beyond the history, structure, and borders of the US nation-state. As we have mentioned briefly and will discuss more in the ensuing sections, the US nation is but an element, albeit a unique product, of the discontents of Western liberal modernity and, particularly, the salience of race to modern social formations. The settler colonial logics of the US nation-state, as Jodi Byrd (2011) has conveyed, also inform and fuel its historic, current, and imperial outreach the world over. This, in sum, represents some of what we are attempting to capture via the concept "decolonial international," that is, a method to account for occupation as a logic for or through which racialized lives are made expendable.[1]

There are other elements of the current conjuncture of black radical possibility that deserve critical scrutiny. Direct actions are also essential considering the growing emphasis on healing and on creating spaces within which the historically excluded feel safe or valued. A defining element of the postcolonial condition is therapy, processes through which the colonized are encouraged to feel included or that there is some form of refuge to be offered if we are patient and trusting enough. By this, we mean that colonial authorities are increasingly mandated to offer space and resources for the colonized to heal, to overcome rage, in ways that make them more pragmatic and instructional, that prepare them to be more worthy of being listened to within the protocols of liberal reform, and thus that make their lives better capable of mattering to a broader spectrum of the body politic. As much as it remains important to flee that setup, it is also important to sabotage it. Fires, literal and figurative, do that.

The analysis made possible by Ferguson begins with the evidence itself. The proof is often in the seeing, hearing, and feeling—in observing how protests are organized and how racialized subjects are able to instantly witness and make a decision about events of dispute and respond to them straightaway. We as scholars are similar to organizers and activists, in that how we know something is dependent not on the visual but on a range of archives. We attain and produce knowledge not just from how we gaze on social movements voyeuristically but also from how we participate in them. As critical ethnic studies scholars, especially as scholars with deep and familial roots in communities that have been imperiled by racial/colonial violence, we work outside and within the academy. Witnessing is not only a form of direct observation; it is how we can image our methodological approach in terms of ethnography attached to radical politics. In the tradition of radical history, such an approach ties the theoretical and analytical positions of thinking through a future politics and theoretical possibility. That white supremacy has become so visible through media and digital technologies makes this all the more complicated and perhaps even unwieldy as a racial analysis. Our commitment to working across and often against the professional and methodological protocols of academia is galvanized by the tone set by what is only the most recent roll call of black or brown lives destroyed, a list that includes Trayvon Martin, Oscar Grant, Akai Gurley, Eric Garner, Tamir Rice, John Crawford, Sandra Bland, Walter Scott, Freddie Gray, Alton Sterling, Philando Castile, Luis Alfonso Torres, Anastasio Hernández Rojas, Joe Nieves, Andy López, and countless others whose names often go unmentioned.

To the Streets

At Ferguson and in the other protests it inspired, it was difficult not to acknowledge how those direct actions unfolded in a moment of spectacular and global racial/colonial/imperial violence. The fires of Ferguson were connected to a broader matrix of insurgent acts against racial capitalism the world over, mobilizations and clashes in Paris, Baltimore, London, Chicago, Gaza, Oaxaca, Baton Rouge, Rio de Janeiro, and Unis'tot'en territory. Those direct actions did not parallel one another. They are relationally interconnected by and within global racial capitalism. Connecting those insurgencies either in the heat of social protests or in their wake, we believe, revitalizes the global and decolonial vision inherent to a black radical tradition that we have been inspired by and hope to build on.

October 2014 was a month of protest leading toward the National Mobilization and Justice for All March in Ferguson.[2] That summer had been rife with tension. The Israeli war on Gaza and the display of mass Palestinian death reported via livestream had set an unbearable tone. What the mainstream news media refused to show was available with a few clicks and a fast Internet connection. The massive death and destruction in Gaza was overwhelming. In response, we and tens of thousands of people took to the streets of Chicago on July 26, demanding an end to the bloodshed in Gaza and expressing a willingness to shut down the commerce of our home city if the attack continued. It was one of the largest political protests in Chicago's history and was made possible, to a large extent, by social media. At the forefront of the march were Palestinians belting out passionate political slogans and chants and displaying incredible art that conveyed the despair faced by the residents of Gaza. On this day Chicago's Palestinians were out in full force. A broad range of Arabs, South Asians, blacks, Latinx, and whites were also present. Boricuas had a strong presence, drawing strong connections between the occupation of their home island and Palestine. Chicago, by no means a refuge from racial-colonial violence, did not need to be shocked into consciousness. Concurrent with the protest for Palestine was another surge in gun violence in Chicago's black and brown communities, with daily death tolls read out on the evening television news accompanied by the images and sounds of black and Latinx women mourning, all elements of suffering produced by coloniality. As if that was not enough, there was an epic uptick in forced deportations of Mexican and Central American immigrants in cities including Chicago, elevating the despair and fear of Latinx denizens. These were all conditions that helped frame and inspire the measures of frustration that characterized the July 26 march.

Three months later, in the middle of October, we joined the march in Ferguson. The heat was coming down. Cops were everywhere and nowhere. And as we walked to the place where Brown breathed for the last time, there

Figure 1. National Mobilization and Justice for All March, Ferguson, MO, August 30, 2014.
Photo by Junaid Rana

was an air of unrest and defiance, with strands of planned organization and unplanned spontaneity. It was organic, a strong and yet unspoken consensus of what united us, what allowed for us all to place our own bodies at risk. There was talk of marching to the police station. Speakers representing multiple constituencies spoke as Brown's family came to mourn collectively with this large presence on the street at what had previously become an impromptu commemorative site. Suited bodyguards drawn from the Nation of Islam's security forces escorted the family of Brown to the center of the marchers who had gathered to pay respect, and eulogies were given by the family, politicians, and clergy. The energy was with the marchers.

We marched and made friends, sharing the mic, posters, and chants. And then the rain came. We ducked for cover on the streets where, days earlier, buildings had been torched. To witness it was surreal. Makeshift canopies had been set up to sell protest and memorial T-shirts—an element of the planning. With the rain clearing and people dispersed, we followed one crowd that was walking in the direction of the police station. Word reached us that an initial group had already made it to the station and was taking up posts for what would be an encounter for the rest of the day. Protest was erupting in many sites and in many forms. That was the plan. As we walked on a side road to the station, the crowds seemed to be walking into a park that we had cut through earlier that morning. A group of young black men and trans folk stood at the edges of the park, asking those who were walking in why the march had stopped here instead of the police station. From the security personnel, we heard that local senior leaders were going to speak and that a live message would be broadcast from Al Sharpton and Louis Farrakhan. The idea was that for some of the families and the elderly this would be a rest stop. The young folks were getting riled up. Bringing some militancy to the march, they asked why we were following these leaders of the past and not taking it to the streets with a more direct and insurgent action. The face of the new leadership was young, trans, queer, and black and not interested in waiting around for a photo op. Some of us could not wait, would not wait, and so we continued to march toward something, an alternative to what was interpreted as appropriation.

As the crowd began to gather at the police station, first in a parking lot across the street and then with numbers in front of the building where police officers had cordoned off a line, the strategy turned to disrupting the flow of traffic. Young black folk who had been part of the initial masses began taking the street, followed by the entire crowd as the numbers of supporters swelled. It was an important galvanizing point, bolstered by a chartered bus full of protesters arriving as the encounter with the police became tense. From this description the protesters might sound young, but it was a multigenerational, family affair, with everyone from young kids to the elderly, and it was also black, brown, and white. At the front line of the direct action were black women who wielded the mic to choreograph the protesters. In the crowd was a group of Palestinians who had driven all night to be a part of the protests. Part of the Palestinian contingent was from the East Coast and others had come from elsewhere in the heartland. From the beginning of the unrest at Ferguson and the resulting uprising, there was solidarity, whether on social media or through the actual bodies of protesters, and the Palestinian struggle was part of the political symbols of protest of black death. Gaza and Ferguson are linked, and this link was made evident in the visual and audible archive of that moment, in the bodies of the marchers themselves and in their willingness to risk health and safety.

One could call it solidarity, and regardless of how analogies between Gaza and Ferguson might seem unsuitable, that day it seemed like the same playing field, the expendability of black and Palestinian bodies made clear as related, if not connected. And here, in such moments and examples, where expressions of solidarity are manifested organically or in spontaneous moments of rage against a global white supremacy, black politics (as filtered through African American history) represents a set of liberatory and decolonial politics that go beyond a conventional wisdom regarding racialized blackness and beyond the racial formation of the US nation-state. We argue that this decolonial analytic is a central component to a future struggle that draws on radical political histories. As a starting point, settler violence is global and interdependent on the subjugation and expendability of numerous subject populations that speak to a range of colonial experiences and forms of occupation and from which a political solidarity should and must emerge. For example, the settler colonial formation that depends on black and Palestinian subordination is also the possibility of black political liberation as internationalist liberation, or what we are calling decolonial internationalism. With this we call attention to how black politics is often an axis or pivot from which reform or revolutionary social movements originate, to how insurgent connections are either made or how they can be impeded. A decolonial internationalism is an insurgency against the rubric of white supremacy and maintains a global outlook through the radical political work of solidarity and ultimately an analytics of liberation. It is not so much place-bound, as compared to a global condition it recognizes particularity and specificity.

That seemed clear to us again a few months later. On November 24, 2014, we were among a few hundred people gathered outside the Chicago Police Department's headquarters in Bronzeville, a historically African American neighborhood on Chicago's Near South Side. We came together to anticipate the grand jury ruling in the Brown case, which would decide whether Ferguson police officer Darren Wilson would face charges for Brown's murder. This ruling was only rumored to be scheduled for release that very chilly evening. We, however, were prepared to respond with direct action. We represented a coalition of blacks, whites, Arabs, Latinx, straights, queers, and trans folks who were uneasy with the status quo and who had been busy organizing on various fronts across the city. The clothing and signage of those of us in attendance bore Marxist, black, anarchist, queer, trans, feminist, Palestinian, Native American, and Latinx symbols of resistance.

The night carried on with no news. It was bitterly cold, around 15 degrees Fahrenheit. We were running out of things to chant, speakers to speak, and ways to keep warm. The crowd began to dissipate. The verdict was finally announced over a megaphone, and the crowd began to stir with unrest. Officer

Figure 2. Palestinian solidarity with Ferguson. Ferguson, MO, August 30, 2014. Photo by Junaid Rana

Wilson was exonerated. We took to the streets with no real plan other than that we should march into the core of the city and disrupt its commerce. We marched eastward from the police headquarters down Thirty-Fifth Street and toward Lake Shore Drive. We dodged vehicles and joined arm in arm to deter traffic and shut that highway down. Much of our solidarity on that day was manifested physically, in our willingness to overcome the cold and risk injury to disrupt the status quo.

Many of us continued our march into the city center. As fatigue and the cold set in, it was hard not to meditate on the meaning and significance of our actions, of the health risks we were enduring to challenge white supremacy with strangers, risks that our bodies were actively reminding us of. One thing that began to stand out, at least for some of us, was that it was intriguing to engage in a strategy of occupation (taking over a major roadway) in a space that for indigenous peoples was and is an occupied territory, an urban settler colonial formation wrought via genocidal violence.

This juxtaposition, between what a political order was designed as (a settler colonial formation) and what we were asking for it to do (make non-

Figure 3. Mass demonstration in solidarity with Palestine, Chicago, IL, July 26, 2014. Photo by John Márquez

Figure 4. Rally for Michael Brown at Chicago Police Department Headquarters, Chicago, IL, November 24, 2014. Photo by John Márquez

white lives matter), seemed even more intriguing as our coalition marched past the Battle of Fort Dearborn Park at Eighteenth Street while en route to shut down Lake Shore Drive in solidarity with Brown. This public park was created to commemorate the Fort Dearborn massacre, an originating moment in the development or manifest destiny of Chicago as a modern and liberal city. Just over two centuries ago, Chicago's western frontier was a militarized border between what European settlers considered to be their civil society and the scene of nature or the savage wilderness that surrounded them, with the threat of the surround or of indigenous peoples having been the impetus for the settlers' construction and defense of Fort Dearborn.

Our path took us past yet another reminder of the settler colonial logics of our city. This time, it was a famous statue that also commemorates the Fort Dearborn Massacre by depicting a large and muscular white male settler slaying natives with his sword while he protects a terror-stricken white woman and child behind him. White guardian angels are depicted as flying above the scene to signify manifest destiny. This statue adorns a large stone section of a bridge over the Chicago River near the famed Magnificent Mile of commerce where consumers from around the world flock to shop and recreate.

To clarify, the Fort Dearborn massacre is commemorated in Chicago, in its civic iconography, as an incident justifying the white civilizing mission of European settlers in the region and the conditions of violent repression, removal, and segregation that have characterized this city and its founding. Fort Dearborn is for Chicagoans what the Alamo is for Texans. Each has been mythologized within a settler colonial imaginary as a space or moment where white pioneers sacrificed their lives for the future of their Western modernity, for the future of a just and democratic society (that has yet to appear), and in the face of a relentless attack of savages (Potawatomis or Mexicans) who obstructed their manifest destiny. This ever-present threat of the surround, as Stefano Harney and Fred Moten (2013), Luana Ross (1998), and others have described, represents the justification for extraviolent law enforcement to be deployed and military apparatuses to be constructed and defended as trademark characteristics of a settler colonial state's ethics.

As we recount these scenes and acts of the initial and pivotal moments of the Ferguson rebellion, what comes to the forefront is how a number of points would continue in the protest movement that developed and how they address the concerns of political theory and the black radical tradition. These points are, first, the use of social media as an organizing tool; second, the youth-oriented strategies of organizing that have reignited the direct-action challenge to white supremacy; third, the solidarities of struggles that are confronting militarized death and genocide; and, fourth, settler colonialism and occupation are the terms under which the militarized and state-sanctioned violence of premature and social death has become a global condition (Patterson 1982; Cacho 2012). And while we recount these points to outline a political practice after Ferguson, we also maintain that these points are central to how social movements and the black radical tradition continue to make demands for social justice and the interpretive and analytical ground from which liberatory and decolonial struggle will carry on.

Black Liberation Means Collective Liberation

In moments of crisis, black politics has a prismatic effect, as made evident by the surge in activism in 2014 driven by movement building associated with BLM. We, in previous publications, and others have conceptualized the black radical tradition as unique for how it brings together expressions of solidarity between spaces and struggles (Rana 2007; Márquez 2013; Daulatzai 2012). This is evident not only in the archive of direct actions but also in the global/political influence of black music genres such as hip-hop and reggae on youth subjectivities and on radical urban collectives in particular. There are challenges and possibilities opened up by this mode of critique. On the one hand, a fallback position for concepts of racism that rely on a black-white narrative helps produce the histories of other groups as tangential at best, a condition often referred to as the black-white binary. John D. Márquez (2016) refers to this as a "regressive mutation" of the black-white binary. A fundamental critique of theories of race for the past few decades has been this same reliance on a race-as-blackness approach, when a more complex and rich theory of race and racism has accounted for a range of racializations that encompass histories of immigration, genocide, and settler colonialism—the interrelated dynamics and histories that we have emphasized as the foundation for our decolonial approach and its emphasis on disavowal.

More recently, the reaction to such shifts has resulted in a putative return to this regressive mutation. This logic, for example, is evident in the slogan "All lives can't matter until black lives matter," which has been popularized by BLM activism following Ferguson and tends to lend itself to a vision of the US nation-state as capable of reform, a vision that furthers the violent and imperial occupation of indigenous lands on this continent or on others. Again, while we support the pushback against those who criminalize BLM for being divisive or disrupting the mythology of a postracial America, we also acknowledge the limitations imposed by this analytic. There is some substantial claim to understanding the depth of black suffering under the heels of white supremacy. However, this cannot be used as an all-encompassing claim to understanding everything from queer/trans social death to native genocide, without rendering the plights of groups outside of the African American experience or, to that extent, outside of the United States as tangential, at best, to how we understand and resist white supremacy.

Under the race-as-blackness approach, the notion of a repair or reform of black-white tensions and the mainstreaming of African American social movements in particular are thus often envisioned as political progress in the United States, lauded as pragmatic or incremental outcomes by liberal scholars who try to make sense of or rationalize insurgent acts in their wake. Thus in this post–civil rights conjuncture, what might be viewed as a radical change within historically white institutions or as changes within white liberal minds, made evident by the belated inclusion of African Americans into positions of power or influence, are not necessarily equivalent to the radical critiques of power that we have mapped on the streets of Ferguson and Chicago and that identify the US nation-state as the arbiter of racial/colonial violence, not its potential remedy. On the other hand, such distinctions are important for the analysis of dissent in terms of political possibility and the idea of insurgent transformation and what Robin D. G. Kelley (2016), in following Harney and Moten (2013), calls black study and black struggle, perspectives that we feel better capture the generative elements of black politics and that, in fact, make the black-white binary quite useful for fomenting a more dynamic, extranational, and critical challenge to white supremacy. This is what we refer to as the prismatic effect of black politics. A return to political education—to how we unpack, sustain, and reinforce the energy of our direct actions—is a place from which we locate ourselves in the neoliberal university, and we join in this call for a rethinking of strategy and the premise and breadth of our theoretical concepts outside of or beyond colonial institutions and their therapeutic protocols.

The notion of blackness as a signifier for other forms of raciality and imperial domination through white supremacy raises a number of theoretical and practical questions. If, for example, antiblackness is a particular formation of necessary social death for the system of liberal modernity to continue (Roberts 2015), and if white supremacy is understood as a colonial relation that confers antagonism through genealogy and analogy, how are we to understand the mystification of black suffering in relationship to, say, Muslim suffering or, through an imposed secularity, that of Palestinian suffering, immigrant suffering, or indigenous suffering? This is to say not that all suffering should be visible in a particular way but rather that some forms of suffering are made invisible as part of the machinery of racial capitalism and white supremacy. These are particularly global terms that shift and pivot in meaning yet share a vocabulary and logic of domination. They are also not the same form of suffering, nor can they be simply analogized for comprehension in what marks a definitive limit of comparative ethnic studies as a field. Rather, analogy is what gives such terms their theoretical force and, at times, reveals the layers from which they operate. It is in this sense that we push against the notion of antiblackness as foundational and primary to white supremacy. The primacy of antiblackness in relation to racial capitalism should signal a range of questions regarding such a narrative of suffering, the first of which we might borrow from Stuart Hall (1993): What is this *black* in antiblackness?

The risk in this strategy is that the ongoing and concurrent persecution of Muslims or Mexicans as natural enemies of the state or as figures of racialization who are deemed to be deserving of violent and militarized repression is implied as an afterthought to what is determined to be radical critique rather than as pillars that help frame and sustain white supremacy. The fact that indigenous genocide is so often acknowledged only as an injustice of the past rather than as a foundational logic from which such white supremacy has been instantiated exacerbates this limitation, a limitation that made it intriguing (to say the least) to chant "Black lives matter" as we marched passed the Battle of Fort Dearborn Park.

It is unreasonable to say, therefore, that antiblackness, which has been drawn from a lineage to slavery and the entirety of its apparatus, is the conceptual base from which white supremacy sublimates anti-Muslim, anti-immigrant, and anti-indigenous racial hierarchies (Spillers 2003). We say that despite the prismatic effect of black politics that we've witnessed in moments of direct action. This, we believe, represents an often underinterrogated gap between solidarities expressed in moments of crisis and the intellectual work needed to make sense of and thus strengthen those bonds, making them more immune from the imperatives of domestic and neoliberal reform. Given how the depth of destruction and mass death concurred with a growing list of black and brown lives destroyed by police terror in the United States, a radical intellectual project requires us to interrogate the relationship between, say, BLM activism and settler colonialism. To do so shifts the frame from which activism and politics emerge and even the point of foundational violence in the *ongoing* colonial experience. It thus also requires us to imagine an insurgent critique of white supremacy in the contemporary war on terror, which has used the racial figure of the Muslim to obscure the reach and destruction of US empire, a power/knowledge interface that also produces the United States–Mexico border as a space deserving of heightened surveillance and militarization, exacerbating the expendability of Mexicans and native peoples of that region. This is also to point out that the rhetoric and violence of anti-Muslim racism is not simply a fact of a political consolidation against Islam and Muslims but is an invigoration of white supremacy and the violences of racial capitalism as a whole.

To be sure, there has been some significant debate regarding these connections. Such connections, however, seem tenuous. Again, many have displayed a willingness to place their own lives at risk to make these connections, and yet there seems to be more intellectual work needed to honor those acts and reinforce the connections that they have made vivid. The BLM campaign is burdened by a liberal teleology that would have *black* stand in for a notion of humanity rather than stand for the radical claim it simultaneously purports to be as the possibility of decolonial liberation—and perhaps there is a dialectical politics here that works through the often-heralded process of reform and revolution that not only Killer Mike but also social movement historians such as Barbara Ransby (2015, 2016), Keeanga-Yamahtta Taylor (2016a, 2016b), Martha Biondi (2016), and others have gestured toward. While these two strategies (reform and revolution or, moreover, the reforms spun by what are often considered to be radical acts) are often at odds with each other and require separate rubrics and approaches, in this essay we advance a perspective that comes from thinking through colonial occupation as a global condition, as a condition produced by and through what Denise Ferreira da Silva (2008) describes as the "analytics of raciality," that is, conditions that refer to the mono-epistemic stranglehold of Western modernity (especially teleological liberalism) on political imaginaries, and the response of the radical and decolonial internationalism that this comprehensive theorization of race and modernity mandates.

This dialectic of reform and revolution, a pervasively popular topic among social movement historians, tends to reinforce a domestication of black politics, a kind of appropriation that we believe dilutes the radical potential inherent to direct actions. Rhetorics regarding radical or revolutionary change are commonly appropriated and used to describe how activists force the US nation-state to repair itself via internal reforms. What often gets described as radical within the US political culture regarding race—the emphasis on incremental progress made possible by direct actions—can thus also be read as insidious when one considers the settler colonial origins of the US nation-state and its related imperial outreach the world over, the genocidal logic of occupation that we center in our analysis. In other words, the more a narrative of repair or reform is conveyed as a result of our direct actions, the further distracted we are from diagnosing the inherent limitations of the US nation-state and especially its origins in conquest and slavery. This domestication, moreover, speaks directly to the discontents of neoliberal adjustments.

The term *neoliberalism* often refers to a particular political economic conjuncture and, namely, the advent of a post-Fordist and global capitalism. We refer to neoliberalism also for its ethical contours, for the style or modicum of racial governance it signifies, a postcolonial method to deter a more critical dissent via the belated inclusion or mainstreaming of social movements and their rhetorics since the civil rights movement of the mid-twentieth century. The advent of what Michelle Alexander (2010) describes as "the new Jim Crow" is not the sole limit of neoliberal adjustment and post–civil rights rhetorics of progress. It also verifies the limitations of colonial recognition and treaty making that Glen Coulthard (2014), Dian Million (2013), and others have exposed as pillars of how racial capitalism has been and is furthered on this continent via genocidal logics, putting an added strain on the impetus and logic of liberal reform.

Neoliberalism has thus exacerbated the inherent limitations of the US nation-state, a liberal politics of rhetorical racial uplift and incremental reform spun in the wake of what has been narrated as a successful civil rights movement of the mid-twentieth century. This modality of politics that sees the US nation-state as capable of racial justice, and as a stand-alone flagship for equality the world over, presents new infrastructures such as those intertwined with the terror industrial complex that are born out of the logics of prisons and warfare (Rana 2016). In the global war on terror, it is precisely this shift to a militarized economy that has fundamentally changed the social and cultural relationships of racial capitalism and that has inspired our intellectual project to refine the connections that we witnessed on the ground and in moments of insurgent protest as of late. The visual and audible archive that we both witnessed and participated in at Ferguson and in Chicago in 2014 gave us a strong indication that important connections were or are being made between the mass suffering in Gaza, the violence created at and by militarized borders separating the United States from the "Third World," and the antiblack and antibrown violence that has been exacerbated as a result of post–Cold War hypercarceralism in US cities.

The surveillance of neighborhoods and programs such as stop and frisk and "broken windows" are inextricable from the drone killings and targeted assassinations of the war on terror, just as they are from the militarization of the United States–Mexico border. This global mapping of white supremacy—the global reach of US and Western European imperialism and its emphasis on security, surveillance, and military threat—is manifested and evident in the increasingly blurred line between law enforcement and militarism, a blurriness that forces us to discuss Guantánamo as a component of our broader discussions regarding what Angela Davis (1999) has famously dubbed "the prison industrial complex." Again, these are examples of the systemic and intended expendability that connects Ferguson, Gaza, Chicago, and the United States–Mexico border. While Paul Gilroy (2014) has made gestures to this global arrangement of power via his conceptualization of a post–Cold War and penal "securitocracy," it is imperative to highlight even further precisely which kinds of bodies have always already been amid the racial-colonial architecture of Western modernity in the current conjuncture.

The diversity of 2014's direct actions thus requires a theorization of race not as a socially constructed obstruction to the United States' liberal telos. Recent and critical theorizations of race are quite useful in this regard. Barnor Hesse (2007) and Ferreira da Silva (2008), for example, offer distinct and yet related conceptualizations of social death. Each illuminates the genealogy of this phenomenon not only within the specific historical developments of racialized groups in modern and liberal nation-states (the ascription of race meanings to bodies) but also within the anthropocentric nature or configuration of European Enlightenment thought and thus the rights-granting or rights-denying characteristics of modern nation-states. Race, according to these models, is not a mere aberration, an obstruction, or the kind of liberal "dilemma" that Gunnar Myrdal (1944) once called it. Its social salience lies in how it structures what Hesse describes as nothing other than a colonial relationship, a governing protocol through which political progress is mapped by the capacity of nonwhite peoples to convince whites that their lives matter, a framework that we have been unable to reform ourselves out of because it is not designed to live up to its promise of universality. Hesse's and Ferreira da Silva's models each map the limits of liberal reform, demonstrating how the very concept of modern liberalism is informed by and thus laden with racial meanings. Each lends itself to the acts of disidentification we've witnessed in insurgent actions as of late and unsettles the dialectic between revolution and reform that we discussed earlier.

The Black Radical Tradition and the Decolonial International

Activist connections between intensified policing and urban black and brown communities, the militarization of borders, and the Israeli war on Palestine are not coincidental. Nor are they parallel phenomena to be compared or cited in a list of unfortunate outcomes of democracy's imperfections. Those connections are related, interdependent, and increasingly based in social science that draws on culturalist ideas of place and people—in other words, culture is used as a weapon to kill and harm (Price 2016). This, we argue, is inherent to the racial/colonial architecture of European modernity, as conveyed by Hesse's and Ferreira da Silva's models, and can be traced across a continuum of systemic racial violence with impunity. It also reflects the current conjuncture within which militarism and hypercarceralism coincide with discourses regarding incremental repair and progress.

In memorializing four police officers who were shot and killed by an African American military veteran with significant disabilities while they were providing security at a peaceful BLM event in Dallas, President Obama (2016) defended BLM by suggesting that Americans "cannot simply turn away and dismiss those in peaceful protest as troublemakers or paranoid." Here Obama was describing the BLM movement as a rational component of the political process, as offering a valid if not useful critique of structural racism, of the kinds of obstruction that he and other liberals believe can be remedied via policy, the kinds of liberal reforms (and the social movements that birthed them) that helped get him elected.

The domestication of social movements, via neoliberal projects or adjustments, requires that those movements and the histories they are associated with be ethnically compartmentalized from one another and bound both literally and figuratively by US borders. Neoliberal multiculturalism in the United States is essentially a system to manage difference (Ferguson 2012; Melamed 2011). It selects when and why a racialized group's history and struggle shall be added to mainstream political discourse, placed on display, and honored or venerated for how it improves the liberal mind-set, for how it steers us closer to a democratic and just consensus, and for how it helps make the United States an exceptional nation of the world. This protocol is rooted in identitarian frameworks for acknowledging when and where white supremacy has obstructed democracy. It is especially rooted in the impetus to repair black-white tensions, the effects of slavery and its afterlife that Obama refers to in his public support for BLM.

Despite our focus on the liberal telos of the BLM movement, we find it imperative to acknowledge some of its radical components nonetheless.

BLM organizers, for example, have made the claim that they are "not your grandfather's civil rights movement." In saying so, they were offering, primarily, a critique of the heteropatriarchal dynamics of the civil rights activism of the mid-twentieth century. We support this intervention, highlighting how the BLM movement's nonhierarchical approach is significant for how it includes voices and positionalities that are too often marginalized due to heteropatriarchy. This represents a radical change in how we examine or participate in social movements, regardless of their scope and goal. We also, however, find it useful to question what such voices are being included into, does such inclusion represent a radical shift? A more inclusive civil rights movement, rather than a radical imagination otherwise, is always captured in a liberal telos. It retains, we suspect, a vision or understanding of the United States as having a legitimate authority or capacity to resolve the discontents of racial capitalism. The duration of antiblack violence and criminalization, in addition to the settler colonial foundation of US empire, places a significant strain on this capacity to provide universality.

What, then, are radical politics that are not merely inherent to the BLM movement's rhetoric but that are also made possible by the rupture witnessed at Ferguson? Does the BLM movement, for example, fulfill or reflect the dynamism that we've witnessed on the ground? Does black politics post-Ferguson, as signified by the mainstreaming of the BLM movement, reflect a radical departure from the analytics of raciality? Or does it feed into a paradigm that renders Latinx, Arab, and indigenous struggles as, at best, supplemental or, at worst, invisible within political discourse regarding race and its salience? These questions derive not only from the social movement archive but also from the value we place on the political cultures that preceded us, a US Third World Left and the black radical tradition that is associated with it.

"There can be no real freedom until the imperialist—world-enemy-number-one—has been stripped of his power. . . . We recognize this when we admit that the United States is no longer a nation but an empire" (Newton 1972: 40–41). Written in the late 1960s by Huey P. Newton, cofounder of the Black Panther Party for Self-Defense, these words represent a radical tradition of black politics, a component of a decolonial international, and the kinds of critical dissent that belated inclusion and other neoliberal reforms have aimed to curb. Against such pressures, and as an attempt to breathe new life into it, we locate ourselves within that tradition and vision. Here we also follow in the theorization of the United States as an empire-state, a settler colonial formation from which racialization must be understood (Jung 2015). This move from the domestic politics of the United States to a global outlook is precisely the form from which we are arguing that a decolonial international can take shape.

As an affront to the appropriating logics of neoliberalism, this tradition and vision is not additive or supplementary to what is conventionally identified as race politics in the United States but is seeking transformation that is open to exploring possibility as the means of insurrection and liberation. Rebooting our own sense of political education is certainly one of the avenues from which we enter into how we work toward struggle and radical organization (Okihiro 2016). The work is not to merely resuscitate the black radical tradition but to build upon and refine it. By turning to what we are calling a decolonial internationalism, we acknowledge that the occupation of these lands established a foundation for the now global reach of US empire, that there is thus also a sense of a global struggle against ongoing occupation not only as a reality of state domination but as a condition that we must wrestle ourselves away from. The synergy we witnessed in the direct actions of 2014 suggests that, for many, antiblackness and occupation remain inseparable within a more insurgent critique of racial capitalism. Those moments, for us, convey that decolonial possibility is lurking and happening every day.

Notes

1   Here we also find Glen Coulthard's (2014) recuperative theorization of Marx's "primitive accumulation" useful for thinking about settler genocide and the white supremacist modalities of governance that are produced on and in their wake.
2   On the organization of these events, see Ferguson Action 2016.

References

Alexander, Michelle. 2010. *The New Jim Crow: Mass Incarceration in the Age of Colorblindness.* New York: New Press.
Anzaldúa, Gloria. 2015. *Light in the Dark / Luz en lo oscuro: Rewriting Identity, Spirituality, Reality.* Durham, NC: Duke University Press.
Biondi, Martha. 2016. "The Radicalism of Black Lives Matter." *In These Times*, August 15.
Byrd, Jodi. 2011. *The Transit of Empire: Indigenous Critiques of Colonialism.* Minneapolis: University of Minnesota Press.
Cacho, Lisa Marie. 2012. *Social Death: Racialized Rightlessness and the Criminalization of the Unprotected.* Nation of Newcomers: Immigrant History as American History. New York: New York University Press.
Coulthard, Glen Sean. 2014. *Red Skin, White Masks: Rejecting the Colonial Politics of Recognition.* Minneapolis: University of Minnesota Press.
Daulatzai, Sohail. 2012. *Black Star, Crescent Moon: The Muslim International and Black Freedom beyond America.* Minneapolis: University of Minnesota Press.
Davis, Angela. 1999. *The Prison Industrial Complex.* CD-Audiobook. San Francisco, CA: AK Press.

Dussel, Enrique. 1977. *Niveles concretos de la* ética *latinoamericana (Concrete Levels of Latin American Ethics).* Vol. 3 of *Filosofía* ética *de la liberación (Ethical Philosophy of Liberation).* 3rd ed. Buenos Aires: Megápolis.

El Kilombo Intergaláctico. 2008. *Beyond Resistance: Everything; An Interview with Subcomandante Insurgente Marcos.* Durham, NC: PaperBoat.

Ferguson Action. 2016. http://fergusonaction.com/ (accessed August 15, 2016).

Ferguson, Roderick. 2012. *The Reorder of Things: The University and Its Pedagogies of Minority Difference.* Minneapolis: University of Minnesota Press.

Ferreira da Silva, Denise. 2008. *Toward a Global Idea of Race.* Minneapolis: University of Minnesota Press.

Gilroy, Paul. 2014. *Race and Racism in "The Age of Obama."* London: British Library.

Hall, Stuart. 1993. "What Is This 'Black' in Black Popular Culture." *Social Justice* 20, nos. 1–2: 101–14.

Harney, Stefano, and Fred Moten. 2013. *The Undercommons: Fugitive Planning and Black Study.* New York: Minor Compositions.

Hesse, Barnor. 2007. "Racialized Modernity: An Analytics of White Mythologies." *Ethnic and Racial Studies* 30, no. 4: 643–63.

Hong, Grace Kyungwon. 2015. "Neoliberalism." *Critical Ethnic Studies* 1, no. 1: 56–67.

James, Joy. 1996. *Resisting State Violence: Radicalism, Gender, and Race in U.S. Culture.* Minneapolis: University of Minnesota Press.

Jung, Moon-Kie. 2015. *Beneath the Surface of White Supremacy: Denaturalizing U.S. Racisms Past and Present.* Stanford Studies in Comparative Race and Ethnicity. Stanford, CA: Stanford University Press.

Kelley, Robin D. G. 1996. *Race Rebels: Culture, Politics, and the Black Working Class.* New York: Free Press.

Kelley, Robin D. G. 2016. "Black Study, Black Struggle." *Boston Review,* March 7. http://boston review.net/forum/robin-d-g-kelley-black-study-black-struggle.

Kreps, Daniel. 2015. "Run the Jewels on Ferguson: 'Riots Work.'" *Rolling Stone,* August 6. rolling stone.com/music/news/run-the-jewels-on-ferguson-riots-work-20150806.

Maldonado-Torres, Nelson. 2008. *Against War: Views from the Underside of Modernity.* Durham, NC: Duke University Press.

Márquez, John D. 2013. *Black-Brown Solidarity: Racial Politics in the New Gulf South.* Austin: University of Texas Press.

Márquez, John D. 2016. "Juan Crow: Progressive Mutations of the Black-White Binary." In *Critical Ethnic Studies: A Reader,* edited by Critical Ethnic Studies Editorial Collective, 43–62. Durham, NC: Duke University Press.

Melamed, Jodi. 2011. *Represent and Destroy: Rationalizing Violence in the New Racial Capitalism.* Minneapolis: University of Minnesota Press.

Melamed, Jodi. 2015. "Racial Capitalism." *Critical Ethnic Studies* 1, no. 1: 76–85.

Mignolo, Walter. 2003. *The Darker Side of the Renaissance: Literacy, Territoriality, and Colonization.* 2nd ed. Ann Arbor: University of Michigan Press.

Million, Dian. 2013. *Therapeutic Nations: Healing in an Age of Indigenous Human Rights.* Tucson: University of Arizona Press.

Muñoz, José Esteban. 1999. *Disidentifications: Queers of Color and the Performance of Politics.* Cultural Studies of the Americas 2. Minneapolis: University of Minnesota Press.

Myrdal, Gunnar. 1944. *An American Dilemma: The Negro Problem and American Democracy.* New York: Harper and Brothers.

Newton, Huey P. 1972. *To Die for the People: The Writings of Huey P. Newton.* San Francisco: Writers and Readers.

Obama, Barack H. 2016. "Speech Honoring Slain Police Officers in Dallas, Texas." *CNN,* July 12, streaming video, 38:17, available at cnn.com/2016/07/12/politics/dallas-shooting -obama-george-w-bush/ (accessed March 8, 2017).

Okihiro, Gary Y. 2016. *Third World Studies: Theorizing Liberation.* Durham, NC: Duke University Press.

Omi, Michael, and Howard Winant. 2015. *Racial Formation in the United States.* 3rd ed. New York: Routledge.

Patterson, Orlando. 1982. *Slavery and Social Death: A Comparative Study.* Cambridge, MA: Harvard University Press.

Price, David H. 2016. *Cold War Anthropology: The CIA, the Pentagon, and the Growth of Dual Use Anthropology.* Durham, NC: Duke University Press.

Quijano, Anibal. 2000. "Coloniality of Power, Eurocentrism, and Latin America." Translated by Michael Ennis. *Nepantla: Views from South* 1, no. 3: 533–80.

Rana, Junaid. 2007. "The Story of Islamophobia." *Souls: A Critical Journal of Black Politics, Culture, and Society* 9, no. 2: 148–61.

Rana, Junaid. 2016. "The Racial Infrastructure of the Terror-Industrial Complex." *Social Text* 34, no. 4: 111–38.

Ransby, Barbara. 2015. "Ella Baker's Radical Democratic Vision." *Jacobin,* June 18. www.jacob inmag.com/2015/06/black-lives-matter-police-brutality.

Ransby, Barbara. 2016. Response to "Black Study, Black Struggle," by Robin D. G. Kelley. *Boston Review,* March 7. http://bostonreview.net/forum/robin-d-g-kelley-black-study-Black -struggle.

Roberts, Neil. 2015. *Freedom as Marronage.* Chicago: University of Chicago Press.

Robinson, Cedric J. 1983. *Black Marxism: The Making of the Black Radical Tradition.* London: Zed Books.

Rodríguez, Dylan. 2011. "The Black Presidential Non-slave: Genocide and the Present Tense of Racial Slavery." In *Rethinking Obama,* edited by Julian Go, 17–50. Political Power and Social Theory 22. Bingley, UK: Emerald Group.

Roediger, David R. 2008. *How Race Survived U.S. History: From Settlement and Slavery to the Obama Phenomenon.* New York: Verso.

Ross, Luana. 1998. *Inventing the Savage: The Social Construction of Native American Criminality.* Austin: University of Texas Press.

Spillers, Hortense. 2003. "Mama's Baby, Papa's Maybe: An American Grammar Book." In *Black, White, and in Color: Essays on American Literature and Culture,* 203–29. Chicago: University of Chicago Press.

Taylor, Keeanga-Yamahtta. 2016a. *From #BlackLivesMatter to Black Liberation.* Chicago: Haymarket Books.

Taylor, Keeanga-Yamahtta. 2016b. Response to "Black Study, Black Struggle," by Robin D. G. Kelley. *Boston Review,* March 7. bostonreview.net/forum/black-study-black-struggle /keeanga-yamahtta-taylor-keeanga-yamahtta-taylor-response-robin.

Vargas, João Costa. 2010. *Never Meant to Survive: Genocide and Utopias in Black Diaspora Communities.* Lanham, MD: Rowman and Littlefield.

Wynter, Sylvia. 2003. "Unsettling the Coloniality of Being/Power/Truth/Freedom: Towards the Human, after Man, Its Overrepresentation—an Argument." *CR: The New Centennial Review* 3, no. 3: 257–337.

Minkah Makalani

Black Lives Matter and the Limits of Formal Black Politics

> I can't breathe. I can't breathe. I can't breathe.
> I can't breathe. I can't breathe. I can't breathe.
> I can't breathe. I can't breathe. I can't breathe.
> I can't breathe. I can't breathe.
> —Eric Garner

> We love you, Ms. Lezley.
> —Female protester to Lezley McSpadden,
> mother of Michael Brown

> Burn this motherfucker down. Burn this bitch down.
> Burn this bitch down. Burn this bitch down.
> Burn this bitch down. Burn this bitch down.
> Burn this bitch down. Burn this bitch down.
> Burn this bitch down. Burn this bitch down.
> Burn this bitch down.
> —Louis Head, stepfather of Michael Brown

Early responses to the Black Lives Matter (BLM) movement from black public figures, intellectuals, journalists, and elected officials ranged from thoughtful reflection on its emergence and core demands to romantic hopes for a new civil rights movement, criticisms of its decentralized organizational structure and lack of identifiable leadership, censure for its lack of clear policy proposals, and even a dismissiveness around a perceived

The South Atlantic Quarterly 116:3, July 2017
DOI 10.1215/00382876-3961472   © 2017 Duke University Press

lack of civility and unwillingness to engage in meaningful dialogue. TV personality Oprah Winfrey, for example, lamented that BLM activists needed "some kind of leadership to come out of this to say, 'This is what we want. . . . This is what has to change, and these are the steps that we need to take to make these changes, and this is what we're willing to do to get it'" (quoted in Somashekhar 2015). While it would be easy to dismiss Winfrey as a marginal figure in black politics, she captured an increasingly popular view. Barbara Reynolds (2015) complained that, as a former civil rights activist, she found it difficult to support BLM activists given their indecorous dress and incivility. In contrast, the historian Peniel E. Joseph (2015) considers the BLM's demands concerning police violence and the corresponding protests "one of the most profound social-justice movements" since the civil rights movement, yet he echoed Winfrey's criticism when he suggested that the central flaw of BLM was its failure to rise to the challenge of our political present, by which he meant the failure to "craft specific and detailed policy goals, at the federal, state and local levels, that will connect creative protest and moral passion to game-changing legal and legislative changes." Joseph (2016) would later cite the policy platform put forward by the Movement for Black Lives (M4BL), a united front of various BLM organizations, as seemingly emerging in response to such criticisms.[1] Such criticisms suggest that black political movements, to be considered legitimate, must engage in reasoned, rationally ordered practices that are legible within the dominant political order.

The focus on organizational bureaucracy, leadership, policy, and civility reflects an ethical understanding of black politics that remains preoccupied with recognition within the prevailing social order. If we take politics to mean not merely the nature of rule or simply efforts by groups to gain advantage within given fields of association (racial groups, communities or neighborhoods, cities, states, or nation-states) but also attempts to adjust or alter a group's position within that field, we can see where the concern with the organizational and affective character of black politics assumes critical importance. A liberal black politics demands that any attempt to influence how black people are positioned within the political order structures its goals and practices so that they align with the operations of formal political rule. The emphasis here is not simply electoral politics or the mechanism by which groups might propose new laws or changes to existing laws or mount efforts to transform civil codes in the service of a desired outcome. Rather, it also entails delimiting the range of claims, proposals, and behaviors to those that are deemed acceptable to the prevailing political order; this is less a common sense than a set of protocols that guide the procedures and practices of governing.

Liberal black political engagements can occur either through participation in those processes and institutions (voting in elections, holding public office, proposing policies, etc.) that are constitutive of the formal or through forms of popular protest and social activism that are designed to bring about adjustments to and transformations of those political institutions and practices. The central feature of either orientation (electoralism or social movements) is their mutual acceptance of the legitimacy of the prevailing order. Whether focused on electoral power or social transformations, much of black political discourse remains guided by a series of assumptions that include, but are not limited to, a notion of proper political action and behavior that has the potential to elicit broad-based public support and empathy, which is commonly, if somewhat mistakenly, understood as a politics of respectability. This entails, as well, the sense that altering dominant political structures can occur only through reasoned participation in its institutions. As such, theatrical confrontations that challenge those in power and are designed to disrupt public events and white social space (protests blocking thoroughfares and highways, black brunch demonstrations, die-ins) reject civil public debate. Whatever value there may be in those "creative protests" of police killings of black people would seem to reside in how well such anger translates into political participation, where candidates for elected office offer the possibility of pursuing practical reforms. Black politics seems capable of understanding BLM only in those terms that are on offer from dominant state apparatuses, whose protocols, procedures, and logics for redress are rooted in the same structures of liberal democratic governance that underpin the police's claim of the state's right to domestic sovereign violence.

The broad-based response from black people to George Zimmerman's killing of Trayvon Martin, to the police killings of Eric Garner in Staten Island, Michael Brown in Ferguson, and Freddie Gray in Baltimore, suggests something of the challenge confronting black politics. The acquittal of Zimmerman, and its illustration of the precarity of black life, prompted three queer black women, Alicia Garza, Patrisse Cullors, and Opal Tometi, to launch #BlackLivesMatter, which they envisioned as "an ideological and political intervention in a world where Black lives are systematically and intentionally targeted for demise" (Garza 2014). What is key in the declaration "Black lives matter" is that it refuses any simplistic call for increased electoral participation, policy proposals, and the expansion of democratic protections as an adequate response to "extrajudicial" killings.

M4BL's policy platform has drawn praise from some as a sign of the movement's maturation, a compliment that simultaneously suggests that the BLM movement had heretofore acted rather childishly, that it can only be taken seriously to the extent that its demands assume a form generally intelligible to a political elite who might then operationalize its proposals within prevailing governing structures. Yet this platform hardly reflects a desire to incorporate BLM into the political mainstream. As M4BL signatories explain, their platform is strategic. Given the nature of their grouping, they openly admit that not all of their "collective needs and visions can be translated into policy," which in itself stems from their belief that "policy change is one of the many tactics necessary" to move them toward the world they envision, "a world where freedom and justice is the reality." Consisting of calls for reparations, an end to state killings of black people, social justice, and political power for black people, the M4BL policy proposals actually exceed the realm of possibility within established political norms. As such, those who would now recognize BLM as a legitimate movement on the basis of its policy platform do so by ignoring the signatories' belief that, rather than reform, they are after "a complete transformation of the current systems," which, they state, "place profit over people and make it impossible for many of us to breathe" (M4BL 2016). This is in line with what Garza (2014) had previously described as the central goal of BLM, which was to build a movement that affirms the lives of "Black queer and trans folks, disabled folks, Black-undocumented folks, folks with records, women and all Black lives along the gender spectrum," lives excluded from the civil rights discourse of access, opportunities, and inclusion that guides much of the thinking of the black political elite. Indeed, one might well say that such proposals, either as policy or as the political demands of a mass movement, are unreasonable given the unlikelihood that these will ever be adopted, though that should hardly be seen as a negative.

How might we think about the declaration "Black lives matter," if we view it as demanding something that might well prove impossible? I have in mind Richard Iton's (2008: 13) observation that modernity "implies and requires antonymic and problematic others—[that] it, to put it bluntly, needs 'the nigger.'" Iton acknowledges that it is reasonable for those deemed "other" to desire to be seen as normal. While such a vindicationist impulse is not unexpected, he questions whether a group excluded or marginalized as other can "viably challenge their circumstances without questioning the logic and language of their exclusion" (13). This observation anticipates the central demands of the BLM movement. "Black lives matter," as a political language capturing the queer, the trans, the convicted, the disabled, the undocumented, and the gender nonconforming, actually insists on a radical transformation. Put differently, the statement "Black lives matter" operates through its acknowledgment of the racial reality that black lives *do not* matter. This is not to impugn or dismiss the claim as such but to underscore that its demand for black lives *to* matter involves an indictment of the sociopolitical order in which black people's incorporation into white racial democracy occurs through their marginalization, exploitation, and exclusion. "Black lives matter," then, against the backdrop of a liberal black political ethics, presents us with "the nigger" as the figure of a black radical politics—the paradigmatic noncitizen that suggests the impossibility of conjoining blackness and citizenship, a proposition that itself raises a foundational question for the US liberal democratic project: Can the United States survive if black lives, in fact, do matter?

Western Political Thinking of the Exception

A major current within the civil rights movement organized local communities and engaged in political education initiatives as part of a larger campaign to dismantle the institutional and cultural structures of white supremacy. A central belief of this movement, one might even say its guiding conviction, which has long since gained ascendency, is a view of racism as a singular flaw in an otherwise ethically sound liberal democracy. Still, efforts around housing, jobs, welfare rights, racial terror, and state violence often involved levels of community organizing and programs in political education that facilitated more radical formations, such as the Lowndes County Freedom Organization and the Mississippi Freedom Democratic Party, two formations whose voter registration campaign and electoral strategies targeted white racial supremacy in county and state government. Indeed, it was in the 1966 March Against Fear, a march to the Mississippi state capital initiated by James Meredith to encourage people to register to vote, that Black Power emerged as a political project. Nevertheless, at its most basic, the civil rights movement sought to improve the daily lives and secure the basic citizenship rights of black people, goals that relied on compelling congressional actions, presidential executive orders, and federal intervention in local governance and winning key court decisions.

A central paradox in civil rights struggles, however, is that a primary focus was to pursue forms of redress by the state for injuries incurred from the state. Jim Crow laws, voter suppression, and the actions of Southern legislators and police forces became, at best, symbols of Southern backwardness, and, at worst, the failure of certain legal institutions, local municipalities, or their representatives to live up to the promise and possibility of US democracy. One consequence of this was to narrow attention to racial injustices to the actions of liberal individuals, bad citizens, or, at best, rogue agents of the state, leaving virtually untouched the constitutive structural elements of the US democratic project that, one might argue, ensured that black life does not matter.

That the civil rights movement was able to secure black people's basic citizenship rights, that it was, in purely juridical terms, able to expand the range of liberal democratic privileges and protections to those foundationally excluded from its purview, has meant to some that its core moral claims, its organizational structures, its political methods, and its spectacular mobilizations and confrontations represent, not a baseline for how groups might seek redress, but the ethical claims, the manner of mobilization, the negotiation, and the compromise required of any engagement with formal political processes. What has come down from the 1960s, then, is less a tradition than a template, the final form of black politics. A core feature of this template involves what Juliet Hooker (2016: 454) describes as the transformation of black democratic suffering into democratic exemplarity, which has as its goal "making the entire political community more just and free." This understanding of black politics renders any deviation from that template, or even the suggestion of an alternative to our liberal democratic present, as, at best, misguided, if not utopian (which is to say irresponsible), or, even worse, a sharp departure from a humanistic project.

The dominant mode of black politics thus confines itself to a range of demands that depend on a delimited rhetorical field and field of action, which has the effect of leaving unexamined a more radically oriented black politics that has issued from the elaboration of black life within a state of exception. As political speech, the declaration "Black lives matter" focuses attention on the mechanisms by which black lives do not matter. To be sure, to assert that black lives matter is to assume a legitimated field wherein black life can be incorporated into the prevailing structures of political association and governance. Yet in its radical register, the declaration involves moving beyond registering a flaw in policing that body cameras or educational programs might easily address. To insist on a world where black lives do matter brings into view those mechanisms by which blackness continues to provide a baseline for a racialized US democracy, where blackness remains visible as the point below which whites must never fall.

Giorgio Agamben's (1998: 10–11) discussion of "bare life" as reflecting not so much basic biological life but the premise of political life that reveals a condition to which "we are all potentially exposed" helps in unraveling the intimacies between modern democratic governance and totalitarian rule, although his turn to the Nazi camp as the paradigmatic example of the moment of collapse elides the very modes of coloniality that remain unremarked in his thinking. I will return to this point of Agamben's thinking later. What I want to highlight here is that the declaration "Black lives matter" echoes a longer-running commentary on, and a rejection of, the protocols of sovereign rule, where thinking about the exception presents colonialism, plantation slavery, and genocidal violence in Africa, the Americas, and India as long-standing features of the modern. From this tradition of black thought, we can see the state of exception not as something arrived at and thus not a state of exception at all. Rather, it appears as something akin to what Achille Mbembe (2001: 29–30) calls a *régime d'exception*, where there is not so much a departure from but an absence of common law, where political rule is designed merely to command subjects, rather than negotiate with citizens within a context of consensual governance. In such a setting, there is no regard for the means by which the modern, the rulers who command, upon encountering their constitutive other, generally in various "states of nature," might bring about their civilization. For Mbembe, this involves a collapsing of the means and ends of rule as civilizing, which, as others have noted of modernity, may necessarily entail violence.

We are therefore confronted with the question of what forms of black politics and political thought open up to us if we view an emergency as representing less the bringing about of an exception than that which illuminates an already operative exception. To draw on Walter Benjamin's (1968: 257) observation that "the tradition of the oppressed teaches us that the 'state of emergency' in which we live is not the exception but the rule," what insights might we gain by viewing Ferguson, Baltimore, and Milwaukee as issuing from a tradition for which the paradigmatic emergency was a prior, longer-standing reality? What if these protests reflect a form of political discourse largely unintelligible to black elites and the larger political structures, for whom this is merely lawlessness and rioting, yet still one whose perspectives insist, if we can follow Benjamin a bit further, that we "attain to a conception of history that is in keeping with this insight" (257)? It seems that it is primarily in thinking through black political thought that we find the conceptual tools for addressing these questions.

Head, Apologies, and Apologia

In discussing the problem of the human in contemporary critical thought, Anthony Bogues (2012: 34) observes that "it is a critical task of radical thought today to work with the speech of those who have been historically excluded from the history of thought," a practice that requires "coming to grips with the speech and practices" of those peoples who are marginalized within or excluded from the social order as productive of thought. This involves taking seriously those claims, actions, and practices that seemingly depart from or stand outside of what is acceptable given prevailing social norms. I want to extend Bogues's thinking, particularly his explicit departure from Agamben's approach to the exception through a foregrounding of the colonial, wherein he focuses on those who exist in a Fanonian zone of nonbeing. While I am not suggesting that Ferguson and Baltimore are colonial contexts, the sovereign practices of those municipalities nonetheless operate within the matrix of coloniality, where the black residents of Ferguson and Baltimore are those on whom "practices of violence [are] conducted that ma[ke] them not sites of exception but rather sites in which regularized performances of violence as power [are] enacted" (Bogues 2012: 34). In other words, I am after how the actions and speech of those in Baltimore and Ferguson reveal the seeming exception as, in fact, the rule of rule.

Within days of Ferguson police officer Darren Wilson's shooting and killing of Brown, an eighteen-year-old unarmed black man who had recently graduated high school, local residents and activists from around the country descended on West Florissant Avenue in the St. Louis suburb. The response of the local police department was to have officers in military-grade riot gear and armored vehicles, using flash grenades and tear gas, confront protesters. One week after Brown's body lay lifeless in the street for four and a half hours, after police repeatedly destroyed memorials that local residents had erected to Brown on the spot where he was killed, Missouri governor Jay Nixon declared a state of emergency in Ferguson. Although the state of emergency imposed a curfew that made it illegal to be out after midnight, protests continued, as did clashes with local and state police, even after Nixon called in the National Guard. Yet, in what many saw as an unprecedented move, on November 17, 2014, Nixon declared another state of emergency, this time in anticipation of the St. Louis County grand jury's decision on whether to indict Wilson. Some might have considered Nixon's second state of emergency prescient. Indeed, on November 25, when it was announced that the grand jury had decided against handing down an indictment of Wilson, Ferguson erupted.

After witnessing their son's body lying in the blistering August heat, handling his transition, burial, and an unimaginable level of grief, Brown's mother, Lezley McSpadden, and stepfather, Louis Head, had to hear not only that there would be no indictment but, possibly more troubling, that St. Louis County prosecutor Robert McCulloch had purposefully undermined any possibility of an indictment. Their range of emotions came together in a moment of grief, anger, and rage when McSpadden, in tears and atop a car, addressed a crowd gathered outside the Ferguson courthouse. McSpadden made it clear that after having endured the loss of her son, she felt that the grand jury's decision demonstrated a complete lack of care. "They ain't never gonna care. I been here my whole life, I ain't never had to go through nothing like this," she told the crowd. As McSpadden began to break down in tears, cries of "fuck the police" were mixed in with a young woman yelling, "We love you, Ms. Lezley," a uniquely Southern black form of address for an honored community member, especially a mother (McDonald 2014).

McSpadden's justifiable anger and indignation helps us bring into view the central paradox of turning to the state as the agent offering repair for the actions of the state. When CNN reporter Sunny Hostin asked McSpadden why she addressed the crowd, she explained, "We heard this and it was just like, like I had been shot. Like you shoot me now" (quoted in Ford and Levs 2014). McSpadden refused to consider police officer Wilson, county prosecutor McCulloch, and the grand jury as separate from one another or apart from the state. Police killings are not, in such a formulation, the action of individual police officers who represent the state but do not constitute the state as such. Rather, they are considered parts of a whole. When McSpadden says, "Like you shoot me now," she brings McCulloch's handling of the grand jury into the same frame as Wilson, where she identifies both as the "you" who shot her son *and* her. The "you" here works to capture the state as the party causing injury. To confront such a scenario, one has to ask how a private "citizen" might reconcile the incongruity of turning to the state to carry out repair of an injury that the state caused.

It was in this vortex of emotion that Head climbed onto the car to comfort his wife and then screamed out, "Burn this bitch down," delivering it at a pitch that many would all too easily explain away as an "excited utterance." Yet Head repeated his incendiary plea eleven times, which, while unintentional, echoed Garner's plea, also uttered eleven times, "I can't breathe." The resonance of Head's "excited utterance" with Garner's pleas is that it resists the disciplining impulse to render it as thoughtless anger. Indeed, Head acted somewhat deliberately. An Al Jazeera America camera recorded him saying moments before he climbed onto the car, "If I get up there, I'm gonna start a riot. Burn this bitch down" (quoted in America Tonight Digital Team 2014).

As Head would later describe his "outburst," "I screamed words that I shouldn't have screamed in the heat of the moment" (quoted in Alcindor and Bacon 2014), an apparent apology born of the necessities of our political present, where the legitimacy of one's grief and anger, one's claim to injury, especially if one is black, depends on one's expression of that grief on the terms sanctioned by the social order. Central to such a demand is that people design their expression of grief so as to cause minimal disruption to that order. Head, McSpadden, and their advisers certainly understood this in having Head issue an apology, particularly given the efforts to charge him with inciting a riot. The response from black political elites revealed the continued sway of a civil rights approach that seeks to maintain a moral ground by putting forth the unimpeachable citizen exemplar of sacrifice. Such an approach requires a disavowal of Head's "outburst" as a mistake, mere thoughtless anger.

Rather than attempt to explain away Head's anger, I want to suggest that we can see in his shouting "burn this bitch down" an adequate response to his slain son *and* to Eric Garner's pleas; his is an anger that, as if speaking to Frantz Fanon's observation, "we revolt simply because, for many reasons, we can no longer breathe," expressed a desire for the total destruction of the racial state. Doing so enables us to dwell on the possibilities that his defiant call holds for thinking through a mode of black politics that refuses the prevailing protocols and logics governing public demands for reparative justice. My interest is not to explain Head's or any other seemingly "extreme" expression of anger as a departure from black politics. What we find in such expressions, which include the uprisings in Ferguson and Baltimore, is a critique that exceeds the sensibilities of liberal black political discourse precisely in their suggestion of the incompatibility, or possibly the constitutive exclusion, of the black as noncitizen, the paradigmatic other.

By taking Head as engaged in political discourse, I want to see in his apology more than an attempt to negotiate the protocols of legitimate or acceptable speech. Given the social function of apology—admission of a violation and an agreement or promise to avoid any such future violation—those apologizing recognize their transgression of a social or political norm and locate guilt for that violation in their own actions or words.[2] This was certainly part of what Head intended when he said, "I humbly apologize to all of those who read my pain and anger as a true desire for what I want for our community." Still, we might better view his statement as an apologia—a defense or justification of his "outburst."[3] Head went on: "But to place blame solely on me for the conditions of our community, and country, after the grand jury decision, goes way too far and is as wrong as the decision itself. To declare a state of emergency and send a message of war, and not peace, before a grand jury decision was announced is also wrong" (quoted in Alcindor and Bacon 2014).

I want to consider Head's apologia as centering on a critique of the racial state through his identification of Governor Nixon's November 17, 2014, state of emergency order as the context in which he expressed his pain and anger. The fundamental injury in this instance becomes the actions of the state itself, though not simply because the grand jury refused to indict Wilson, or even because county prosecutor McCulloch worked to ensure that the grand jury would not return an indictment. Whereas Agamben might consider Nixon's two state of emergency orders the moment an exception appeared, Head invites us to bring into view a longer-running exception already in place. As such, his original "outburst" brings to mind not so much a desire to destroy property or "our community" but the institutional orderings of the local municipality in which black people experienced a perpetual exception. Head's invective thus reflects a knowledge born from experiencing Ferguson as a *régime d'exception*. Unlike in Mbembe's (2001) framing, where the departure from common law occurs when privileged individuals and companies constitute for themselves a "form of sovereignty," in Ferguson there was no departure as such, as the posture that the municipality of Ferguson assumed toward its black residents was that of a sovereign toward its subjects who existed outside the compact of consensual governance.

The Department of Justice's (DOJ) report on Ferguson offers insight into how the city's revenue-generating strategy allowed local police and courts to elaborate an exception. As the report outlines, generating revenue through policing black residents "fostered practices in the two central parts of Ferguson's law enforcement system—policing and the courts—that are themselves unconstitutional or that contribute to constitutional violations" (DOJ 2015: 27). Where for the police these policies led to practices that "resulted in a pattern and practice of constitutional violations" (27) of black residents' First and Fourth Amendment rights, the local courts assumed as their primary goal maximizing revenue rather than "administering justice or protecting the rights of the accused" (68). The DOJ (2016: 24) investigation of the Baltimore police discovered a similar "pattern or practice of making stops, searches, and arrests in violation of the Fourth and Fourteenth Amendments" where they lacked "reasonable suspicion of people who [were] lawfully present on Baltimore streets," which in turn "escalate[d] street encounters and contribute[d] to officers making arrests without probable cause." The DOJ's (2015: 27) concern in both instances lay with the erosion of "police legitimacy and community trust" that made "policing in Ferguson less fair, less effective at promoting public safety, and less safe," a concern the DOJ (2016: 29) repeated in its Baltimore report, where it identified the practice of unlawful stops and searches as working to "erode public confidence in law enforcement and escalate street encounters."

The DOJ reports on Ferguson and Baltimore take as a core concern the erosion of black trust in the police, where the level of distrust helps to escalate encounters between black people and the police. This is no minor problem. Amy E. Lerman and Vesla Weaver (2014) explain that this eroding trust in the police and the state more generally gives rise to what they call custodial citizenship, where citizenship is transformed from a mode of civic engagement through democratic structures into a series of maneuvers designed to minimize encounters with the state. This sense of needing to evade encountering the state certainly seemed to have guided Garner's, Gray's, and Brown's respective encounters with the police officers who killed them. The DOJ (2016) report on Baltimore is littered with incidents where black people breaking no laws attempt to evade and avoid encounters with the police. What the DOJ reports do not question, and it would have been surprising if they had, is whether the erosion of black people's trust in the agents of the state, and thus the state itself, was of recent provenance. In light of Joel Olson's (2004: xv) observation that "American democracy is a white democracy, a polity ruled in the interests of a white citizenry and characterized by simultaneous relations of equality and privilege . . . in relation to those who are not white," we might question whether there is a basis for black citizenship to be anything other than custodial, with a corresponding fugitive orientation toward (or away from) state apparatuses.[4] To put the question differently, is it useful to approach the problem of the "erosion" of black trust in the state as one that the state can solve?

To answer this question demands that we give attention to how the state approaches the issue of police violence. One feature of both the DOJ's (2015: 48; 2016: 74) reports on Ferguson and Baltimore that deserves attention is their reliance on the US Supreme Court's 1989 *Graham v. Connor* decision that provides the legal framework for how to assess police officers' use of force. The key passage from that ruling (*Graham v. Connor*, 490 U.S. 386, 396 (1989)), quoted in both reports, holds that police officers' use of force must be judged based on whether "the officers' actions are 'objectively reasonable' in light of the facts and circumstances confronting them," wherein the central element of such an assessment is "the perspective of a reasonable officer on the scene," rather than "the 20/20 vision of hindsight." The part of the ruling that neither report references, however, holds that such an assessment is to be made "without regard to [the officer's] underlying intent or motivation." The effect of this ruling, which allows for the use of force if the officer determines that a "suspect poses an immediate threat to the safety of the officers or others," is that the officer is the sole body capable of determining whether force, and what degree of force, is necessary—"even if it may later seem unnecessary in the peace of a judge's chambers" (*Graham*, 490 U.S. at 396). *Graham* thus provides the legal justification for police officers to exercise violence, but outside the judgment or oversight of any other governmental body; the police become, in effect, the sovereign, and they are the ones who decide. This is not the suspension of law that Agamben describes as a moment that democracies arrive at—thus marking their historiographical distinction from totalitarian regimes. Rather, the context in which black people exist is itself the exception.

Notwithstanding the insights we might gain from the DOJ's investigations into the Ferguson and Baltimore police departments, these reports follow a pattern whereby the state is the agent offering repair for actions of the state. In finding fault with local police departments or municipal courts, the issue is rendered a strictly local one. That the police practices described in Ferguson and Baltimore are also found in Philadelphia, Cleveland, New Orleans, and Milwaukee (all police departments under consent decrees) never seems to present the possibility that what the DOJ has "uncovered" in any of these departments is less an aberration from the norm than the norm itself. Indeed, rarely have such findings resulted in the prosecution of local police officers for corruption. Under *Graham*, police officers are virtually unprosecutable.

We are confronted, then, with the Ferguson and Baltimore uprisings mounting what we might describe as an ontological challenge to the guiding premise of black politics as a liberal engagement that pursues redress so that black life can matter within US liberal democracy. Rather than the suspension of law during an emergency, or an aberration from legitimate modes of governance, what Ferguson and Baltimore bring into sharp relief is that the police, even before the juridical armature of *Graham*, exercised the sovereign right to kill. It is in this context that we should read Head's "outburst," his unacceptable, nonsensical speech, as making a fundamental claim about the nature of Western democracies. Head's words reveal how Ferguson is less a zone of exception, an aberration arrived at, than an example of a constitutive element in the operation of democracy. Head thus reflects a politics largely rejected in dominant black political discourse, yet one that suggests something of the nature of US democratic governance as constituted through an exception.

Coloniality and Democracy

Coloniality offers an analytical lens through which to unravel and read Head's invective as exemplary of a form of black radical thought that is rejected by black political elites. *Coloniality* should not be seen as a synonym for *colonialism*. Iton (2008: 301) suggests that a far more productive approach is to view colonialism, slavery, genocide, the postcolony, and citizenship as among a series of conveniences available "within the broader matrix of coloniality." While black political elites would dismiss Head's invective as nonsense, I want to argue that it gestures toward or expresses a desire for a politically unimaginable future. This argument involves two moves. First, I attend to coloniality as a frame for the political realities of black people in the United States. This is not a novel observation, but one that reflects a largely disregarded account of black political reality in the United States as an internal colony. A central feature of the internal colonization thesis, as it was loosely known, was a critique that regarded the guiding logic of civil rights struggles for citizenship rights as accepting Western liberal democracy as a sound political structure with minor flaws, and which suggested that citizenship represented another form of coloniality. What is crucial about this understanding of coloniality is how it considers the present as issuing from a much longer set of practices and modes of rule that are rooted in colonial institutions yet extend beyond what some might view as a strictly colonial context.

The second move entails approaching utterances like Head's—those generally dismissed as unreasonable, irrational, and unintelligible as thought—as what Bogues (2003) calls "redemptive prophecy." Redemptive prophecy is employed in the colonial context by those who are entirely unlike the black educated elite—those "rooted in the subsoil of the African diaspora in the West" (16), who operate in a zone of nonbeing where "the formal public spaces of political action are sometimes the unlikely sites for the examination of forms of resistance and struggle" (17). In the US context, Bogues's argument that a black redemptive prophecy engages in social criticism of racial and colonial oppression can be traced in the internal colonization thesis developed by Black Power intellectuals, which reflected a critical shift in thinking about power that I want to argue anticipates the core of Head's invective.

In 1967 Jack O'Dell, a longtime Communist, civil rights activist, and editor of the black radical periodical *Freedomways*, made a compelling observation about colonial structures and the constituting of the United States. Focusing specifically on the American Revolution as an anticolonial struggle, O'Dell (2012: 129) noted that "the de-colonization of the American mainland achieved by the Revolution of 1776, which at the same time left the institution of slavery intact, meant, in effect, that the African population in America remained a colonized people." The failure to end slavery, O'Dell continued, meant that the American Revolution, itself an anticolonial revolution, resulted in the new nation that, in its formation, "consolidat[ed] its state power and sovereignty on the basis of preserving the slavery variety of colonialism. . . . The new American Republic did not completely uproot its own colonial heritage" (129). In describing plantation slavery as a colonial institution, O'Dell was not, however, merely relegating slavery to a colonial holdover but rather was situating it as a central feature of the colonial orderings of the postindependence US state. The plantation represents a colonial ordering constitutive of modern society, where questions of freedom, mastery, and regimes of the (hu)man took shape. With the defeat of Reconstruction, there was not merely the failure of a fulsome democratic experiment, as W. E. B. DuBois ([1935] 1998) would put it. It ensured the "colonial-captive position of the black population in America" and the exercises of power through racial violence that O'Dell (2012: 130) argued compared "favorably with what the European colonialists . . . were doing on the African continent during the same period."[5]

Regardless of how one might assess O'Dell's claim, of greatest importance here is his insistence on blurring the colonial violence of empire and its institutions and the forms of republican governance that might suggest a unique historical plantation experience. O'Dell's insistence on plantation slavery as a colonial institution implicates not merely a domestic institution but a central feature of the Westphalian order—the nation-state. The result is not, as Jared Sexton (2010) might view it, a disavowal of slavery as a prior structure instituting social death. Rather, it suggests an attempt to think through the violence of modernity.

In the classic work *Black Power*, Kwame Ture (Stokely Carmichael) and Charles V. Hamilton ([1967] 1992) identified urban ghettos as the political and economic structures of internal colonial control that sustained white supremacy. Ture had already drawn on Fanon ([1963] 2004) in order to discuss institutional racism (or a system of racial oppression, as opposed to individual acts of racism) as a form of colonial violence (Wald 2012: 190–91).

In *Black Power*, he and Hamilton extended the point to rethink black social movements as struggles that stood in opposition to realizing a liberal democratic dream. Seeing the United States itself as an empire, they declared that the only "place for black Americans in these struggles . . . is on the side of the Third World" (Ture and Hamilton [1967] 1992: xix), where, quoting Fanon directly, they argued that one could approach "starting a new history of Man" (Fanon [1963] 2004: 238).[6] Robert L. Allen, in his work *Black Awakening in Capitalist America* ([1967] 1990: 14), parted with Ture and Hamilton to consider black America's transformation "from a colonial nation into a neocolonial nation . . . subject to the will and domination of white America." Rather than the civil rights movement having granted black America full equality, Allen emphasized what today we might usefully see as the postcolonial condition of black America that, like many newly independent African colonies, assumed incorrectly that "they were being granted equality and self-determination" (14).

The arguments of Allen, as well as Ture and Hamilton, contrast with Agamben's (1998: 10–11) more recent provocation concerning "modern democracy's decadence and gradual convergence with totalitarian states in post-democratic spectacular societies." Agamben's focus on the camp involves a corresponding historiographical distinction between totalitarianism and modern democracy that inheres precisely through his elision of coloniality—the geopolitical nodes and long-standing features of the modern, the states of exception that stood as the rule on which liberal democracy proceeded, the locus where that historiographical *and* historico-philosophical link between totalitarianism and democracy precedes by some centuries the Nazi extermination camp. There is also a conceptual limit in Agamben's focus on the Nazi camp as the moment of collapse, the "hidden matrix and *nomos* of the political space in which we are still living" (166). The camp represents "the space that is opened when the state of exception begins to become the rule" (168–69).[7] On this view, we might see Benjamin's state of emergency as rule, and the single catastrophe perpetually piling debris before the angel of history, beginning to accumulate through coloniality, that is, in 1492.

Coloniality thus allows, if in a limited way, for us to approach Head's demand to "burn this motherfucker down" as speaking in a prophetic register that, in the realm of nonelite black political discourse, disregards the neat temporal and geographic distinctions common in normative political theory. In so doing, the concern is less with a given genealogy of black thought in which we might position Head—though this may well prove fruitful. Rather, it is to find in those observations and ways of seeing that issue from those "rooted in the subsoil of the African diaspora" in the United States, a politics that resonates with a longer tradition of black radical thinking of the colonial and simultaneously insists on the central ethical claims about freedom implicit in the declaration "Black lives matter."

What I am after here is an approach to Head's invective that recognizes how it resonates with similar critiques that issue from a similar region of what Bogues calls this diasporic subsoil. I have in mind specifically the hip-hop artist Nas's 1994 album *Illmatic* and in particular the track "The World Is Yours," where the Queens-based MC considers the tenuous possibilities of black life that are simultaneously ignored and heavily surveilled. Nas (1994) renders this dynamic in one exceptionally dense stanza:

> To my man Ill Will, God bless your life
> To my peoples throughout Queens, God bless your life
> I trip, we box up crazy bitches
> Aiming guns at all my baby pictures
> Beef with housing police, release scriptures that's maybe Hitler's.

In these lines, Nas captures the deep ties between life and death. After invoking the name of his deceased childhood friend Ill Will, Nas's lyrics descend into apparent nihilism—wanton murder, children engaged in gunplay—as a way to approach something quite different. This line forms part of a couplet that draws in housing police who "release scriptures that's maybe Hitler's." The reference here is to a provision in the 1988 Anti-Drug Abuse Act that required public housing authorities to include in all leases a clause that made any drug-related activity grounds for eviction (Weil 1991). During the 1990s, public housing authorities across the country routinely evicted entire families if a single resident, especially a dependent teen, was charged with a drug offense. Yet Nas complicated his critique by also underscoring how these are the same police, as the state, who fail in their obligation to reduce violence. As Lisa L. Miller's (2014) discussion of Brown reminds us, state violence entails an array of "social risks which the state itself shapes, limits, expands, or diminishes," such as unemployment, poverty, access to firearms, and infant mortality, all of which depend on whether we are talking about the citizen or the subject. It is not inconsequential that in the opening verse of "The World Is Yours," Nas invokes anticolonial struggle: "I sip the Dom P., watching *Gandhi* 'til I'm charged." Drawing on Miller, we can thus see Nas as registering the normalcy of gun violence and murder not through the simplistic trope of "black-on-black violence" but as focusing attention on the range of state violence as both failure and killing. This is what makes Nas's equating the housing police with Nazis compelling, as it draws a link between the ghetto and the Jewish ghettos in Eastern Europe, thus the ghetto and the concentration camp, which in turn calls into question any identification of the Nazi extermination camp as the paradigmatic site of collapse. Indeed, given Agamben's exclusive reliance on European philosophers such as Hannah Arendt and Michel Foucault, it is not surprising that he misses a more profound theoretical commentary on the exception that we find occurring among Black Power theorists, who are themselves, as possibly Nas was, drawing on important Caribbean anticolonial thinkers.

Aimé Césaire's *Discourse on Colonialism* ([1950] 2000: 31) offers a critique of the colonial underpinning of modernity by declaring that the two central problems of Western civilization are "the problem of the proletariat and the colonial problem." Importantly, it was in this same work that Césaire echoed earlier black radicals who rejected any sense of distance between democratic European powers engaged in empire and fascism. Describing the fascism of Hitler's Nazi regime as the "boomerang effect" of colonialism, Césaire argued that Europe had tolerated "Nazism before it was inflicted on them," because until then "colonialist procedures . . . had been reserved exclusively for the Arabs of Algeria, the 'coolies' of India, and the 'niggers' of Africa" (36). Fascism, then, was not the product of an abhorrent mind or a more general aberration from modernity that required a special response.[8] Likewise, C. L. R. James in his essay "Dialectical Materialism and the Fate of Humanity" ([1947] 2013) forecast what he considered the decline of Western civilization by noting that the totalitarian regimes of Nazi Germany and Soviet Russia were emblematic of the modern social order. In this way, James, and Césaire after him, departed from Arendt's more well-known articulation of the "boomerang" thesis as the result of late nineteenth-century racial thinking that issued from European imperialism. Rather than root their notion of the convergence of democracy and fascism in economics, as one might expect of Marxist thinkers, they expressly located it in the political. "Only a shallow empiricism can fail to see," James ([1947] 2013: 371) argued, "that such monstrous societies are not the product of a national peculiarity (the German character) or a system of government ('communism') but are part and parcel of our civilisation." James (1973: 71–72) would recast this claim slightly, though importantly, in a 1960 lecture in Trinidad, where he insisted, "When I speak about the barbarism, the degeneration and the decay of Western civilization, I do not separate East from West, and Fascism from Democracy. I take the whole as symptomatic of what is taking place today."

The Challenge to Black Politics

Ferguson thus raises the question of what insights are available if we attend to a tradition of political thought for which emergency was a prior, long-standing reality.[9] Head's call to destroy Ferguson, which I take here to mean a state structure that exacted its power through violence on his and McSpadden's son, Brown, echoes an articulation of the black radical tradition's more developed arguments about the imbricated nature of democracy and coloniality. Such a view underscores the limits of a liberal black politics that assumes that black life can matter, if by mattering we understand the question of blackness not as the paradigmatic other, "the nigger," but as juxtaposed to the citizen, a party to the constitution of the state but constituted as its subject.

I want to see countervailing claims about the black citizen as equally a problem of political imagination. These insights suggest a need for something entirely new, which I would frame not in terms of futurity but what I call the politically unimaginable. The politically unimaginable concerns less bringing the future into focus than how one might exceed the limits of the current political or social order. Where Richard Rorty (2007: 107) describes "imagination not as a faculty that generates mental images but as the ability to change social practices," which entails a new deployment of already given and legitimated "marks and noises," available procedures and ideas— thought that remains within given political and social norms—the unimaginable takes up what he dismisses as "foolish, or perhaps insane." My concern here occupies similar conceptual terrain as Iton's (2008: 16–17) discussion of the "black fantastic," in particular his efforts to bring "into the field of play practices and ritual spaces that are often cast as beyond the reasonable and relevant—to the point, indeed, of being unrecognizable as politics. . . ." Where the imaginary constricts the range of possibility to what is reasonable, proper, and makes sense, the unimaginable, by contrast, refuses this normative range of possibility and begins precisely with that which is impossible or nonsensical as thought and culls from the experiences of peoples and movements those worldviews, practices, and knowledges that enable us to move beyond the already available.[10]

The politically unimaginable is precisely what a liberal black politics finds itself unable to grapple with in Ferguson. We might even say that there is no way for liberal black politics to incorporate a Ferguson. This is in large part because the activists of Ferguson seem to reject the parameters of black electoral politics, national black leaders, and even progressive venues of political discourse.[11] As a decentralized movement led by black women that locates police violence within larger structures of the state, and poverty, it presents a challenge to formal black political practices that seek access and power within those very structures. The result is that BLM and Ferguson, whose demands are generally beyond possible within the current political order, are largely unintelligible to those outside its organizational practices and political discourses.

If we ever do burn this motherfucker down, we would rightly be concerned with what we might build in its place. I am not suggesting that we should grope toward a clearly outlined, rationally ordered future that would realize a utopia, not if our aim is to get beyond coloniality. But burning this motherfucker down at least offers the possibility insisted on by the insights of the oppressed into the limits of modern rule.

Notes

I would like to thank Debra Thompson, Ed Baptist, and Russell Rickford for helping me think through some of the arguments that appear here. I would also like to especially thank Juliet Hooker and Barnor Hesse for their critical feedback on initial drafts of this project. Earlier versions were presented at the 2015 Western Political Science Association meeting, and the Black Politics–History–Theory Workshop, titled "After #Ferguson, After #Baltimore: The Challenge of Black Death and Black Life for Black Political Thought," sponsored by Northwestern University's Center for African American History.

1 Joseph (2016) mentions specifically an August 2015 exchange where Hillary Clinton told BLM activists, "You're going to have to come together as a movement and say, 'Here's what we want done about it.' . . . Because in politics, if you can't explain it . . . it stays on its shelf" (for footage of this exchange, see Merica 2015). Joseph expressed the sense among many that this exchange reflected a general failing of BLM until its 2016 policy statement (M4BL 2016). What has been lost in most commentary about this exchange is Clinton's own obvious and utter failure to have any policy ideas of her own that might address state-sanctioned police killings of black people, let alone a clear policy that might offer any manner of remedy for the damage done by the 1994 crime bill that then president Bill Clinton pushed through and by her strident advocacy of that bill as a safeguard against the now thoroughly debunked myth of black teenage superpredators.

2 The *Oxford English Dictionary* (*OED*; 2017) provides the following primary definition of *apology*: "the pleading off from a charge or imputation, whether expressed, implied, or only conceived as possible; defence of a person, or vindication of an institution, etc., from accusation or aspersion." Obviously, in public life (especially with politicians and public figures) we often see something radically short of this. Especially in terms of racist language or actions, it is more common for a black person responding to racism, if that response is deemed unacceptable, to offer an apology, while the one who committed a racist act or made a racist statement is able to qualify an apology thus: "I apologize if I / my comments / my actions offended anyone," or "I apologize if anyone was offended by my comments/actions." The rhetorical gesture conveys no sense of regret

or a commitment to repair and has the effect of locating the offense in the actions of the one who feels offended or violated, not in the actions or words of the one apologizing; thus an offense occurs only if someone was offended or injured, allowing for the possibility that no one was, in fact, offended or injured or, at a minimum, impugning those who took offense or felt violated, as it is their taking offense or feeling violated that brings about the injury rather than the act that no reasonable person would have otherwise taken issue with. For a discussion of governmental apologies, see Nobles 2008.

3   The sole *OED* (2017) definition of *apologia* bears little resemblance to its etymological root, *apology*: "a written defence or justification of the opinions or conduct of a writer, speaker, etc."

4   On black fugitivity, see Harney and Moten 2013 and Hesse 2014.

5   On the historico-philosophical conflation of the European to the paradigmatic human, see Wynter 2003.

6   For an illuminating treatment of the influence that Fanon's discussion of colonial violence had on Ture's distinction between individual and institutional racism, see Wald 2012: 190–91.

7   While in the hands of Benjamin (1968) such a starting point allowed him to produce some of the more penetrating observations about the conceptual demands of a dialectical analysis of the exception and the historical insights to issue from those who suffer exceptions as rule, it is less clear why scholars covering similar terrain have not looked beyond, or back before, the camp as their conceptual limit. Thus Agamben, in his keen insights into the exception's constitutive centrality to democracy, follows a rather general practice of starting his observations with the concentration camp. Edith Wyschogrod (1985: ix), whose conceptualization of the death-world I find to hold important insights into the structure of coloniality, identifies "nuclear annihilation and the creation of the concentration camp" as paradigmatic twentieth-century horrors. Even as an empirical question, there is a strict delimiting of thought around the camp. Critical reviews of David Olusoga and Casper W. Erichsen's *The Kaiser's Holocaust* (2011) generally dismiss their location of German death camps and genocidal violence in early twentieth-century Namibia with the Herero genocide. On the question of race and the exception that starts from the Herero genocide to interrogate Hannah Arendt's thinking, see Lee 2007.

8   For a discussion of this thinking by Amy Ashwood Garvey, C. L. R. James, and George Padmore in London, see Makalani 2011: 203–7. See also Robinson 1983 and Kelley 2000: 19–21.

9   Michael Hanchard (2006) makes a similar claim regarding the state of exception in diasporic contexts, though he does not explore this point as fully as he does others in his examination into blackness."

10   See also Sheldon Wolin's (2009: 18) discussion of imagination. My argument shares many of Bogues's (2012) concerns with a radical imagination, or what Gary Wilder (2009) calls strategic utopianism. Both Bogues and Wilder take up the problem of freedom to suggest that it is a practice that involves creativity, is rooted in experience, and is open-ended rather than a given set of claims with an already determined outcome.

11   For a thorough discussion of this generational conflict that informs my thinking here, see Taylor 2016.

References

Agamben, Giorgio. 1998. *Homo Sacer: Sovereign Power and Bare Life.* Translated by Daniel Heller-Roazen. Stanford, CA: Stanford University Press.

Alcindor, Yamiche, and John Bacon. 2014. "Michael Brown's Stepfather Apologizes for Violent Rant." *USA Today,* December 3. www.usatoday.com/story/news/nation/2014/12/03 /louis-head-apology-burn/19827121.

Allen, Robert L. (1967) 1990. *Black Awakening in Capitalist America: An Analytic History.* Trenton, NJ: Africa World Press.

America Tonight Digital Team. 2014. "What Michael Brown's Stepdad Said before Climbing onto the Car." Al Jazeera America, December 3. http://america.aljazeera.com/watch /shows/america-tonight/articles/2014/12/3/what-michael-brownsstepdadsaidbefore heclimbedontothecar.html.

Arendt, Hannah. (1951) 1976. *The Origins of Totalitarianism.* New York: Harcourt.

Benjamin, Walter. 1968. *Illuminations: Essays and Reflections.* Translated by Harry Zohn. New York: Schocken Books.

Bogues, Anthony. 2003. *Black Heretics, Black Prophets: Radical Political Intellectuals.* New York: Routledge.

Bogues, Anthony. 2010. *Empire of Liberty: Power, Desire, and Freedom.* Hanover, NH: University Press of New England.

Bogues, Anthony. 2012. "And What about the Human? Freedom, Human Emancipation, and the Radical Imagination." *boundary 2* 39, no. 3: 29–46.

Césaire, Aimé. (1950) 2000. *Discourse on Colonialism.* Translated by Joan Pinkham. New York: Monthly Review Press.

DOJ (Department of Justice). 2015. *The Ferguson Report.* New York: New Press.

DOJ (Department of Justice). 2016. "Investigation of the Baltimore City Police Department." August 10. www.justice.gov/opa/file/883366/download.

DuBois, W. E. B. (1935) 1998. *Black Reconstruction in America, 1860–1880.* New York: Free Press.

Fanon, Frantz. (1963) 2004. *The Wretched of the Earth.* Translated by Richard Philcox. New York: Grove.

Ford, Dana, and Josh Levs. 2014. "Michael Brown's Mother: 'This Could Be Your Child.'" CNN, November 27. www.cnn.com/2014/11/26/justice/ferguson-grand-jury-reaction.

Foucault, Michel. 1995. *Discipline and Punish: The Birth of the Prison.* Translated by Alan Sheridan. New York: Vintage Books.

Garza, Alicia. 2014. "A Herstory of the #BlackLivesMatter Movement." *The Feminist Wire* (blog), October 7. www.thefeministwire.com/2014/10/blacklivesmatter-2.

Hanchard, Michael. 2006. *Party/Politics: Horizons in Black Political Thought.* New York: Oxford University Press.

Harney, Stefano, and Fred Moten. 2013. *The Undercommons: Fugitive Planning and Black Study.* New York: Minor Compositions.

Hesse, Barnor. 2014. "Escaping Liberty: Western Hegemony, Black Fugitivity." *Political Theory* 42, no. 3: 288–313.

Hooker, Juliet. 2016. "Black Lives Matter and the Paradoxes of U.S. Black Politics: From Democratic Sacrifice to Democratic Repair." *Political Theory* 44, no. 4: 448–69.

Iton, Richard. 2008. *In Search of the Black Fantastic: Politics and Popular Culture in the Post–Civil Rights Era.* New York: Oxford University Press.

James, C. L. R. (1947) 2013. "Dialectical Materialism and the Fate of Humanity." In *Caribbean Political Thought: The Colonial State to Caribbean Internationalism*, edited by Aaron Kamugisha, 371–98. Kingston: Ian Randle Publishers.

James, C. L. R. 1973. *Modern Politics*. Detroit: Bewick Editions.

Joseph, Peniel E. 2015. "Time for #BlackLivesMatter to Turn Protest into Policy." *Root*, January 7. www.theroot.com/articles/culture/2015/01/_blacklivesmatter_turning_protest _into_policy.

Joseph, Peniel E. 2016. "Black Lives Matter's Big Steps." Opinion, CNN, August 3. www.cnn .com/2016/08/03/opinions/black-lives-matter-movement-report-joseph.

Kelley, Robin D. G. 2000. "A Poetics of Anticolonialism." Introduction to Césaire, *Discourse on Colonialism*, 7–28.

Lee, Christopher. 2007. "Race and Bureaucracy Revisited: Hannah Arendt's Recent Reemergence in African Studies." In *Hannah Arendt and the Uses of History: Imperialism, Nation, Race, and Genocide*, by Richard H. King and Dan Stone, 68–86. New York: Berghahn Books.

Lerman, Amy E., and Vesla Weaver. 2014. *Arresting Citizenship: The Democratic Consequences of American Crime Control*. Chicago: University of Chicago Press.

Makalani, Minkah. 2011. *In the Cause of Freedom: Radical Black Internationalism from Harlem to London, 1917–1939*. Chapel Hill: University of North Carolina Press.

Mbembe, Achille. 2001. *On the Postcolony*. Berkeley: University of California Press.

McDonald, Brent. 2014. "Michael Brown's Mother, Stepfather React." *New York Times* video, 1:30. November 25. www.nytimes.com/video/us/100000003254183/michael-browns -mother-reacts.html.

Merica, Dan. 2015. "Black Lives Matter Videos, Clinton Campaign Reveal Details of Meeting." Politics, CNN, August 18. www.cnn.com/2015/08/18/politics/hillary-clinton-black -lives-matter-meeting.

M4BL (Movement for Black Lives). 2016. "Platform." http://policy.m4bl.org/platform (accessed July 12, 2016).

Miller, Lisa L. 2014. "Racialized State Failure and the Violent Death of Michael Brown." *Theory and Event* 17, no. S3. http://muse.jhu.edu/journals/theory_and_event/v017/17.3S .miller.html.

Nas. 1994. "The World Is Yours." *Illmatic*. Columbia Records. Compact disc.

Nobles, Melissa. 2008. *The Politics of Official Apologies*. New York: Cambridge University Press.

O'Dell, Jack. 2012. *Climbin' Jacob's Ladder: The Black Freedom Movement Writings of Jack O'Dell*. Edited by Nikhil Pal Singh. Berkeley: University of California Press.

Olson, Joel. 2004. *The Abolition of White Democracy*. Minneapolis: University of Minnesota Press.

Olusoga, David, and Casper W. Erichsen. 2011. *The Kaiser's Holocaust: Germany's Forgotten Genocide and the Colonial Roots of Nazism*. New York: Faber and Faber.

Oxford English Dictionary Online. 2017. "apologia, n." and "apology, n." *OED.com*.

Reynolds, Barbara. 2015. "I Was a Civil Rights Activist in the 1960s. But It's Hard for Me to Get behind Black Lives Matter." PostEverything, *Washington Post*, August 24. www.washington post.com/posteverything/wp/2015/08/24/i-was-a-civil-rights-activist-in-the-1960s -but-its-hard-for-me-to-get-behind-black-lives-matter.

Robinson, Cedric. 1983. "Fascism and the Intersection of Capitalism, Racialism, and Historical Consciousness." *Humanities in Society* 3, no. 6: 325–49.

Rorty, Richard. 2007. *Philosophy as Cultural Politics.* Vol. 4 of *Philosophical Papers.* Cambridge: Cambridge University Press.

Sexton, Jared. 2010. "People-of-Color-Blindness: Notes on the Afterlife of Slavery." *Social Text* 28, no. 2: 31–56.

Somashekhar, Sandhya. 2015. "Protesters Slam Oprah over Comments That They Lack 'Leadership.'" *Post Nation* (blog), *Washington Post*, January 2. www.washingtonpost.com /news/post-nation/wp/2015/01/02/protesters-slam-oprah-over-comments-that-they -lack-leadership.

Taylor, Keeanga-Yamahtta. 2016. *From #BlackLivesMatter to Black Liberation.* Chicago: Haymarket Books.

Ture, Kwame [Stokely Carmichael], and Charles V. Hamilton. (1967) 1992. *Black Power: The Politics of Liberation.* New York: Vintage Books.

Wald, Priscilla. 2012. "American Studies and the Politics of Life." *American Quarterly* 64, no. 2: 185–204.

Weil, Lisa. 1991. "Drug-Related Evictions in Public Housing: Congress' Addiction to a Quick Fix." *Yale Law and Policy Review* 9, no. 1: 161–89.

Wilder, Gary. 2009. "Untimely Vision: Aimé Césaire, Decolonization, Utopia." *Public Culture* 21, no. 1: 101–40.

Wolin, Sheldon. 2009. *Democracy Incorporated: Managed Democracy and the Specter of Inverted Totalitarianism.* Princeton, NJ: Princeton University Press.

Wynter, Sylvia. 2003. "Unsettling the Coloniality of Being/Power/Truth/Freedom: Towards the Human, after Man, Its Overrepresentation—an Argument." *CR: The New Centennial Review* 3, no. 3: 257–337.

Wyschogrod, Edith. 1985. *Spirit in Ashes: Hegel, Heidegger, and Man-Made Mass Death.* New Haven, CT: Yale University Press.

Shatema Threadcraft

North American Necropolitics and Gender:
On #BlackLivesMatter and Black Femicide

Feminists (Spelman 1982; Young 1990; Gatens 1996) have long concerned themselves with Western approaches to the body as well as the relationship between the body and politics and the impact of both on women. While these approaches and ways of thinking about the body are important and worthy of black feminist exploration, I think the most important issue regarding the relationship between the body and politics today is the growing concern with how that body politic produces its dead: that the body that we are thinking about, the body that receives the most attention in contemporary racial politics, is a deceased one. Contemporary racial politics is most focused on the politics of black death, on necropolitics, and relatedly on the very important work of exposing the state's efforts—often, as activists have fairly successfully pointed out, with considerable assistance from the mainstream press—to assure its citizens that it has produced the "right kind" of dead. In practice this means that the body around which blacks can most easily rally members to the cause of racial justice in this moment, the body around which we can organize, is a dead one. It is crucial that those concerned with the status of black women in society reckon with how we

The South Atlantic Quarterly 116:3, July 2017
DOI 10.1215/00382876-3961483   © 2017 Duke University Press

should respond to the centrality of necropolitics on the contemporary political stage, to this focus on the politics of death and the ensuing contests over the meaning of the bodies of the dead in the wake of the production of dead black bodies. There are benefits and burdens, inclusions and exclusions, in centering the politics of death within black politics, in giving dead bodies pride of place in black politics, and even within that necropolitics to centering the slain body. A focus on the slain body privileges how cis men die, how young men die, how able-bodied blacks die, over all other black dead.

In what follows I consider the ways that the Black Lives Matter movement and those sympathetic to its narrative regarding the production of the bodies of the black dead have brought strategies employed in an earlier US necropolitical struggle, the US antilynching campaign, together with technological innovations. They have achieved considerable success in comparison to a fairly recent necropolitical struggle, the struggle against femicide at the Mexico–United States border outlined by Melissa Wright, which preceded the advent of those innovations the Black Lives Matter movement has used to great effect. However, while I recognize and celebrate these successes, I am deeply concerned that the movement may ultimately fail black women. I would therefore like to reflect on how this necropolitical movement, if it is not properly intersectional, may do little to change the problematic ways that state power intersects with the black female body as well as the production of the bodies of black female dead.

As may now be clear, I have reservations about privileging the slain black body in politics. For one thing, blacks have more than the bodies of the slain around which to organize, even within a strictly necropolitical sense. On this point, I have stated elsewhere (Threadcraft 2016b) that residential conditions in black neighborhoods are described as "pathogenic" in themselves, producing "excess death." Public health scholars (Williams and Collins 2001: 405) have acknowledged that "racial residential segregation is the cornerstone on which black-white disparities in health status have been built in the US." They argue that "segregation is a fundamental cause of differences in health status between African Americans and whites because it shapes socioeconomic conditions for blacks not only at the individual and household levels but also at the neighborhood and community levels" (405). Consider, as well, the points Clint Smith (2016) makes in an essay titled "Racism, Stress, and Black Death":

> According to a study by the American Psychology Association, "more than three in four black adults report experiencing day-to-day discrimination and nearly

two in five black men say that police have unfairly stopped, searched, questioned, physically threatened or abused them." Living under the perpetual and pervasive threat of racism seems, for black men and black women, to quite literally reduce lifespans. Black people face social and economic challenges—often deriving from institutionalized racism—in the form of disparities in education, housing, food, medical care, and many other things. But the act of interfacing with prejudice itself has profound psychological implications, resulting in the sorts of trauma that last long beyond the incidents themselves.

Perhaps just as important, according to research published this past December in the journal *Psychoneuroendocrinology*, simply perceiving or anticipating discrimination contributes to chronic stress that can cause an increase in blood-pressure problems, coronary-artery disease, cognitive impairment, and infant mortality. Black Americans do not have to directly experience police brutality to experience the negative health ramifications of its possibility. And that fear is not something grounded in paranoia. As President Obama noted in his speech after the deaths of [Alton] Sterling and [Philando] Castile, these disparities in treatment at the hands of the police are well-documented.

There is a great deal to be said about the health effects of discrimination. First, blacks do not have to be physically injured by police to be brought closer to death. Second, blacks do not even have to encounter police to be harmed by their presence. Third, we must consider racism as part of the environmental conditions in black neighborhoods. The health data reveal a great deal about the operation of this form of power, how its impact extends beyond the discrete encounter to touch the bodies of all in the space. Naa Oyo Kwate and I address this health threat in a separate piece (Threadcraft and Kwate, forthcoming). In what follows, however, I would like to return to a point I have also made before regarding gender and necropolitics.

Black women have been subject to a host of practices that have much more in common with Achille Mbembe's necropolitics than with Michel Foucault's biopower and normalization but are nonetheless not identical to the phenomenon Mbembe describes (Threadcraft 2016a). Black women are subjected to disproportionate sexual assault, community violence, and public sexual aggression. They are disproportionately targeted for long-acting contraceptives and child removal policies. Power, specifically white power, intersects with the black female body to produce its preferred forms of racialized feminine embodiment—the assaulted and terrorized body, yes—but when held in comparison to how power intersects with the black male body, far more rarely does it produce a dead black female body. I would like to return to the topic of how power intersects with the black female body below as, given this and the extraordinary amount of attention given to the dead body in contemporary racial politics, we must decide how black politics can/should be reformulated in light of the gendered distinctions in how power intersects with the black body.

Sex Worker, Narco, Thug:
Resisting Contemporary North American Necropolitics

Protests against recent police murders of unarmed black men have brought questions that have long been topics of conversation within black communities to the forefront of mainstream politics. The visibility of these issues was evident in events like the #BlackLivesMatter debate during the 2016 Democratic presidential campaign, as well as a White House town hall meeting on the topic (Hirschfeld Davis 2016). Notably, criminal justice reform topped Democratic presidential nominee Hillary Clinton's "racial justice" platform (Hillary for America 2016b). After the #BlackLivesMatter movement brought considerable pressure to bear on both her campaign and that of her rival Bernie Sanders, Clinton pledged to bring "law enforcement and communities together to develop national guidelines on the use of force by police officers, making it clear when deadly force is warranted and when it isn't and emphasizing proven methods for de-escalating situations" (Hillary for America 2016a). She also stated that it is important to acknowledge that "implicit bias still exists across society." She promised to use executive power to combat said implicit bias and pledged to commit "$1 billion in her first budget to find and fund the best training programs, support new research, and make this a national policing priority." She also pledged to collect and report national data—as at this point it is concerned citizens who have collected what data exist—in order "to inform policing strategies and provide greater transparency and accountability when it comes to crime, officer-involved shootings, and deaths in custody." Members of Clinton's campaign team, and specifically her "deputy millennial vote director" Jamira Burley, explicitly credited #BlackLivesMatter for this shift, saying, "The fact that the Black Lives Matter movement and other criminal justice reformers have held her feet to the fire has helped her become a lot more sensitive to how she shows up in those spaces" (quoted in Beckett and Lartey 2016).

What these debates, town halls, and Democratic presidential platforms demonstrated is that, finally, the nation, and not simply blacks, now questions how state power intersects with the black body in this country and why that power so often produces a dead body. Critically, in all of this discussion, a media-savvy group of protesters began to convince others of their understanding of the meaning of the bodies of the dead the state produced. The loose structure of Black Lives Matter activism—as, to take part, one can do as little as compose a tweet and as much as take nonviolent direct action that may lead to arrest and detention—is both a benefit and a curse. The movement has benefited from the rise of phenomena such as "black Twitter," and the fact that many members of that community concur with the meaning Black Lives Matter assigns to the bodies of the dead rather than the state's assertion of what the bodies mean—that they are thugs deserving of death— black Twitter, like #BlackLivesMatter, accepts that the dead are the product of the disproportionate and illegitimate use of police force against black bodies. They have thus gone on to disseminate the Black Lives Matter narrative regarding the meanings of the bodies of the dead. But, as the movement also depends on the ability of each dead body to resonate with the wider black community, it has become clear that all black bodies do not produce equal amounts of community outrage. It is thus not clear how the movement can respond to existing hierarchies and prejudices in the wider black community regarding the meaning of the living, which holds fast to bodies, even in death.

Mbembe (2003) examines the importance of the politics of death in the exercise of power in his article "Necropolitics" and notes that this power is particularly salient in the control and management of subject peoples and marginalized populations. He holds that "the ultimate expression of sovereignty resides, to a large degree, in the power and the capacity to dictate who may live and who must die" (11). Mbembe goes on to say: "Hence, to kill or to allow to live constitute the limits of sovereignty, its fundamental attributes. To exercise sovereignty is to exercise control over mortality and to define life as the deployment and manifestation of power" (11–12).

He asks readers, then, "What place is given to life, death, and the human body (in particular the wounded or slain body)? How are they inscribed in the order of power?" (12). Mbembe's impressive analysis of the politics of death considers how necropower intersects with a generic body and remains silent on how the phenomenon intersects with male and female bodies, respectively.

Wright (2011), in her examination of the gendered necropolitics at the Mexico–United States border, grapples with Mbembe's important question and argues, first, that the politics of gender and the politics of death go hand in hand and, second, that states often play a decisive role in assigning meaning to the bodies of the dead in the successful operation of necropower. States engage in efforts to convince those within their borders that the proper body for the subjects in question is, in fact, a deceased body. I whole-heartedly agree with Wright's first point and see it as especially relevant in the US case. Wright is also correct in drawing attention to the fact that the successful operation of necropower requires the work of assigning meaning to the bodies of the dead. The state expends effort, uses its resources, to define how the subject lived and therefore what the subject was, thereby labeling a given subject as deserving of death, a subject whose proper embodiment is, in fact, a deceased body. In the Mexican case Wright probes, state officials did so both with the death the state itself produced and with the deaths it failed to stop, assigning subjects the labels of sex worker and narco and thereby legitimizing their deaths. In the US context, the same was true of lynching, with efforts to affix the mark of the rapist to the body of the dead; with contemporary police slayings we also see concerted efforts to affix the mark of the thug to the black body.

In the incidents Wright examines, as dead bodies piled up, the question became this: Do the dead bodies in Ciudad Juárez demonstrate that the state is failing, as activists contend, or that the state is that much stronger, as government elites contend? With femicide and the male victims of narcoviolence, the state asserted that the female dead were simply sex workers and the male dead were involved in the drug trade, respectively. In both circumstances, the dead bodies were certainly no cause for alarm and were even cause for celebration—their deaths were, then, evidence of a strong state.

A few words on *femicide*. It refers to the murder of women because they are women. Diana E. H. Russell heard the term as early as 1974, used it publicly at the First International Tribunal on Crimes Against Women in 1976, and originally defined it as the hate killing of women by men. Russell eventually settled on the killing of females because they are female. In her testimony she stated: "From the burning of witches in the past, to the more recent widespread custom of female infanticide in many societies, to the killing of women for so-called honor, we realize that femicide has been going on a long time" (Russell 2011).

It has indeed.

Mexican activists concerned about the female dead challenged the state's claims that all dead women were sex workers, but, in this, they confronted the very strong association between working women and "working" women, between female workers and sex workers. Because of these associations, of the tendency to see a woman in public as a "public woman," state officials could readily explain the women's deaths as a kind of public cleansing that rid the body politic of their contamination, their deaths helping to restore the moral and political balance of society. The logic, drawing heavily on the gendered divisions between public and private and a notion that public space is properly male space, operated this way: a woman who was dead must have been in public, out of her proper place in private, for a woman in public is a public woman, a sex worker, and thus now properly embodied in the dead body she possessed, deserving her death, possessing a dead body indicted the subject as a sex worker—death was all the proof one needed of her transgressions into public space and sex work, and her death should not trouble women who are not sex workers, women who did not transgress, should not trouble properly private women. Officials also asserted that keeping women at home would keep them safe—and here ceded any role for the state itself in protecting them, since women were by definition safe at home. The activists countered that the subjects, the women, were not sex workers—not that there was anything wrong with that—but were good daughters, working in factories to support their families, and therefore lethal violence against them was evidence of a severely weakened, if not failed, state. The activists, however, mounted this challenge largely without the benefit of social media and smartphones.

In the US context, it appears that the #BlackLivesMatter campaign has gained considerable ground in one aspect of a long-standing necropolitical struggle: it has gained ground not in stopping the production of dead bodies, as that continues apace and may yet increase, but in the extremely important contest over the meaning of the bodies of the black dead. It has gained ground, and now a growing number of people ask, "Is the proper body for the subject who finds himself in the grip of state power a deceased one?" In comparison to struggles between the state and activists over meaning around femicide and narcoviolence, the #BlackLivesMatter campaign has been more successful in challenging the state's preferred meaning regarding the bodies of the dead. It has also gotten many who once opposed it to make at least verbal concessions to the Black Lives Matter cause. It has been able to do this in part due to technological innovations, such as smartphones and social media, but in particular because of the rise of black Twitter. But while technology has been important, I see the movement's successes as a result of its ability to blend old and new, new technology with strategies deployed in an older US necropolitical campaign, the antilynching campaign, specifically; it has, whether consciously or not, brought together many of the strategies employed by the United States' most iconic necropolitical warrior, one Ida B. Wells, along with the aforementioned technological innovations.

From the Antilynching Campaign to #BlackLivesMatter

Wells's pioneering necropolitical activism lives on in the contemporary #BlackLivesMatter movement in three very important ways. First, in challenging the meaning assigned to the bodies of the black dead in her time, Wells ([1892] 1991) outlined the consecutive excuses white supremacists offered for why they murdered blacks, and by doing this alone she managed to trouble the meaning assigned to the bodies of the dead. She asked her readers to recall that white supremacists asserted that the lynched black dead were race rioters. When that was proved false she reminded her audience that white supremacists then claimed that the dead were "negro dominators," attempting to subordinate whites politically. This excuse also did not hold. Finally, she pointed out, the murderers and their apologists hit on rape, and this meaning stuck. With "rapist" attached to the dead black body, the subject's status as dead was legitimized, and those who slay the subject were shielded from criticism. In death, the subject, the rapist, was now appropriately embodied. Second, Wells ([1892] 1991) not only pointed out the suspect nature of this moving-meaning target—as obviously the murderers and their supporters were simply justifying what they had done after the fact and attempting to see what excuse worked—she also called out "the malicious and untruthful white press" for its role in perpetuating lynching by circulating false stereotypes of black people. Third, she documented the actual circumstances of lynching to present a story far different from the narrative those in power circulated. The murders were much harder to justify once she documented and compiled evidence of blacks lynched for infractions such as stealing chickens and "sassing" whites.

The Black Lives Matter campaign and those sympathetic to its cause have made use of all these strategies. They have challenged white attempts to attach the meaning "thug" to the body of the black slain, understanding the work that this word was doing and how it functioned to justify police killings, much as Wells challenged the meaning "rapist." They have also challenged the state's assertion that *thug* should mark the line between he who lives and he who must die, here going a step further than femicide activists who have simply argued that the deceased female subjects were hardworking women not working girls. They have called out the mainstream press for aiding and abetting the state's efforts to affix this meaning to the bodies of the dead. And they have documented the circumstances of blacks' deaths at the hands of police, in a context in which the state has long refused to do so.

They have done the above aided by technological innovations, including smartphones and social media. Smartphones, in particular, have helped to amplify what turns out to be the important phenomenon of witnessing in evoking outrage over the production of dead bodies. Social media has been particularly important in disseminating Black Lives Matter's counternarrative regarding the bodies of the dead. Alicia Garza first uttered and disseminated the phrase "black lives matter" in response to the acquittal of George Zimmerman in the murder of Trayvon Martin. Yet recall the massive social media campaign that led to the eventual arrest and prosecution, if sadly not the conviction, of Zimmerman, after police initially failed to arrest him. I dare say that without social media there would be no Black Lives Matter.

Consider the phenomenon that is "black Twitter." Black Twitter may represent a virtual black counterpublic, rising again after a period of decline, as noted by Michael C. Dawson (1994). Twitter itself is a technological innovation all but tailor-made to accommodate black oral traditions such as signifying and playing the dozens. The contemporary necropolitical struggle has had the good fortune to arise in a cultural context in which a higher percentage of blacks use Twitter (26 percent of all black Internet users as compared to 14 percent of whites [Duggan and Brenner 2013]); use Twitter more times per day than whites (Jones 2013); and, arguably, though I would venture objectively, use Twitter far better than all other groups. On the last point, in the words of André Brock (2012: 545), "Black Twitter came to online prominence through creative use of Twitter's hashtag function and subsequent domination of Twitter's 'trending topics.'" Brock writes: "Twitter's discourse conventions, ubiquity, and social features encouraged increased Black participation; Black Twitter is Twitter's mediation of Black cultural discourse, or 'signifyin.' In particular, Black hashtag signifying revealed alternate Twitter discourses to the mainstream and encourages a formulation of Black Twitter as a 'social public'; a community constructed through their use of social media by outsiders and insiders alike" (530). Blacks' exceptional use of Twitter has allowed black counterdiscourse on a variety of topics to register and register consistently within mainstream discourse. Among the topics to register is blacks' long-standing counterdiscourse regarding police brutality and lethal state violence against blacks. Black Twitter has been so successful at driving the conversation, by dominating trending topics each week, that the mainstream media has often been forced to respond.

Whereas Wells took aim at white supremacists' and the mainstream press's attempts to attach the meaning "rapist" to the body of the black dead in the Jim Crow era, the current black necropolitical insurgency has set its sights on the mark "thug" and how this mark serves as a justification for death. Rashad Robinson, executive director of Color of Change (2017), the nation's largest online racial justice organization, committed to creating "a more human and less hostile world for Black people in America" summed up the problem and why it is such an important front in the current necropolitical contests: "'These young people have their bodies criminalized even after death.' Criminalization occurs when images chosen by media consciously or unconsciously create a justification for why people of color are killed" (quoted in Lewis 2014). The campaign has taken on the malicious stereotypes regarding blacks circulated by the mainstream press, and here CNN and even the *New York Times* become Wells's *Evening Scimitar*. According to the *Root*'s Yesha Callahan (2014a):

> The vicious slaying of Michael Brown by Ferguson, Mo., police has once again shown that the narrative the media paints surrounding black people in America more often than not includes depicting us as violent thugs with gang and drug affiliations. . . .
>
> Trayvon [Martin], who was killed by George Zimmerman, was depicted as a gold-grill-wearing, weed-smoking teenager in the photos used by the media. There were no photos of Trayvon smiling with his family members or being just your average happy teen, which his family members said he was. Similarly, the photos of Brown that have been picked up by the media included him throwing up a peace sign, which conservative media has translated into a "gang sign."
>
> You'd be hard-pressed to find mainstream media showing Brown at his high school graduation or with members of his family.

In response to the above, Callahan reported the creation of the hashtag #IfTheyGunnedMeDown to make a statement regarding how the media circulated a biased narrative when it came to reporting the slayings of black men and women. Twitter users responded to the hashtag and posted photos of themselves in respectable clothing—that is, in formal wear, including military uniforms and graduation gowns—alongside photos of themselves in less respectable attire and, not coincidentally, in clothing that is closely associated with "urban" youth, although it is also worn by broader segments of the US population. The campaign posed the question: "If police gunned me down, what photo of me would the media circulate after my death?" (Callahan 2014a).

The question resonated. Lewis reports that the campaign drew nearly two hundred thousand responses to the hashtag. It was followed by the hashtag

#NoAngel in the wake of John Eligon's *New York Times* profile of Brown. Eligon (2014) wrote, "Michael Brown, 18, due to be buried on Monday, was no angel, with public records and interviews with friends and family revealing both problems and promise in his young life." Callahan's (2014b) response to the article is emblematic of the outrage it evoked on social media:

> What the f——k is wrong with the New York Times? I'll tell you what's wrong: In most mainstream media, victims of color continue to be victimized and criminalized even in death. As I read the article, my anger rose—not only as a parent of a young black man but also because just two weeks ago I wrote a blog post about #IfTheyGunnedMeDown, which discussed the imagery the media choose to use when it comes to black men. And this New York Times article is clearly a prime example of that.

Eligon's article birthed the hashtag #NoAngel. The #NoAngel backlash led to a fairly weak but decidedly *Times* "mea culpa." The BBC reported that, at first, the *Times* stuck by its account, but after the hashtag #NoAngel got three thousand mentions in less than a day, the *Times* public editor, Margaret Sullivan, admitted that the piece was not "ideal" and that "'no angel' was a blunder" (quoted in Waldman 2014). Forcing the Gray Lady to change her tune is no small feat and demonstrates the power black Twitter has been able to yield in amending the narrative in the mainstream press.

That was not the only time that reporting sparked controversy. The *Huffington Post*'s Kimberley Richards (2015) wrote that CNN faced a backlash for describing Freddie Gray as "the son of an illiterate heroin addict," in the second paragraph of an article on the trial of one of the police officers charged with Gray's death. Richards went on to report that "a torrent of people on social media pointed out that such a description has nothing to do with the allegations against the officers, but instead demeans Gray's family." The social media backlash was successful, as the company removed the description and acknowledged its "mistake."

Online activism against media representations have also led to questions regarding how whites, and often white perpetrators of mass violence, are portrayed in the press. For example, Twitter responded when CNN referred to a Planned Parenthood shooter as an "older gentleman" (@ThomboyD 2015). The *Washington Post*'s Janell Ross (2016) wrote of Cliven Bundy and his followers:

> As of Sunday afternoon, The Washington Post called them "occupiers." The New York Times opted for "armed activists" and "militia men." And the

Associated Press put the situation this way: "A family previously involved in a showdown with the federal government has occupied a building at a national wildlife refuge in Oregon and is asking militia members to join them."

Not one seemed to lean toward terms such as "insurrection," "revolt," anti-government "insurgents" or, as some on social media were calling them, "terrorists." . . .

It is hard to imagine that none of the words mentioned above—particularly "insurrection" or "revolt"—would be avoided if, for instance, a group of armed black Americans took possession of a federal or state courthouse to protest the police. Black Americans outraged about the death of a 12-year-old boy at the hands of police or concerned about the absence of a conviction in the George Zimmerman case have been frequently and inaccurately lumped in with criminals and looters, described as "thugs," or marauding wolf packs where drugs are, according to CNN's Don Lemon, "obviously" in use.

Ross calls out a clear double standard for reporting on whites and blacks.

US necropolitical activists have thus gone further than their Mexican counterparts, who did not challenge the status of sex workers as a justification for death, instead asserting that the women were not that. Even if the word *thug* successfully attaches to the body of the slain, activists in the US context have worked to ensure that this meaning is no longer sufficient to mark the line between he who lives and he who must die—they have challenged this particular claim of sovereignty. Some have gone so far as to assert that *thug* is the new N-word, with all its implications. As Jamelle Bouie (2014) has observed, "The word 'thug' has become an 'accepted way of calling somebody the N-word.' You saw it, for instance, during the Trayvon Martin controversy, where defenders of the shooter, George Zimmerman, were quick to label Martin a 'dangerous thug' for ordinary teenage behavior, like cursing or smoking marijuana." This is an excellent point, for if the mark "thug" legitimizes death and *thug* simply means "black," all with black skin are premarked for death. If *thug* and *black* are collapsed and all black bodies are thereby always marked for death, their deaths are prelegitimized. With blackness the proper packaging for all dead bodies, the death factory can continue its production at current levels, and the state can simply stamp them "thug" after their production.

Finally, like Wells, activists have collected the actual circumstances of each death at the hands of police in order to advance activists' narrative regarding the meaning of the body of the dead. For example, lists of all the reasons blacks can be killed often circulate on social media platforms to make the larger point that it is blackness itself that makes one worthy of death in the US necropolitical order. But there are also more systematic efforts to document black death. In the Mapping Police Violence project and an initiative of Campaign Zero, an organization committed to ending lethal police violence through limiting police contact, improving community inter-actions, and ensuring police accountability, we have nothing if not a modern Red Record (Sinyangwe 2016). Mapping Police Violence tracks the number of blacks killed by police each month, compares the percentage of those who were unarmed at the time of their deaths to that of white unarmed victims, and documents blacks' greater likelihood than that of whites of being killed by police each month (at the time of this article it was three times greater). In a further effort to destabilize the state's narrative regarding the meaning of the bodies of the dead, the website also presents statistics that demonstrate that blacks' greater likelihood of death at the hands of police is unconnected to higher crime rates and reports that, for example, levels of crime are not correlated with the likelihood of police killings. Newark and St. Louis are cases in point. They have similar populations and similar demographics and murder rates, yet police have killed no black men in Newark since 2013 and sixteen in St. Louis in the same period. The activists have thus made great strides by adapting Wells's strategies to the social media age.

When and Why We Should Say Her Name

I am impressed by all that #BlackLivesMatter activists have accomplished and how successfully they have been able to intervene in the politics of death in the United States. However, I would like to turn to some of the challenges they have faced and also to what I see as potential problems with centering the politics of death and the body in black politics. Although much of the above demonstrates that the Black Lives Matter movement has been able to capitalize on the ways that members of the black community have proved to be genuinely, objectively exceptional, the discussion below will show that the movement has also had to contend with the ways that blacks are not, in other words, how they are also ordinary, completely run-of-the-mill, like every other community, that is, homophobic and sexist. As I have stated else-where (Threadcraft 2016a), possessing a female body can be problematic in the US necropolitical context, as female embodiment itself appears to work against activists recognizing one's body as a body with which necropower has intersected. Female embodiment (as well as gender-nonconforming embodiment and trans embodiment) heightens the risk that any given subject's dead body will not be counted, will go unrecognized (Threadcraft 2016b). Those concerned with violence against black women, like the members of the #SayHerName campaign, have pointed out that women's deaths receive less attention and activism. The deaths of lesbian, gay, bisexual, and transgender (LGBT) people of color and trans persons of color also receive less attention and activism. But while this is disconcerting, the lack of said recognition provides an opportunity to reflect on whether joining in the struggles surrounding the politics of death is actually best suited for bringing attention to the problematic ways that state power intersects with the black female body.

I would add that if, after reflection, those concerned with the status of black women concede that—given this moment—it makes sense to take part in the necropolitical struggles receiving so much attention, they must take seriously the significant distinctions between homicide and femicide and what that will mean regarding an intersectional approach to confronting black femicide. It is not obvious that those concerned with the forces endangering black women's lives must adopt a strict "what happens to men also happens to us" approach to the politics of death, and they should not. If activists concede to centering the politics of death in black politics, they will have to find ways to overcome the challenges presented by the public/private divide and how that divide deprives their cause of a key resource that Black Lives Matter activists have been able to mobilize to great effect: witnessing. The spectacle of public, violent death, where technology facilitates the multiplication of witnessing so that a nation sees the lethal violence, when before it had only heard about it, and is therefore motivated to act, has been invaluable to the success of #BlackLivesMatter. Much of the extraordinary guerrilla power of Black Lives Matter in the face of a much more powerful meaning-making apparatus—the US state—has come from the ability to transmit images of the slaughter. This has served to rally others to accept the #BlackLivesMatter movement's narrative regarding the meaning of the bodies of the dead. Activists concerned with stemming black femicide should reflect on the fact that the movement has relied on amplifying the spectacle of death in a context in which black women suffer from a severe spectacular violent death deficit. Femicide does not lend itself to being captured in the same way. Therefore, they must ask themselves what can stand in the place of this public spectacle, when what they are dealing with are a greater number of wholly private murders. What, then, will motivate people to rally around the bodies of our black female dead?

I do not want to suggest that #BlackLivesMatter members are unaware of the issues I raise here. Garza and Patrisse Cullors, and Opal Tometi (all of whom identify as queer women of color) are recognized as founders of the #BlackLivesMatter movement (Cobb 2016). Officially, the movement is committed to black women and trans-affirming. The #BlackLivesMatter (2016) website states, "We are committed to building a Black women affirming space, free from sexism, misogyny, and male-centeredness." It also states, "We are committed to being self-reflexive and doing the work required to dismantle cis-gender privilege and uplift Black trans folk, especially Black trans women who continue to be disproportionately impacted by transantagonistic violence." What's more, the organizing aims of the Movement for Black Lives are radically comprehensive and call for nothing less than a total transformation of American society; the process by which the collection of organizations that make up the formal movement arrived at these aims was almost unassailable. Kelley (2016) writes that

> On August 1 the Movement for Black Lives (M4BL), a coalition of over sixty organizations, rolled out "A Vision for Black Lives: Black Power, Freedom, and Justice." . . . It lays out six demands aimed at ending all forms of violence and injustice endured by black people; redirecting resources from prisons and the military to education, health, and safety; creating a just, democratically controlled economy; and securing black political power within a genuinely inclusive democracy. Backing the demands are forty separate proposals and thirty-four policy briefs, replete with data, context, and legislative recommendations.

Kelley continues:

> It was the product of a year of collective discussion, research, collaboration, and intense debate, beginning with the Movement for Black Lives Convening in Cleveland last July, which initially brought together thirty different organizations. It was the product of some of the country's greatest minds representing organizations such as the Black Youth Project 100, Million Hoodies, Black Alliance for Just Immigration, Dream Defenders, the Organization for Black Struggle, and Southerners on New Ground (SONG). As Marbre Stahly-Butts, a leader of the M4BL policy table explained, "We formed working groups, facilitated multiple convenings, drew on a range of expertise, and sought guidance from grassroots organizations, organizers, and elders. As of today, well over sixty organizations and hundreds of people have contributed to the platform.". . . If heeded, the call to "end the war on Black people" would not only reduce our vulnerability to poverty, prison, and premature death but also generate what I would call a peace dividend of billions of dollars. Demilitariz-

ing the police, abolishing bail, decriminalizing drugs and sex work, and ending the criminalization of youth, transfolk, and gender-nonconforming people would dramatically diminish jail and prison populations, reduce police budgets, and make us safer. "A Vision for Black Lives" explicitly calls for divesting from prisons, policing, a failed war on drugs, fossil fuels, fiscal, and trade policies that benefit the rich and deepen inequality, and a military budget in which two-thirds of the Pentagon's spending goes to private contractors. The savings are to be invested in education, universal healthcare, housing, living wage jobs, "community-based drug and mental health treatment," restorative justice, food justice, and green energy.

However, the movement depends very much on others accepting and disseminating Black Lives Matter's preferred narrative regarding the overreach of state power and pushing for change in light of it. Kelley (2016) notes that "A Vision for Black Lives" was not drafted with the expectation that it would become the basis of a mass movement. Observers have noted that, although the movement was founded by queer women of color and many of the movement's most prominent activists identify as queer, black communities around the country have shown differing levels of concern based on the gender, sexual orientation, and gender identity of the slain (West 2016). The movement now struggles with the ways that the communities to whom it appeals evince different levels of concern that map onto existing social hierarchies vis-à-vis violence, including lethal violence against black men, black women, black trans men, and black trans women. And in this struggle, it has confronted the hierarchies of social status that contribute to how people respond to murder. So blacks face the problem not only of relative white indifference to black death, of whites caring less about murdered blacks, but also of black men and women caring less about murdered black women, of cis blacks caring less about slain trans blacks, and so on. Beth Richie (2012), for example, says that black community members have long tolerated direct physical assaults, sexual abuse and aggression, emotional manipulation, and social alienation of black women that they do not countenance against black men. Cis blacks also tolerate high levels of harassment and violence against trans blacks, just as they tolerate the disproportionate murder of trans women of color.

The activists who launched the #SayHerName campaign, like those in the broader #BlackLivesMatter movement, also attempt to intervene at the level of socially accepted meanings given to the bodies of the dead, but they struggle to have names such as Sandra Bland, Rekia Boyd, Tanisha Ander-

son, and those of other women who have been murdered by police repeated
as often, and in truth carry as much meaning, as the names of Martin, Gray,
Castile, Sterling, and Brown. Indeed, Brown's name carries so much meaning that it can stand as a synonym for the entire Black Lives Matter movement. But black women will be disadvantaged in trying to win recognition
by arguing that the same thing that happens to black men happens to them,
as that is not entirely the case. Far fewer black women, for example, than
black men are killed by police; however, black women are being slain at an
alarming rate, alongside a host of other challenges they face. That is, the
problem is far more complex for black women. #BlackLivesMatter activists
have derived benefit from the stark simplicity of their most memorable and
widely disseminated goal—ending the disproportionate murder of blacks by
police. Black women will benefit from no such simplicity, as the issues of
police violence and murder themselves are far more complex for women.
Activists concerned with black women can never articulate the situation
simply. The intersectional complexity means that if those concerned with
how power acts on the black female body want to keep the focus on the state
and state violence in a way that is gender inclusive, they cannot focus exclusively on death and the production of dead bodies. However, if activists want
to keep the focus on death, they must heed earlier feminist critiques regarding mainstream liberalism's blind spots and biases that regard the state as
the only dangerous force in a woman's life; if they are going to take part in
the politics of death, they cannot privilege the state as the death-distributing
mechanism. Often the state is not the biggest threat of violence in a woman's
life. That is not to let the state off the hook, as this does not mean that the
state cannot be indicted and that women are not endangered by the state's
inaction in the face of violence against them.

 #SayHerName activists attempt to enter the conversation around the
politics of death and at the same time broaden the conversation around how
power intersects with the black body. Kimberlé Crenshaw and Andrea J.
Ritchie (2015) wrote the report *Say Her Name: Resisting Police Brutality against
Black Women*. Crenshaw says that "although Black women are routinely
killed, raped, and beaten by the police, their experiences are rarely foregrounded in popular understandings of police brutality." Ritchie adds, "Black
women are all too often unseen in the national conversation about racial profiling, police brutality, and lethal force. . . . This report begins to shine a light
on the ways that Black women are policed similar to other members of our
communities, whether it's police killings [or] 'stop and frisk'" (Crenshaw and
Ritchie quoted in African American Policy Forum 2015).

The report's name is something of a hook to seize the moment of concern with lethal police force, however, as Crenshaw and Ritchie immediately move to broaden the discussion to include gender-specific forms of police violence. Ritchie points out that the report "also pushes open the frame to include other forms and contexts of police violence such as sexual assault by police, police abuse of pregnant women, profiling and abusive treatment of lesbian, bisexual, transgender, and gender nonconforming Black women, and police brutality in the context of responses to violence—which bring Black women's experiences into even sharper focus" (quoted in African American Policy Forum 2015). Therefore, they are attempting to seize the moment of considerable interest in the use of lethal force by police officers to drive attention to other forms of police misconduct against women. Here Crenshaw, Ritchie, and others who are concerned about violence against black women have seized on an extraordinary moment given the amount of attention police killings have received, to drive attention to the problem of violence against black women. But the entry point they have chosen may put them in a bind.

If activists must emphasize the similarities between black men's and black women's experiences over their differences to get others to care about what happens to women at all, and thus join in struggles within this variant of the politics of death—by calling attention to police murders of women to get activists to care about women at all—then they risk not having the right kind of resources devoted to ending the things police disproportionately do to black women. Ritchie is right about the broader issues facing black women. And here the scope of the problem is enormous. Consider the following: police sexual misconduct is the second-largest category of reported police misconduct after police brutality. It is also an underreported crime—a hidden crime, routinely unreported, where identified cases are recognized as only "the tip of the iceberg." It is thus quite possibly the largest category of police misconduct. Scholars (Stinson et al. 2015: 682) report that "the sexual nature of these offenses and the absence of official data have hampered the study of the phenomenon." Matt Sedensky and Nomaan Merchant (2015), writing for the Associated Press, state: "In a yearlong investigation of sexual misconduct by US law enforcement, the Associated Press uncovered about 1,000 officers who lost their badges in a six-year period for rape, sodomy and other sexual assault; sex crimes that included possession of child abuse images; or sexual misconduct such as propositioning citizens or having consensual but prohibited on-duty intercourse." The article goes on to point out: "The number is unquestionably an undercount because it represents only those officers whose licenses to work in law enforcement were revoked, and not all states take such action. California and New York—with several of the nation's largest law enforcement agencies—offered no records because they have no statewide system to decertify officers for misconduct." It may go without saying that in a context in which blacks and other communities of color are overpoliced, this misconduct disproportionately affects women of color. In an essay titled "The Color of Lawlessness: Sexual Abuse by Police, Nationwide," Chagmion Antoine (2016) points out that "racial profiling also takes gender-specific forms that often lead to sexual assault." Antoine cites a 2006 report by the United Nations Human Rights Committee (McClary and Ritchie 2006: 31), which found that "women of color experience particular impacts of current law enforcement policies and practices across the U.S." The report states:

> For instance, women are routinely profiled as drug couriers by law enforcement officers in the context of the U.S. government's "war on drugs," leading to arbitrary stops, strip searches, and detentions. The high prison sentences meted out for drug-related offenses in the U.S. also provide law enforcement officers with increased leverage for extortion schemes such as those in which officers routinely demand sexual acts in exchange for leniency. . . .
>
> . . . Additionally, racial profiling of women of color has branched out from streets and airport lounges to more gender-specific contexts, including delivery rooms across the nation, where drug-testing of pregnant women fitting the "profile" of drug users—young, poor, and Black—has given rise to a new race-based policing phenomenon of "giving birth while Black." Similarly, "mothering while Black" gives rise to more frequent allegations of child abuse and neglect against Black women, be it for perceived neglect resulting from poverty or for alleged failure to protect their children from witnessing abuse against them [the mothers] in the home. (31, 32)

This profiling extends to domestic and intimate partner violence in other ways as well, as the report notes:

> While racial profiling and use of force against women of color takes many of the same forms as it does with men of color, racial profiling also takes place in gender-specific contexts—such as implementation of mandatory arrest policies, in which women of color are disproportionately perceived to be perpetrators of domestic violence rather than survivors—and takes gender-specific forms. (32)

So if resources are funneled solely to ending the lethal use of force by police, it may do little to change how this form of state power intersects with the black female body.

However, if those concerned with black women also decide against extending the scope of protest over the problematic deployment of state power against the black body to encompass gender-specific forms of abuse and instead concede what I agree is the extraordinary power of this necropolitical moment and therefore remain most focused on the politics of death, then they run up against the distinctions between homicide and femicide and what those distinctions mean for what is necessary in stemming the production of dead black bodies and, furthermore, what I see are the problems this distinction will present for rallying others to end black femicide. Crenshaw and Ritchie are keen to drive attention to fatal black intimate partner violence, yet this issue is missing one important component that #BlackLivesMatter activists have used to great effect: spectacle.

Homicide masquerades as a general, sex-blind phenomenon covering all murder, but in some ways the androcentrism of the term is warranted. First, men and boys are, disproportionately, victims of murder. The US Department of Justice (Cooper and Smith 2011: 3) reports that between 1980 and 2008, males, including juveniles under fourteen and teens between fourteen and seventeen, were 77 percent of murder victims. Second, men and women are killed in different ways, by different people, with men more likely to be killed in what are quite literally more "spectacular" circumstances, in ways that are public and in view. Scott A. Bonn (2015) reports: "Men are most likely to be killed by a friend or an acquaintance in a public place such as the street or a sporting event. This is due in part to the fact that men are more likely than women to be in public places that increase their victimization risk such as a bar or pool room." Their deaths are therefore more likely to be witnessed—and in the twenty-first century, filmed—and perceived as disruptions to the public order and, as such, perceived as part of a problem that society should devote collective resources to solving. Third, men and boys are much more likely to be killed during concurrent illegal activity; they were 90 percent of drug-related and 95 percent of gang-related homicides between 1980 and 2008 (Cooper and Smith 2011: 10) and, again, these are the kinds of deaths that register as threats to the public order. Significantly, they are killed by nonintimates, although they are often killed by acquaintances. In this broader context—with men more likely to be killed period, to be in a public space when killed, and to be killed during criminal activity—men are far more likely to be killed by police and today are more likely to be killed by police on tape.

Femicide is a different phenomenon. The term may strike some as feminist linguistic overreach, but *femicide* is as apt as *homicide*. First, as the above makes clear, only 23 percent of those murdered are women and girls, and they are not killed in the same contexts that men are, nor are they killed by the same people. They represent 63.1 percent of those killed by intimates and 81.7 percent of those killed in sex-related murders (Cooper and Smith 2011: 10). They are, therefore, killed in the course of things that have come to define the private sphere in many cultures, not least of all our own. They are also likely to be killed during an argument and not during the commission of a felony. Women are killed in private, without witness or only witnessed by politically voiceless minors; they are killed in the home, that space long considered a man's castle. Their deaths are unlikely to register as threats to the public order. Their deaths are unlikely to register at all.

More broadly, Russell (2011), one of the earliest adopters of the term *femicide*, states:

> Examples of femicide include the stoning to death of females (which I con-
> sider a form of torture-femicide); murders of females for so-called "honor";
> rape murders; murders of women and girls by their husbands, boyfriends,
> and dates, for having an affair, or being rebellious, or any number of other
> excuses; wife-killing by immolation because of too little dowry; deaths as a
> result of genital mutilations; female sex slaves, trafficked females, and prosti-
> tuted females, murdered by their "owners," traffickers, "johns" and pimps,
> and females killed by misogynist strangers, acquaintances, and serial killers.

The above does not necessarily mean that those concerned about the lives of black women have to abandon the politics of death. The bodies of black female dead are being produced. The black female dead are also being produced and produced at a rate as impressive as the most arresting Black Lives Matter sta-tistics. This is the case because, if murder is something of a male problem, it is also a black problem in the United States, with blacks six times more likely to be murdered than whites. In fact, despite murder's status as a male prob-lem, black women are killed at higher rates than white men and have been for decades (Miller 2014). It may come as little surprise that—in a context where blacks are more likely to be killed, period, women are more likely to be killed by intimates, and police disproportionately profile, sexually assault, and arrest black female victims of domestic violence—black women make up a dispro-portionate percentage of those who are slain in the course of domestic and intimate partner violence. The Bureau of Justice Statistics (Catalano et al. 2009: 3) reported that, in 2007, black women were almost four times more likely than white women to die at the hands of a current or former boyfriend. Beth Richie (2012: 26) writes that "black women are killed by a spouse at a rate twice that of white women. However, when the intimate partner is a boyfriend or girlfriend, this statistic increases to four times the rate of their white counterparts." And while it is alarmingly true that a black man is killed by police, security guards, and others operating as vigilantes every twenty-eight hours, it is also true that, on average, a black woman is killed by her intimate partner every nineteen hours (Eisen-Martin 2013; Violence Policy Center 2015: 6).[1] What this means is that if those who are concerned with the status of black women agree to take part in necropolitics, this necropolitics cannot continue to privilege spectacular public murders at the hands of state agents. That will not stem the production of dead black female bodies.

The reader might reasonably ask: Is not the above a black-on-black crime deflection? No, it is not. First, the problem of impunity is a major factor here, much as it is for lethal police violence. That is not the case with black homicides and the crimes leading up to said homicides, all of which are punished and punished severely by the state. Intimate partner murder is the most predictable form of murder, and the perpetrator often escalates his abuse in ways that go unpunished until the final lethal act of violence. Experts (Women's Justice Center 2010) have found that if prior acts of violence are evaluated using a "lethality index," it is fairly easy to determine whether or not someone will ultimately murder his partner. Prior incidents of choking, for example, are a huge red flag. Let me state that again: lethal intimate partner violence is predictable; we can know if it will happen in advance. These deaths, then, are the result of police (and prosecutorial and judicial) inaction in response to violence against black women. As the United Nations Human Rights Committee noted, often black female victims of domestic violence are punished themselves, either by being arrested or by having their children taken away, decreasing the likelihood that they will ask for help when they experience violence. They are punished because someone has enacted violence against them.

I also want to be clear that I see this situation as a problem of state failure and not of black male deviance. I believe the solution lies in state building, in confronting the problems of racialized uneven development. Alongside police, prosecutorial, and court inaction, there are further inactions that endanger black women's lives. Carolyn M. West (2004: 1487–89) writes:

> The race of abusers and victims was not associated with partner homicide risk after controlling for demographic factors. Instead, the strongest sociodemographic predictor was the abuser's employment. . . . Black men are overrepresented among the unemployed, which may contribute to black women's elevated murder rate.

Earlier in West's essay, she writes

> Alternatively stated, a consistent demographic profile of victims and perpetra-
> tors has emerged: African American couples who are young, undereducated,
> impoverished, unemployed urban dwellers. Based on these findings, it should
> not be concluded that Black Americans are biologically or culturally more
> prone to violence than other ethnic groups. Rather, these results suggest that
> African Americans are economically and socially disadvantaged, which places
> them at greater risks for IPV [intimate partner violence].

Therefore, the problem of disproportionate black intimate partner femicide is a complex problem at the intersection of black community and police
relations—which include disproportionate police physical and sexual violence against blacks, combined with the ongoing reluctance of state agencies
to prevent forms of violence that involve a man and his woman in his castle
and that do not threaten the public order. There is the problem, as well, of
relying on police officers to end intimate partner violence, given police officers' own documented greater likelihood of domestic and intimate partner
abuse and therefore their greater willingness to condone the abuse of intimate partners. There are also larger problems of unemployment and underemployment as well as gun control.

On Making the Private Public

I have mentioned the problem that a lack of spectacle presents in rallying
people to act against femicide. A potential solution may be to draw attention
to how the private can become public. Feminists who seek to do so have
begun to demonstrate the links between domestic and intimate partner violence and terror. When it comes to terror, those most concerned with threats
to the public order are being forced, however slowly, toward conceding feminist critiques regarding the danger of evaluating public and private violence
differently. Salamishah Tillet, Soraya Chemaly, Melissa Jeltsen, and Pamela
Shifman have pointed out that some of this private violence eventually goes
public, and they have pushed to redefine domestic and intimate violence as
the terror it is. This move is strategically brilliant, as terror is a problem
toward which we are completely comfortable devoting considerable resources.

For example, in the wake of recent mass shootings and public terror
and major concern regarding their apparent randomness, feminists long
involved with the issue of violence against women and girls saw an opening.
They pointed out, first, that most mass shootings were actually instances of

domestic and intimate partner violence: 57 percent of mass shootings between January 2009 and June 2014 involved a perpetrator killing female intimates and their children, 70 percent of mass shooting incidents occurred at home, and 42 percent involved a current or former intimate partner (Jeltsen 2015). Second, they noted that those who went on to commit acts of random public violence—what we generally think of as terrorism—had practiced by terrorizing the women and children around them first (Shifman and Tillet 2015). In the wake of Omar Mateen's mass murder at Pulse, an Orlando LGBT nightclub and onetime community safe space, Chemaly (2016) not only wrote about Mateen's history of intimate partner violence but also reported that "while the world watched in horror as news poured out of Orlando, a man in New Mexico was arrested in the fatal shooting deaths of his wife and four daughters." Feminists bringing attention to the links between domestic violence and intimate partner violence and "public terror" can help drive more resources toward solving the problem of femicide. The #SayHerName campaign might consider how it could join with or make strategic alliances with efforts to connect intimate partner violence and terror to direct more resources to the problem of the black female dead.

Of course, this approach is not without drawbacks, given the racialized nature of the war on terror. For that reason, the feminists who seek to link intimate partner violence and terror might also benefit from the coalition I suggest and from discussions with pioneering intersectional feminists such as Crenshaw as they, too, foray into the complex waters of the politics of death in North America.

Note

1   The "every twenty-eight hours" claim has been disputed. In the absence of official statistics it is difficult to assess. See Lee 2014.

References

African American Policy Forum. 2015. "#SayHerName: Resisting Police Brutality against Black Women." #SayHerName brief. www.aapf.org/sayhernamereport.

Antoine, Chagmion. 2016. "The Color of Lawlessness: Sexual Abuse by Police, Nationwide." Women Under Siege (blog), May 4. www.womenundersiegeproject.org/blog/entry/the -color-of-lawlessness-sexual-abuse-by-police-nationwide.

Beckett, Lois, and Jamiles Lartey. 2016. "How Hillary Clinton Is Campaigning on Race and Crime: 'She Must Own Her Role.'" *Guardian*, July 25. www.theguardian.com/us-news /2016/jul/25/hillary-clinton-race-crime-justice-reform.

#BlackLivesMatter. 2016. "Guiding Principles." http://blacklivesmatter.com/guiding-principles (accessed November 9, 2016).

Bonn, Scott A. 2015. "White Females Are Rarely Murder Victims or Perpetrators: The Reality of Gender, Race, and Homicide." *Wicked Deeds* (blog), *Psychology Today*, October 12. www .psychologytoday.com/blog/wicked-deeds/201510/white-females-are-rarely-murder -victims-or-perpetrators.

Bouie, Jamelle. 2014. "Richard Sherman Is Right: Thug Is the New N-Word." *Daily Beast*, January 27. www.thedailybeast.com/articles/2014/01/27/richard-sherman-is-right-thug -is-the-new-n-word.html.

Brock, André. 2012. "From the Blackhand Side: Twitter as a Cultural Conversation." *Journal of Broadcasting and Electronic Media* 56, no. 4: 529–49.

Callahan, Yesha. 2014a. "#IfTheyGunnedMeDown Shows How Black People Are Portrayed in Mainstream Media." *The Grapevine* (blog), *Root*, August 11. www.theroot.com/blog /the-grapevine/_iftheygunnedmedown_shows_how_black_people_are_portrayed_in _mainstream_media.

Callahan, Yesha. 2014b. "New York Times Receives Backlash for Calling Michael Brown 'No Angel.'" *The Grapevine* (blog), *Root*, August 25. www.theroot.com/blog/the-grapevine /ny_times_receives_backlash_for_calling_michael_brown_no_angel.

Catalano, Shannan et al. 2009. "Bureau of Justice Statistics Selected Findings: Female Victims of Violence." Washington, DC: US Department of Justice.

Chemaly, Soraya. 2016. "In Orlando, as Usual, Domestic Violence Was Ignored Red Flag." *Rolling Stone*, June 13. www.rollingstone.com/politics/news/in-orlando-as-usual-do mestic-violence-was-ignored-red-flag-20160613.

Cobb, Jelani. 2016. "The Matter of Black Lives." *New Yorker*, March 14. www.newyorker.com /magazine/2016/03/14/where-is-black-lives-matter-headed.

Color of Change. 2017. "About." Colorofchange.org/about/.

Cooper, Alexia, and Erica L. Smith. 2011. *Homicide Trends in the United States, 1980–2008*. Washington, DC: Department of Justice, Bureau of Justice Statistics. www.bjs.gov /content/pub/pdf/htus8008.pdf.

Crenshaw, Kimberlé, and Andrea J. Ritchie. 2015. *Say Her Name: Resisting Police Brutality against Black Women*. New York: African American Policy Forum and Center for Intersectionality and Social Policy Studies.

Dawson, Michael C. 1994. "A Black Counterpublic? Economic Earthquakes, Racial Agenda(s), and Black Politics." *Public Culture* 7, no. 1: 195–223.

Duggan, Maeve, and Joanna Brenner. 2013. "The Demographics of Social Media Users— 2012." Pew Research Center, Internet and American Life Project. www.pewinternet .org/2013/02/14/the-demographics-of-social-media-users-2012.

Eisen-Martin, Tongo. 2013. "We Charge Genocide Again! A Curriculum for Operation Ghetto Storm: Report on the 2012 Extrajudicial Killings of 313 Black People by Police, Security Guards, and Vigilantes." Malcom X Grassroots Movement. mxgm.org/wp-content /uploads/2013/05/we-charge-genocide-FINAL.pdf.

Eligon, John. 2014. "Michael Brown Spent Last Weeks Grappling with Problems and Promise." *New York Times*, August 24. www.nytimes.com/2014/08/25/us/michael-brown-spent -last-weeks-grappling-with-lifes-mysteries.html.

Gatens, Moira. 1996. *Imaginary Bodies: Ethics, Power, and Corporeality*. London: Routledge.

Hillary for America. 2016a. "Criminal Justice Reform: Our Criminal Justice System Is out of Balance." www.hillaryclinton.com/issues/criminal-justice-reform (accessed November 9, 2016).

Hillary for America. 2016b. "Racial Justice: America's Long Struggle with Race Is Far from Finished." www.hillaryclinton.com/issues/racial-justice (accessed November 9, 2016).

Hirschfeld Davis, Julie. 2016. "Obama Warns of Growing Mistrust between Minorities and Police." *New York Times*, July 14. www.nytimes.com/2016/07/15/us/politics/tensions -flare-at-obamas-town-hall-on-race-and-police.html.

Jeltsen, Melissa. 2015. "We're Missing the Big Picture on Mass Shootings." *Huffington Post*, August 25. www.huffingtonpost.com/entry/mass-shootings-domestic-violence-women _us_55d3806ce4b07addcb44542a.

Jones, Feminista. 2013. "Is Twitter the Underground Railroad of Activism?" *Salon*, July 17. www.salon.com/2013/07/17/how_twitter_fuels_black_activism.

Kelley, Robin D. G. 2016. "What Does Black Lives Matter Want?" *Boston Review*, August 17. bostonreview.net/books-ideas/robin-d-g-kelley-movement-black-lives-vision.

Lee, Michelle Ye Hee. 2014. "Fact Checker: The Viral Claim that a Black Person is Killed by Police 'Every 28 Hours.'" *Washington Post*, December 24. www.washingtonpost.com /news/fact-checker/wp/2014/12/24/the-viral-claim-that-a-black-person-is-killed-by -police-every-28-hours/?utm_term=.c1525fd9ca6f.

Lewis, Renee. 2014. "Ferguson Reports Raise Questions on Media Criminalization of Blacks." Al Jazeera America, August 14. http://america.aljazeera.com/articles/2014/8/14/ferguson -media-iftheygunnedmedown.html.

Mbembe, Achille. 2003. "Necropolitics." Translated by Libby Meintjes. *Public Culture* 15, no. 1: 11–40.

McClary, Tonya D., and Andrea J. Ritchie. 2006. *In the Shadows of the War on Terror: Persistent Police Brutality and Abuse in the United States.* Report prepared for the United Nations Human Rights Committee on the Occasion of Its Review of the United States of America's Second and Third Periodic Report to the Human Rights Committee. www.prison legalnews.org/media/publications/15.%20In%20the%20Shadows%20of%20the%20 War%20on%20Terror%20-%20Persistent%20Police%20Brutality%20and%20 Abuse,%20ICCPR%20Coalition%20Report.pdf.

Miller, Lisa L. 2014. "Racialized State Failure and the Violent Death of Michael Brown." *Theory and Event* 17, no. S3. http://muse.jhu.edu/journals/theory_and_event/v017/17.3S.miller .html.

Richards, Kimberley. 2015. "CNN under Fire for Calling Freddie Gray 'Son of an Illiterate Heroin Addict.'" *Huffington Post*, December 1. www.huffingtonpost.com/entry/cnn-freddie -gray-son-of-an-illiterate-heroin-addict_us_565dafafe4b072e9d1c32a77.

Richie, Beth. 2012. *Arrested Justice: Black Women, Violence, and America's Prison Nation.* New York: New York University Press.

Ross, Janell. 2016. "Why Aren't We Calling the Oregon Occupiers 'Terrorists'?" *Washington Post*, January 3. www.washingtonpost.com/news/the-fix/wp/2016/01/03/why-arent -we-calling-the-oregon-militia-terrorists.

Russell, Diana E. H. 2011. "The Origin and Importance of the Term Femicide." December. www.dianarussell.com/origin_of_femicide.html.

Sedensky, Matt, and Nomaan Merchant. 2015. "Investigation Reveals about One Thousand Police Officers Lost Jobs over Sexual Misconduct." *Guardian*, November 1 (edited version of an Associated Press report). www.theguardian.com/us-news/2015/nov/01 /police-sexual-assault-investigation.

Shifman, Pamela, and Salamishah Tillet. 2015. "To Stop Violence, Start at Home." The Opinion Pages, *New York Times*, February 3. www.nytimes.com/2015/02/03/opinion/to-stop-violence-start-at-home.html.

Sinyangwe, Samuel. 2016. "Compare Police Departments." Mapping Police Violence. http://mappingpoliceviolence.org/ (accessed November 9, 2016).

Smith, Clint. 2016. "Racism, Stress, and Black Death." *New Yorker*, July 16. www.newyorker.com/news/news-desk/racism-stress-and-black-death.

Spelman, Elizabeth V. 1982. "Woman as Body: Ancient and Contemporary Views." *Feminist Studies* 8, no. 1: 109–31.

Stinson, Philip M., et al. 2015. "Police Sexual Misconduct: A National Scale Study of Arrested Officers." *Criminal Justice Policy Review* 26, no. 7: 665–90.

@ThomboyD. 2015. Twitter, November 27. https://twitter.com/thomboyd/status/670405964827234304.

Threadcraft, Shatema. 2016a. "The Black Female Body at the Intersection of State Failure and Necropower." *Contemporary Political Theory* 15, no. 1: 105–9.

Threadcraft, Shatema. 2016b. "Embodiment." In *Oxford Handbook of Feminist Theory*, edited by Lisa Disch and Mary Hawkesworth, 207–26. New York: Oxford University Press.

Threadcraft, Shatema, and Naa Oyo Kwate. Forthcoming. "Dying Fast and Dying Slow in Black Space: Stop and Frisk's Public Health Threat and a Comprehensive Necropolitics." *Du Bois Review: Social Science Research on Race* 15, no. 2.

Violence Policy Center. 2015. "When Men Murder Women: An Analysis of 2013 Homicide Data." Washington, DC: Violence Policy Center. www.vpc.org/studies/wmmw2015.pdf.

Waldman, Annie. 2014. "Michael Brown 'No Angel' Controversy." *Echo Chambers* (blog), BBC News, August 25. www.bbc.com/news/blogs-echochambers-28929087.

Wells, Ida B. (1892) 1991. *On Lynchings*. Salem, NH: Ayer Company.

West, Carolyn M. 2004. "Black Women and Intimate Partner Violence: New Directions for Research." *Journal of Interpersonal Violence* 19, no. 12: 1487–93.

West, Crissle. 2016. "You Won't Stop Our Blackness." *The Read*, podcast, July 13. soundcloud.com/theread/you-wont-stop-our-blackness.

Williams, David R., and Chiquita Collins. 2001. "Racial Residential Segregation: A Fundamental Cause of Racial Disparities in Health." *Public Health Reports* 116, no. 5: 404–16.

Women's Justice Center. 2010. "Domestic Violence Homicide Risk Assessment (Data from USDOJ Scale)." http://justicewomen.com/tips_dv_assessment.html.

Wright, Melissa. 2011. "Necropolitics, Narcopolitics, and Femicide: Gendered Violence on the Mexico-U.S. Border." *Signs: Journal of Women in Culture and Society* 36, no. 3: 707–31.

Young, Iris Marion. 1990. *Throwing like a Girl, and Other Essays in Feminist Philosophy and Social Theory*. Bloomington: Indiana University Press.

Barnor Hesse

White Sovereignty (. . .), Black Life Politics: "The N****r They Couldn't Kill"

Police got a choke-hold they use out here man,
they choke n*****s to death. That mean you be dead
when they through. Did you know? N*****s going
"yeah we know," white folks going, "no, I had no
idea." Two grab your legs, one grab your head, then
snap, "oh shit he broke." "Can you break a n****r?
Is it ok?" "Let's check the manual. Yep, page 8,
you can break a n****r. Right there, see?"
"Let's drag him down town."
—Richard Pryor, *Live in Concert*, 1979

The so-called N-word whether invoked in a white
form of violence or as a black relation of affinity, is
derived politically from the repetitions of racial
policing. Its affinity through blackness exists only
because of the violence inspired from its mobilization by whiteness. In this sense, racial policing is as much a structural repetition of American
democracy as are capitalism and liberalism. My
understanding of racial policing also draws on a
motif of repetition described in an interview given
by Denzel Washington a few years ago (Rellek
2010). Washington recalled a troubling moment
when, as a young actor in the mid-1980s, he was
offered and rejected the part of a leading role in a
movie about a black man who has been convicted
of raping a white woman. The black man is given

The South Atlantic Quarterly 116:3, July 2017
DOI 10.1215/00382876-3961494 © 2017 Duke University Press

a death sentence that cannot be carried out because the executioners fail to kill him after trying various methods. The apparent conceit of the movie was the spectacle of watching how many attempts it would take to kill a black man who had committed a capital offence against white womanhood. Whether the condemned black man is actually guilty is unclear. It is also unknown if the movie was ever made, as Washington did not provide any further details nor divulge its title. Instead he told the audience his cynical name for the movie had long been "The N****r They Couldn't Kill" (Rellek 2010).

In radically dissociating himself from the movie, Washington's use of that N-phrase condemned the film as a spectacle of state repetitive violence against the pathologized black male body. However, the N-phrase also implied a rejected cinematic spectacle that drew its narrative from the contemporary criminal justice system that routinely violated, stereotyped, arrested, arraigned, convicted, and incarcerated the black people it policed. Washington's refusal to entertain audiences by playing the role of the black man subject to repetitive state violence underlined his use of that N-phrase to protest a logic of repetition in the killing of black men resistant to being killed by state agencies, with their deaths normalized as social spectacles for white public consumption. The N-phrase suggested that the black bodies subject to repetitive violations were so undifferentiated in the policing relation that they epitomized racially threatening, irrepressible black protests, whose killing could not be socially exhausted by individual black deaths.

This elaboration of "The N****r They Couldn't Kill," however, should not be considered in the exclusively masculine and adult sense in which Washington evokes it. Black men, women, boys and girls, straight, queer, and transgender have all been killed in the political logic of repetition that produces what I call racial policing. By this I mean the routine racial profiling and racial problematization of the black presence, in whatever form, that is aligned with obliging or coercing black social and political assimilation and conformity. For me, this raises three questions of racial policing as repetition: First, what figures of blackness are the police repeatedly trying to kill, insofar as each time they appear to succeed, they apparently fail, and insofar as the killing of black people is prolonged. Second, on what basis is racial policing in both its narrow and expanded senses derived from the repetitions of a white citizenship democracy that condemns and condones these killings? Third, how do we understand this relationship of repetition between racial policing and black politics? These questions suggest that racial policing presents the most fundamental challenge to black political thought.[1]

Police Killings, Black Deaths

There is little in the West's idealizations of Western democracy that does not become a mantra despite evidence that repeatedly belies these idealizations. The Kantian inspired idea that Western democracies do not go to war against each other has a corollary in the idea that Western democracies do not kill their own citizens. These reassuring nostrums conventionally overlook how both ethical projections assume a colonial-racial social order of white individuals as the primordial basis of citizenship. Black citizenship is a problem for Western democracies. This is one way we can read what has been witnessed since 2014 through the high definition of social media in its take on black protests in the United States where the names of Michael Brown, Rekika Boyd, Eric Garner, Aiyanna Stanley Jones, Sandra Bland, Tamir Rice, and so many others before and after, have become black symptoms and symbols of racial policing. The repeatable and unnecessary deaths of black men, women, and children in untimely encounters with urban racial policing, raises all kinds of unasked questions about their racial meaning and the institution of that repetition. "Hands Up Don't Shoot," "I Can't Breathe," "No Justice, No Peace," "Say Her Name," and "Black Lives Matter" are all now political slogans that signify the irrepressible repetition of police violence against black citizens, both male and female, underscored by the rhetorical force of their own repetition. Ferguson, New York, Baltimore, Milwaukee, Chicago, and Charlotte are all now known as racially contested cities where police-related deaths of black individuals have galvanized uprisings and embodied opposition to the socially determined and spatially structured racial demise of black populations. Racial policing is socially dispersed in normalized, routine, institutional practices of disciplining and regulating black people, which, in nonrepresentational terms, is accomplished through enforcing the law and maintaining the order of democracy's white citizenship against alternative or even supplemental claims of black citizenship. How else can we explain the racially coded law-and-order populisms that frequently mobilize specters of black criminal and political threats, which are deserving of elimination or repeated punishment to ensure the security of white civil society and which induce racial panic or backlash among white populations?

It is worth noting that in November 2014, less than three months after the black protests in Ferguson over the police killing of Michael Brown, *USA Today* published its analysis of the arrest records of 1,581 police departments "scattered from Connecticut to California" across the United States (Heath 2014). It reported that while the Ferguson police arrested black people at

three times the rate of other communities, in other US cities the comparative arrest rate for black people was even higher, and in at least seventy police
departments, the arrest rate for black people was "ten times higher than [for]
people who are not black." In March 2015, when the Department of Justice
(2015: 2) published its report on the investigation into the Ferguson Police
Department, they made the following observation:

> This culture within FPD [Ferguson Police Department] influences officer
> activities in all areas of policing, beyond just ticketing. Officers expect and
> demand compliance even when they lack legal authority. They are inclined
> to interpret the exercise of free-speech rights as unlawful disobedience,
> innocent movements as physical threats, indications of mental or physical
> illness as belligerence. Police supervisors and leadership do too little to
> ensure that officers act in accordance with law and policy, and rarely respond
> meaningfully to civilian complaints of officer misconduct.

The report's various references to police obsessions with "compliance,"
"disobedience," "threats," and "belligerence" in the comportment of black
persons was arguably indicative of police desires to supervise and violate black
populations, perhaps ensuring the enduring racial segregation of civil society
remains unbreached by black democratic resistance. In thinking about these
findings of democratically sanctioned repetitions of racial policing, we should
recognize two of its structural urban dimensions noted by the report. First,
Ferguson was predominantly inhabited by black residents and the police force
was largely white. This meant that the institutional relationality of race was
reproduced constitutively as white domination and black subordination. Second, the report's characterization of the police extended beyond the narrow
confines of law enforcement and maintaining social order into a broader
apparatus of liberal-democratic social control that combined racial profiling
with racial hierarchy and racial segregation. This broader characterization of
racial policing indicates there was something structural and repetitive about
the history of race and its policing of black people at work there.

The policing of black people has traditionally preoccupied the social
and political infrastructure of the US liberal capitalist democratic state, but
that history has been mystified. Bryan Wagner (2009) suggests that the "traditional story" of law enforcement in the United States established between
the 1960s and the 1980s obscures the meaning and longevity of the police
force's racial constitution. The traditional story claims that modern bureaucratic policing in the United States was modeled on the 1829 establishment
of the Metropolitan Police in London. It suggests cities like Boston, Philadelphia, and New York were instrumental in creating modern police forces dur-

ing the 1830s and 1840s in relation to racially unmarked white populations. The traditional story takes the form of a white narrative. This describes a story or explanation that avoids any reference to race, seamlessly erasing evidence and memories of social contexts sedimented by white jurisdictions of hierarchy, segregation, and normativity. Consequently, the traditional story routinely forecloses a black historical narrative that exposes the racial antagonisms in the formations of modern policing, recounting the professional development of city police in the slave patrols of the southern states from the 1780s onward. In this black historical narrative, the southern gestations of racial policing were "paramilitary in organization'" and established on a far grander scale than in northern cities (Wagner 2009: 59). Developing this perspective, Wagner (2009: 60) argues that the "first modern police in the United States were created not for the general maintenance of the public peace on the London model, but for a more specific purpose: the restraint of urban slave populations." It involved the application of various state laws concerned with the mobility and conduct of slaves in public places enforceable only by the police. This explains why during the late eighteenth century, police officers in the south "spent much of their time managing the [slave] pass systems in their cities, enforcing curfews and stopping slaves they found in the street to see whether they were on an errand or otherwise authorized to be away from their masters" (60). Indeed, as Wagner reminds us, "capturing fugitives was a primary duty" of these police officers and accounted "for more than half of the slave arrests in many locations" (60). What this elided black narrative of the US police reveals is not so much a policing distinction as a policing imbrication between the foundational performativity of the racial force of law "that can be just and or in any case judged legitimate" and the police racial violence "that one always judges unjust" (Derrida and Anidjar 2002: 233). Both the traditional story and the black historical narrative of the history of the police force in the United States are predicated on, respectively, disguising and exposing democracy as the exclusive real estate of a white citizenship. Their imbrication reinscribes the racial meaning of repetition in its democratic foundations as the white citizen/black citizen doubling of policing in racial law enforcement and racial social ordering. If the first of these citizen iterations reproduces practices of policing against black people, the second reinstantiates orientations of policing by white consent. Racial policing, spawned from a foundational white architecture of US democracy, defined the emergent US states where "the power to police was considered not as a state prerogative but as racial privilege of all whites over all blacks, slave and free" (Wagner 2009: 60). Since the late nineteenth century, this racial order has been normalized in discourses of legality and lawfulness inscribed in whiteness and discourses of illegality and criminalization attributed to blackness. Establishing the grounds for the racial performativity of the police, the repeatable violations of pathologized black populations as a problem to be socially and politically mastered, has historically accumulated in a police accountability that simply bears the impress of the institution of race.

Race and Repetition

The question of race is always a question of its repetition as hierarchy, segregation, and normativity. To ignore this configuration of repetition is to discount how race has always had a policing function. Inscribed within a force of law, the salience of race is an enforceability that obliges conformity and imposes the law of its colonial inheritances. Guaranteed by a violence lying in wait, its origins forgotten but no less preserved in repetition, race is the assembled law of a certain kind of colonial or postcolonial social order. It might be argued that "law is always an authorized force, a force that justifies itself or is justified in applying itself, even if this justification may be judged from elsewhere to be unjust or unjustifiable" (Derrida and Anidjar 2002: 233). Jacques Derrida's reflections on the obscured foundations of legitimacy in law and justness in justice provides an initial way of thinking about race as policing. However, the concept of race as policing is not something that can be understood without identifying the "instituting, founding and justifying moment" of the law of race, which is at the same time an inauguration consisting of a "performative and therefore interpretative violence" (233). It is the inauguration of race and its policing lineage which has become "mystical," insofar as there is a "silence walled up in the violent structure of the founding act" (Derrida and Anidjar 2002: 241–42). Rather than continue to think of race as a scientifically contested ideological idea, socially constructed in relation to perceived biology or ethnicity, concerning disputed physical or genetic markers distinguishing different human population groupings, we should think of it more historically, materially, and relationally. Thinking of race in this way requires conceptualizing it as a Euro-colonial constitutive practice that economically and politically identified and named the populations it violated, assembled, and segregated as discrete races.

Our understanding of race and its institutionalization as policing needs to resist the violence of interpretations that mystify its colonial assembling as segregated demarcations of Europeanness over non-Europeanness. On the basis of these colonial demarcations, race was assembled and tabulated through practices of making and marking white and nonwhite chains of association between corporealities, territories, ecologies, cultures, religions, and histories. Lisa Lowe (2015: 8) explains part of this approach when she argues that "racial classifications and colonial divisions of humanity emerged in the colonial acquisition of territory, and the management of labor, reproduction, and social space." In other words, race under "taxonomic states" (Stoler 2002: 206–8) emerged from the material colonial settler practices of whites territorializing, capturing, enslaving, segregating, disciplining, regulating, terrorizing, intimidating, patrolling, surveying, profiling, and violating non-whites (Hesse 2014a). These myriad constitutive acts of conquest, assemblage, and classification grounded the policing forms of colonial ordering that comprised the practical, liberal, capitalist, democratic lineage of race from the sixteenth century through the twenty-first century. These acts also provided the discursive and political basis on which "liberal and colonial discourses improvised racial terms for the non-European peoples whom settlers, traders, and colonial personnel encountered" (Lowe 2015: 7). With that liberal-colonial, material inheritance of race in mind, we should not dismiss any consideration of the ways in which the colonial settler formations of racial policing resemble in repetition and improvisation the contemporary urban formations of policing black populations in the United States. What defines these limits and possibilities of racial policing is a logic of repetition whose political configuration is usually anchored in US liberal democracy's reoccupation of its colonial settler burial ground.

Claudia Rankine's *Citizen* (2014) is a poetic attempt to grapple with these obscured and yet relentless postcolonial legacies in the everyday racial policing of the black subject. What interests me are her reflections on the police's repetitive, indiscriminate, and disproportionate use of "stop and frisk" to detain, interrogate, inconvenience, search, abuse, and assault black citizens. Rankine gestures heavily to the racial policing repetitions of the United States' colonial-settler inheritance in two refrains. The first occurs where she identifies a familiar racial policing scenario: a black man's car is blockaded and rapidly surrounded by police cars, and he is told to get on the ground. The stop results in the wrong and wronged black person, thereby reproducing a racial policing suspicion that proclaims "and you are not the guy and still you fit the description because there is only one guy who is always the guy fitting the description" (Rankine 2014: 105). Racial profiling and racial suspicion repeat the racially twisted apartheid logic in which every mistaken identity or wronged black citizen is fungible and, at the same time, a potential threat averted as well as a readiness for the fire next time. Racial policing is the latency of terror for black populations. As Christina Sharpe (2016: 86) observes, this terror means black populations fit the description of "the non-being, the being out of place, and the noncitizen always available to and for death." Rankine's (2014: 107) second refrain traces this terror through another repetition, where she writes: "Each time it begins in the same way, it doesn't begin the same way, each time it begins, it's the same." She evinces racial policing in the inevitability of black bodies accumulating in the racial collateral damage that disfigures the rights of black citizens as noncitizens in daily violent encounters with the police's racial ordering of their social lives. That racial policing event never fails to shock, is always to be expected, but always without knowing how, where, or when. However, in drawing our attention to the racial logic of contingency and force in repetitions of racial policing, Rankine exposes but does not explain its indexicality. What is the racial, historical, and political indexicality of the "it," framed as a racial policing event, that always begins in the same way but is never the same?

I want to suggest that the indexical "it" is repetition itself, in this case the form of repetition taken by the racial policing inheritance. Provisionally, we can think of this repetition in terms of what Saidiya Hartman (2007: 6) calls the "afterlife of slavery" that "persists" in the "political life of Black America." What is repeated is "a racial calculus and a political arithmetic" that endangers and devalues black lives. As evidence, Hartman describes "skewed life chances, limited access to health and education, premature death, incarceration, and impoverishment" (6). For me, this suggests that what is repeated is not slavery's replication or its simulation but rather its afterlife, in which the freedom of the black subject emerges through and within the colonial-racial architecture that instituted, sustained, and abolished slavery. The theoretical task becomes one of understanding the configuration and repetition of that colonial-racial architecture in the liberal-democratic capitalist institutions of the United States, especially its procuring and repression of the black citizen as a political subject. This colonial-racial configuration after-slavery can be viewed in Jacques Ranciere's (1999: 29) distinctive political terms as "the police." Suggesting a homology with what I have called racial policing, "the police" is "first an order of bodies that defines the allocation of ways of doing, ways of being, and ways of saying, and sees that those bodies are assigned by name to a particular task." It enables us to see the constitutive policing function of race after slavery that allocated a differential freedom, under a liberal and democratic regime of whiteness, to bodies bearing white and black citizenship, assigned by racial hierarchy and racial segregation, to their respective political subject positions. Ida B. Wells observed this US specificity over a century ago, arguing that there was a racially violent predicament of democracy for the emancipated ex-slave under white jurisdiction. She wrote that, "with freedom, a new system of intimidation came into vogue; the Negro was not only whipped and scourged; he was killed" (Wells and Royster 1997). Wells was describing not only the emergence of the systematic white lynching of black bodies as an addendum to the racial rule of law, but a white political formation of democracy, "growing out slavery," which had become crystallized in the oft repeated slogan: "This is a white man's country and the white man must rule." This idea of white rule was not legislative and representational as embellished in the iconography of Jim Crow, but rather performative and nonrepresentational, designed to deter the political mobilization of black populations and retain the imprimatur of democracy through white institutional and civilian violence. Wells's understanding of lynching as constitutive of *white* democracy, taken together with her observations regarding the failures of white witnesses and white newspapers to condemn it and the federal government's white indifference to it, can also be read as a white democratic formation of racial policing. Wells enables us to conceptualize differential freedom during the afterlife of slavery as derived from the democratic rule of white citizens and predicated on the exploitation, subordination, incorporation, consumption, and violation of black citizens, repeated for the benefit and security of white populations (Wells 1995; Wells and Royster 1997). This recalls Gilles Deleuze's (1994: 18) observation that repetition is a recurrent form of social violence, productive of a certain way of social life: "I do not repeat because I repress. I repress because I repeat. I forget because I repeat. I repress because I live certain things or certain experiences only in the mode of repetition. I am determined to repress whatever would prevent me from living them thus." In this sense, liberal-democratic freedom, through white and black citizenships in the afterlife of slavery, is mediated by a regime of repetition in which race takes the policing form of white privileged citizenship regulating the repression of black citizenship. Race as repetition involves a commitment to the reproduction of white forms of life over, above, and against black forms of life. In other words, the repetition of race is what reproduces the afterlife of slavery as racial policing.

The "Negro Problem's" Problem

What is it about blackness that repeats itself as a political problem for whiteness? In 1890 Fredrick Douglass gave a speech indicting the name and meaning of the so-called *Negro problem*, which signified the white conventional wisdom that the black presence, especially since emancipation, was threatening the racial, social, and political cohesion of the nation. Douglass argued this belief arose from widespread white anxieties and desires to regulate the behaviors and mobilities of black populations across politics, work, education, and religion and in any domain where white people had misgivings and questions concerning the competence or entitlement of black people to participate in the civic freedoms of the nation. Instead, Douglass (Douglass and Daley 2013: 94) insisted that the "true problem" was "whether the nation has in itself sufficient moral stamina to maintain its honor and integrity by vindicating its own Constitution and fulfilling its pledges." In short, given that the "United States Government made the negro a citizen," Douglass asked: "Will it protect him as a citizen?" While Douglass quite rightly pointed out that the government had a duty to protect and ensure the constitutional rights of all its citizens and despaired that this would ever be the case, his reference to the US government *making* the Negro a citizen, also alerts us to something equally important on which he did not dwell. The Negro was not part of the civil society that had been established racially between white men who were in the process consecrated as the embodiment of citizenship (Mills 1997). Through the performative institution of civil society, the originary white citizens had subsequently created black citizens, which meant in the performativity of the democratic nation, the citizenship of black citizens was substantially owned by its white citizens. The white democratic lineage of the Negro problem implied a citizenship that had been conferred by whites on blacks could also be withdrawn. Even if the citizenship of black citizens was simply held in trust by white citizens, it still meant black people could be regulated and policed by the state as well as by white civilians to determine their fitness and readiness for social and political life. Of course, against that insight it has become conventional within liberal discourse to overlook this racial policing dimension attached to the Negro problem in favor of representing it as a rectifiable problem of democracy.

This racial policing problem, expressive of a white citizenship democracy, has confronted black people in the United States since slavery emancipation and the overthrow of Reconstruction. It has the repetitive force of a white democratic conviction that repeats the law of racial rule, normalized as a response to the obduracy of its Negro problem, the routine perception that black people were a criminal or political threat to white civil society. Tellingly, when W. E. B. DuBois ascribed the term "racial revolution" to the end of Reconstruction and the establishment of Jim Crow beginning in 1876, it seemed as much a comment on post-slavery white democracy as on the post-slavery white south.[2] DuBois's concept of racial revolution was an attempt to account for the constitutive meaning and impact of race as governing practices beyond the abolition of slavery. He was describing the emergence of newly distinctive social and political orders of race in assembling the segregations and subordinations of black populations in relation to their ordeals.

DuBois cites two examples of such emergence as flowing from the racial revolution that particularly exemplify the repetitions of racial policing. First, he observed that since 1876 "negroes have been arrested on the slightest provocation and given long sentences or fines they were compelled to work out" (DuBois and Lewis 1995: 698). Second, he noted that "white people paid no attention to their own laws. White men became a law unto themselves, and black men, so far as their aggressions were confined to their own people, need not fear intervention of white police" (700). DuBois revealed an institutional level of racial policing, in which the rule of whiteness prevailed over the liberal rule of law. We can certainly think of these racial policing formations enduring as the white democratic alterity of a black citizenship racially unprotected and violated by the social and political order. In seeking a context for this social and political order I argue below that in each instance of racial policing against the black citizen, the violence inhabiting that white democratic alterity, then as now, accrues in its repetition as white sovereignty.

White Sovereignty Violence

In trying to understand the modern political constitution of whiteness in liberalism and democracy, we quickly find ourselves experiencing repeated denials by whiteness that it has a political constitution. Outside of references to white supremacy as an epithet or an expression of extremist right-wing ideology, it remains the case that the idea of whiteness as a paradigmatic relation of power or domination, or indeed as an ultimate source of political authority in Western polities, is virtually nonexistent in Western political theory and critical theory. In *The Racial Contract*, Charles Mills (1997: 1) argues that "white supremacy is the unnamed political system that has made the modern world what it is today" because, as Mills goes on to suggest, white supremacy "is not seen as a political system at all. It is just taken for granted; it is the background against which other systems, which we *are* to see as political are highlighted" (2). While Mills has heuristically elaborated his understanding of white supremacy as originating in a "racial contract" underpinning or intersecting with the European social contract tradition variously referenced in the theories of consent to state authority, expounded by Hobbes, Rousseau, and Kant, he leaves unexplained the locus of its ontology as ubiquitously unnamed and transparently in the background. In other words, he leaves us to guess at what establishes the authority lineage of white supremacy (i.e., the racial contract) and authorizes any shifts or changes in that lineage. My argument here is that we need the idea of white sovereignty to explain the founding and authorizing violence of white supremacist political systems in colonialism, capitalism, liberalism, and democracy.

The meaning of sovereignty is less fixed by modernity's political and spatial coordinates than derived from the historical contingencies of their different conceptualizations as normative foundations of power and authority (Bartleson 1995; Prokhovnik 2008). However, as Antony Angie (2005: 101) has observed, the Western normative tradition of thinking about sovereignty has usually neglected its relationship with "the colonial encounter and the constellation of racial and cultural distinctions it generated and elaborated." In short, it was always the case that whiteness became the "subject of sovereignty" and non-whiteness, "the object of sovereignty" (Angie 2005: 102)." White sovereignty is the historical assemblage of repeated colonial-racial violence. Borrowing from Achilles Mbembe (2001: 25), we can understand this assemblage of colonial-racial violence in three sovereign, European, and American political forms of repetition: The first was the white settlers' "founding violence" that established the "right of conquest," created the space over which whiteness was exercised, "presupposed its own existence," and "regarded itself as the sole power to judge its laws. The second was a legitimating violence, which through a "self-interpreting language" externalized and imposed whiteness as the architecture of the colonial-racial order, "converting the founding violence into authorizing authority" (25). The third was a reiterative violence, instituted to ensure and "authenticate" the permanent authority of whiteness—it "recurred again and again in the most banal and ordinary situations," thereby "constituting the central cultural *imaginary* that the state shared with society" (25). Accounting for the normalization of white sovereignty as violence should not be considered anachronistic or merely symbolic, since its colonial-racial imprimatur has less to do with the legacies of Jim Crow and the excesses of the far right, than with the liberal democratic failures, if not successes, of Reconstruction repeated and preserved as racial policing in the afterlife of slavery. When thinking about white sovereignty, it is useful to return to Wells's short article, "Lynch Law in America," written in 1900. There, she defines the lynching of black people in Jim Crow society, as the "unwritten law" (1995: 71). This was a racially performative social convention that enforced white democracy by deterring black resistance to white regulation. Its authority resided in the capacity to put "human beings to death without complaint under oath, without trial by jury, without opportunity to make defense, and without right of appeal" (70). Lynching as the unwritten law repeated the white sovereignty that underwrote the white democratic rule of law through the black compliance obliged by the race performativity of white violence.[3] In that instantiation, it also *extruded* black populations from the American democratic rule of law and due process, effectively installing itself constitutionally as the unwritten white addendum to American democracy. Consequently, the unwritten law also underwrote the social disenfranchisement of newly created black citizens within a white democracy, extruding them from any rights, protections, and representation that might question or challenge white sovereignty. The unwritten law in that sense confirmed the violence of white sovereignty as the founding authority of the liberal-democratic system against "negro domination" (Wells and Royster 1997).

It is often forgotten, because never actively remembered, that it was within the lineaments of liberalism and democracy that the rudiments of mainstream white rule were crafted in both representational and performative governance (Saxton 2003; Olson 2004). One of these forms of governance has been referred to several times already as white citizenship democracy. Two of its defining structural features are crucial to clarifying the meaning of repetition in the racial policing of black populations under white sovereignty. The first is what Joel Olson (2004: xix) has described as "white citizenship." Olson (2004: xv-xvi) suggests that once we realize that "racial oppression and American democracy are mutually constitutive rather than antithetical," we will see that "democracy is not just a solution; it is a political problem itself." This reveals the democracy problem for black citizens. Historically and conceptually, the only modern democracy imaginable and perfectible in Western political history and theory has been a universalized, marked or unmarked "white democracy." The white citizen is the location of a valorized structural position within the white democratic polity, a racial "position of equality and privilege simultaneously: equal to other white citizens yet privileged over those who are not white" (Olson 2004: xix). While this valorization of white citizenship is complicated and saturated by structural positions of class, gender, and sexuality, occupants are often too easily enamored by their lifeworlds within whiteness, ensuring that the white citizen prevails through hierarchy and segregation in resisting "any political vision in which his or her privileges are not respected" as "natural rights, a normal condition or a deserved advantage" (Olson 2004: xxi). In short, there is a structural political incentive that has to be overcome if the white citizen is to be dissuaded from actively participating in or refraining from interfering in the racial policing of black citizens.

The second structural feature of white citizenship democracy involves what Hartman has described as a racially "burdened individuality" for the black citizen, resulting from "manhood and whiteness" always operating as "the undisclosed, but always assumed, norms of liberal equality" (Hartman 1997: 115–18). Due to an untrammeled white citizenship surviving different postcolonial incarnations of the United States, what emerged and remained from the Reconstruction period was the liberalism problem for the black citizen. Black individuality was burdened by its inscription in the racial "entanglements of bondage and liberty that shaped the liberal imagination of freedom" (Hartman 1997: 115). Within the terms of white sovereignty, freedom for the emancipated, former slave and enduring black citizen meant it was one thing to be free of slavery, but quite another to be free of the white jurisdiction of the federal government's freed men's bureau that regulated the mobility and labor forms in which that freedom was practiced. Throughout the Reconstruction period, a white citizenship democracy and a racially stipulated liberalism not only conferred upon black people the status of "citizen and subject," "equal and inferior" but also insisted on the "control and domination of the free black population, and the persistent production of blackness as abject, threatening, servile, dangerous, dependent, irrational, and infectious" (116). What is significant about this formulation of racial policing is that its violence is based on the US federal government's mid-to-late nineteenth-century reconstruction of white liberal democracy rather than the southern states' innovations in iconographic white supremacy and legislative racial segregation inaugurated by Jim Crow. In other words, the southern states' Jim Crow movement was basically an authoritarian alternative to the ostensibly more liberal federal and northern states' rule of democracy under white sovereignty. For that reason, it is useful to think together the black experience of racially conferred freedom and racially enforced subjection of the Reconstruction era (1863–77) and the racially analogous black experience of the post–civil rights era (1964–present). In the aftermath of both postcolonial transitions, black freedom was racially profiled and policed, resulting in a black citizenship encoded as the "resubordination of the emancipated" (Hartman 1997: 116). Here we can locate the importance of the argument made by Michelle Alexander's (2010) account of the post-1970s racially coded law-and-order campaigns, war-on-drugs operations, and mass prison incarcerations inflicted against black populations. Although she describes the congealing of these racial policing practices, resulting in extensive curtailments of black liberties and expanding black disenfranchisement, as the "New Jim Crow," there are perhaps more compelling grounds for calling them the "second Reconstruction" (Marable 2007). What is striking about the homology between the earlier Reconstruction (1865–77) and the later Reconstruction eras (1965–present) is their predication on a liberal democratic and capitalist repetition of white sovereignty and its racial policing of obliged black comportment, within the terms of its unwritten law.

Black Power, Black Colony

Colonial-racial violence is the unwritten law of white sovereignty that has continued to characterize the repetitions of racial policing in the post–civil rights era. We see this in the criminal justice system's racial profiling, assaults, torture, mass incarcerations, and killings of black people, despite the dismantling of Jim Crow, enactment of civil rights and voters' rights legislation, and achievement of federal government policy commitments to eliminate race discrimination in housing, education, and employment (Muhammad 2010; Hinton 2016). During the late 1960s and early 1970s, black attempts to understand and deal with this renewed incarnation of white sovereignty were undertaken by thinkers and activists in the black power movement who began to develop the "internal colonialism" thesis (Gutiérrez 2004: 281). This symbolized what might be described as the black power movement's ideological break with the civil rights movement's orientation of black politics. It turned on their radically different understanding of US capitalist democracy as colonial and class antagonistic rather than national and class agnostic, as well as their understanding of its liberal institutions as racially oppressive rather than universally liberating (Hesse 2014b). Despite its subsequent neglect by black political thinkers, the internal colonialism thesis, as a point of departure for thinking about imbrications of race, coloniality, liberalism, and democracy, continues to have contemporary political relevance as an explanation of racial policing, particularly in two areas of analysis. The first concerns what Stokely Carmichael and Charles V. Hamilton (1967: 4) famously described as "institutional racism." Writing during the late 1960s, when *racism* was still a relatively new term and concept in mainstream political discourse, Carmichael and Hamilton were reacting to its liberal polemical uses as epithet and ideology. Rather than treating the indictable question of racial hierarchies and racial segregations as resulting from prejudices, bigotry, antagonisms between different communities, or the mobilization of ideologies, arising from an accident or a peculiar contingency of history, they diverted the meaning of racism from the actions of extremist groups to mainstream institutions. In institutional racism, a "sense of superior group prevails: whites are better than blacks"; it takes the form of a social and racial inheritance drawn from institutional policies and decisions that are developed for reasons of "subordinating a racial group and maintaining control over that group" (Carmichael and Hamilton 1967: 4). The white citizen who derives benefits and advantages from a superior group position comes to think of these benefits and advantages as "normal, proper, customary as sanctioned by time, precedent, and social consensus" (Carmichael and Hamilton 1967: 3–8).

Of course, this kind of analysis has antecedents in similar critiques undertaken by Wells, Douglass, and DuBois. What is different within the black power framework is the added insight that institutional racism resided in the "established and respected forces" of society, routinely enforcing the status of black people as "colonial subjects in relation to white society." Carmichael and Hamilton's idea of "social colonialism" refers to inequalities in resources and wealth, power and authority, and respect and recognition, each of which institutionally and racially entrenches the authority and control of a white citizenship over black citizenship. In short, this "institutional racism" of the post–civil rights era had "another name: colonialism" (Carmichael and Hamilton 1967: 3, 7–16). Whereas analysis and indictment of the contemporary mainstream recognition of racism has, since the 1960s, been restricted to the level of the individual and ideological, particularly when associated with political extremism, considered antithetical to liberalism and democracy, Carmichael and Hamilton's evocation of social colonialism argued there was an imbrication of institutional racism and liberal democracy. However, thinking about racism as racial policing in this democratic institutional way means recognizing that the United States is the "most exemplary model of the embedded colonial/postcolonial structure" that both lacks and resists the language necessary to describe that embeddedness (Iton 2008: 137).

The second area for thinking about racial policing from the internal colonialism thesis that develops a language that is resisted is George Jackson's (1971: 24–25) description of the "Black Colony" under occupation by the "city-state." Jackson, a black political prisoner, argued that the colony was not outside but within the metropole. This argument drew on a reconceptualization of the meaning of racial segregation in residential, employment, and educational terms, specifying the idea of black populations assessed, supervised, and "manipulated" by white institutions. Associated with poverty, the inner city, high crime rates, and intense street policing, black populations experiencing these social, economic, and racial oppressions, argued Jackson, could not redress these issues because "the necessary resources for their solution" were the "personal property of an extraneous minority motivated solely by the need for their own survival" (24). For Jackson, it was precisely the internal colonial relation that also suggested the black political potential for the Black Colony to become transformed, through critical and practical consciousness, into locations for "black revolutionary rage" that could "carry at least the opening stages of a socialist revolution under certain circumstances" (25). Whatever we now make of Jackson's optimistic 1970s preoccupations with revolution and socialism, we should not overlook how his concept of the Black Colony was indicative of the enduring racial state of extruding black people from the resources, securities, and protections of civil society reserved for white citizenship. It also meant because black politics situated in and organized through the Black Colony did not assimilate to submissive comportment required by the violence of white sovereignty, it was systematically pathologized and attacked in the name of law and order, for the benefit and security of privileged white populations. Jackson's anticolonial analyses were associated with the Black Panther Party's focus on the self-defense of black populations and the political need to police the police force who were perceived as an army of occupation. For example, Huey P. Newton (2002: 149), writing against the background of the US war in Vietnam, argued that the experience of black people with constant police brutality suggested a "great similarity between the occupying army in Southeast Asia and the occupation of our communities by the racist police." Significantly, Stuart Hall et al. ([1978] 2013: 386) extended the comparison to the policing of black people in 1970s Britain. They argue that this understanding of the urban Black Colony as under occupation suggests that political analysis forged in "colonial society and struggle" was transferable and adaptable to the "conditions of black minorities in developed urban capitalist conditions." It also meant that black politics was "obliged to adopt a more 'populist' approach to its constituency and, to work from a *community* base" (379). In that framing, "racial oppression" became the "specific mediation" through which violated black populations experienced their "material and cultural conditions of life" and formed their political self-consciousness (379). If we notice the contemporary resonance of Hall et al.'s formulations, it is hard not to speculate whether this historically specific anticolonial response of the black power movement to racial policing continues to have contemporary relevance (Bloom and Martin 2013).

Black Life Politics

Of the many political slogans generated by contemporary US movement against the police killings of black civilians, signified under the discursive banner Black Lives Matter (BLM), one stands out as intriguing though rarely discussed. Although variously phrased, it is popularly recognized as a corrective to mass-media misrepresentations when it states: "This ain't your grandfather's civil rights movement" (Ford 2015) While it should be clear that a

1950s–1960s movement to attain civil rights and voting rights legislation is radically different from a movement that since 2014 has worked to expose and end the police killings of black citizens, we should not mistake a wrong comparison for the wrongness of comparison. Despite its recent emergence, BLM has been confronted with issues similarly faced by the black power movement of the 1960s–1970s (Taylor 2016). These issues include not only how to contend with and interrupt the repetition of racial policing under regimes authorized by white sovereignty, despite incorporation within liberal democracy, but also how to sustain and edify black life beyond the limitations and violations of citizenship. In a strategic sense, if the civil rights movement placed greater emphasis on reclaiming the liberal democratic rights of the black political subject, the black power movement placed greater emphasis on reclaiming the black lives of the black political subject. Clearly, then, the idea of black lives rather than civil rights, human rights, or black rights as the mobilizing fulcrum of BLM is indicative of at least its partial lineage in the black power movement. In taking the black power movement comparison seriously, we need to appreciate that an organization like the Black Panther Party was engaged in a *black life politics* with its activism through direct action on health, food, education, and policing issues as these affected the capacities for black life to survive and flourish. However, this also meant that their own black lives confronted a racial policing that made them subject to concentrated surveillance and targeted assassination by the federal bureau of investigation's counterintelligence program (Nelson 2011; Bloom and Martin 2013). In short, its black life politics was a day-to-day mobilization for black life against black death, which had long-term black life or immediate term black death consequences. It might be said that the Black Panthers' understanding of black political life was a precursor to what Christina Sharpe (2016: 20–22) has recently described as "wake work." This centers on inhabiting a "blackened consciousness" that confronts all the ways blackness has become "the symbol, par excellence, for the less-than-human being condemned to death." At the same time, wake work also involves the recognition that "black lives are lived under occupation" and insists on thinking and pushing through "containment, regulation, punishment, capture, and captivity."

Thinking about the impetus for black life politics in this way shares some affinity with Stefano Harney and Fred Moten's (2013: 19) critique of the political. Though I want to emphasize the idea of black life politics as antagonistic to the Western political (Hesse 2011) and yet operative as politics in the same sense that they write of blackness: "We've been around. We're more than politics, more than settled, more than democratic. We surround democracy's false image in order to unsettle it. Every time it tries to include us in a decision, we're undecided. Every time it tries to represent our will, we're unwilling." This perhaps describes the central predicament of black life politics: it cannot be politics as usual, but it must be politics as unusual. Alicia Garza (quoted in Lowery 2016: 87), who along with two other black queer women, Patrisse Cullors and Opal Tometi, formulated and founded the intervention BLM in 2013, suggests a contemporary rationale and direction for this idea of black life politics where she writes: "Black Lives Matter is an ideological and political intervention in a world where Black lives are systematically and intentionally targeted for demise. It is an affirmation of Black folk's contribution to this society, our humanity, and our resilience in the face of deadly oppression." Significantly, in the evolution of BLM, much like the Black Panther Party of the early 1970s prior to its demise, black women are involved in much of the organizing and occupy many of the leadership roles, and are often its public face (Brown 1994; Taylor 2016). In thinking about a black life politics, unlike "your grandfather's civil rights movement" or even "your grandmother's black power movement," the mobilizing of black women in BLM has underlined the public meaning of black lives in "black women and black girls [and] black LGBTQ folks," all against the background of a "much more deliberate intervention to expose police brutality as part of a much larger system of oppression in the lives of all black working class and poor people (Taylor 2016: 166). Of course, there is a paradox at the center of the BLM movement. Given its naming of white supremacy, rather than individual racism, as the political object of critique, its exhortation "black lives matter" is simultaneously an appeal to the liberal democratic institutions to implement protections and justice and an expression of a resolve to expose and confront those same institutions' constitutive failures to provide civil and political redress. As Richard Iton (2008: 14) has argued, "in the language game staked out by the modern, blacks are uniquely locked into a relationship that allows few possibilities for agency, autonomy, or substantive negotiation." Consequently, BLM is repeatedly caught on the horns of a dilemma, either engaging directly with white sovereignty that represses and violates the idea of the black political subject or engaging indirectly with white democracy, which assimilates and polices the black political subject. If the former engagement makes transformation radically perverse, the latter makes reform radically precarious. Within the horizon of that paradox, BLM will need to consider breaking with the idea of a rights-based politics by increasingly questioning the diminishing legal value of rights and citizenship already attained and emphasize increasing the social value of a black life-based politics that expands the capacities for emancipating the possibilities of black practices from the assimilation of black skin to white masks. What I mean by capacities are black bodily, cultural, gendered (etc.) orientations, political/economic resources and opportunities that can be used or mobilized against the race obligations placed on black life to be comported in line with the social contortions of white sovereignty. The emancipation demanded by black performance from this race performativity begins with capacities that release black life from being diminished in the racial instrumentalities of subordination, segregation, or socialization. It continues with capacities that innovate black practices in lives committed to identities, trajectories, activities, discourses, and cultures beyond the interference of and antagonism toward racial policing. However, as Shatema Threadcraftt (2016: 25–26) has suggested, this innovative black activism must be suffused with an acknowledgment of the "impact of racial domination on black intimate capacities" and a self-reflexivity that eliminates "the violence wrought against some bodies over others—and some capacities of the black body over others." Working through these terms, black life politics can be enacted, that is, performed, in whatever emancipates a black body "from the place assigned to it or changes a place's destination" (Ranciere 1999: 30). Black life politics, it might be said, "makes visible what had no business being seen, and makes heard a discourse where once there was only place for noise; it makes understood as discourse what was once only heard as noise"(30). One of the ways a black life politics of visibility and audibility appears to be already advanced in BLM is through its practical implementation of and theoretical engagements with "intersectionality," enabling and allowing the complexity of black lives inscribed differently and multiply in relations of, for example, gender, sexuality, class, and ethnicity to be seen, heard, and encountered politically (Cobb 2016). The converse of emancipating diverse black lives from their racially determined designations is of course the translation of any expressive blackness into political invisibility and inaudibility, providing white citizenship democracy with its imprimatur as democratically open in its universal representation while democratically closed in its racial performativity.

The fundamental challenge for black life politics, however, lies not only in the emancipation of an edified black life from premature black death, its existential orientation, but in two areas of day-to-day social life. The first is the mobilization of black civic life, developing capacities to frame and contest racial and political issues surrounding black deaths, using social media to construct and disseminate a contemporary archive. So far, BLM activists have engaged in forms of disruption and occupation, turning moments of mundane life in shopping malls and transportation complexes into spectacles of spontaneous protest and political education that affirm a racial-civil disobedience that has become known as *unapologetic blackness*, a term that embodies and signifies a refusal of white sovereignty and an embrace of black expressive cultures. The challenge is to expand this unapologetic blackness to more areas of civic life on a recurrent basis, unsettling and derailing the normalization of the racial social order. The second challenge is the mobilization of black solidarity life, developing long-term capacities to form affinities with diaspora black and nonblack others in overturning the political chain of equivalent violence that extends between white sovereignty, white supremacy, and white citizens democracy. The challenge is to deepen and widen the transnational and multicultural oppositions to institutions and ideologies of white supremacy and white privilege. In short, a black life politics is antagonistic to the political constitution of whiteness as sovereignty, which is predicated on the repetition of racial policing, both procuring the depoliticized black subject and repressing the black political subject for the provision of white security. White sovereignty is confirmed each time the liberal-democratic social order draws on the unwritten colonial-racial law that extrudes black populations from rights, protections, and respect. This racial state of extrusion is the contemporary heritage of the modern-colonial world. Historically all prominent Western states have advanced, defended, and valorized their white sovereignties, whether in republican, liberal, democratic, or fascist terms, while violating non-European colonies and racially segregated nonwhite populations both inside and outside the Western rule of law. This is what is being repeated in each incident that has catalyzed black expressive protestations that black lives matter. Of course, we should also be aware that there is a global dimension to black life politics. For example, the United Kingdom, France, Israel, Canada, Australia, and Brazil are all countries where mobilizations have insisted for decades that black lives matter. There has always been a global ubiquity to a routine police encounter with an unarmed black individual, man, woman, or child that replicates a prior scenario in which the unlawful police killing of a black person reiterates local and national histories of racially punitive policing. The fungibility of the racially policed black body suggests in each additional police killing of a black person that there is an insufficiency in the prior killings that is not resolved by subsequent killings. Its repetition is derived from the police enforcing the racial segregation of an abjectly and violently marked yet constitutively resistant and recalcitrant black population that refuses to yield without mobilizing opposition. Racial policing is acculturated from a white citizen's democratic system of regulating socially and demographically black populations as criminal and political threats. Through the repetition of racial policing, white sovereignty is consecrated in the repression of the black body whose black life politics persists, unapologetically. In other words, this repetition is "the N****r they couldn't kill."

Notes

1   Although the main focus of this article is the United States, many of the arguments about racial policing are applicable to other Western democracies and their relation with black populations. The United Kingdom is perhaps the best known historical example. See John and Humphrey 1972; Hall et al. (1978) 2013; Institute of Race Relations 1987; Gilroy 2002; Hesse et al. 1992; Keith 1993; Bowling 2001; and Patel and Tyrer 2012.

2   As DuBois (1995: 697) observed, the "North was not disposed at this time to defend universal suffrage or even democracy."

3   Nadine Ehlers makes an important argument that race is disciplinary practice that is also performative. Although our understandings of race differ slightly, I draw upon her idea that race is "performative because it is an act that—or more precisely a series of repeated acts—that brings into being what it names" (Elhers 2012: 7). I read this as a naming that recalls the performativity of a racial regime in the moment that it requires and enforces black compliance and subordination.

References

Alexander, Michelle. 2010. *The New Jim Crow: Mass Incarceration in the Age of Colorblindness.* New York: New Press.

Anghie, Antony. 2005. *Imperialism, Sovereignty, and the Making of International Law.* Cambridge, UK: Cambridge University Press.

Bartelson, Jens. 1995. *A Genealogy of Sovereignty.* Cambridge, UK: Cambridge University Press.

Bloom, Joshua, and Waldo E. Martin, Jr. 2013. *Black against Empire: The History and Politics of the Black Panther Party.* Berkeley: University of California Press.

Bowling, Benjamin. 2001. *Violent Racism: Victimization, Policing, and Social Context.* Oxford: Oxford University Press.

Brown, Elaine. 1994. *A Taste of Power: A Black Woman's Story.* New York: Anchor Books.

Carmichael, Stokely, and Charles V. Hamilton. 1967. *Black Power and the Politics of Liberation.* New York: Vintage.

Cobb, Jelani. 2016. "The Matter of Black Lives: A New Kind of Movement. What Will Its Future Be?" *New Yorker,* March 14. www.newyorker.com/magazine/2016/03/14/where-is -black-lives-matter-headed.

Deleuze, Gilles. 1994. *Difference and Repetition.* London: Althone Press.

Derrida, Jacques, and Gil Anidjar. 2002. *Acts of Religion.* New York: Routledge.

Douglass, Fredrick, and James Daley. 2013. *Great Speeches by Fredrick Douglass.* Mineola, NY: Dover.

DuBois, W. E. B., and David L. Lewis. 1995. *Black Reconstruction in America 1860–1880.* New York: Simon and Schuster.

Ehlers, Nadine. 2012. *Racial Imperatives: Discipline, Performativity, and Struggles against Subjection.* Bloomington: Indiana University Press.

Ford, Glen. 2015. "This Ain't Your Grandfather's Civil Rights Movement." *Black Agenda Report* (blog), November 11. www.blackagendareport.com/not_your_grandfather%27s _movement.

Gilroy, Paul. 2002. *There Ain't No Black in the Union Jack: The Cultural Politics of Race and Nation.* London: Routledge.

Gutiérrez, Ramon A. 2004. "Internal Colonialism: An American Theory of Race." *Du Bois Review: Social Science Research on Race* 1, no. 2: 281–95.

Hall, Stuart, et al. (1978) 2013. *Policing the Crisis: Mugging, The State, Law and Order*. New York: Palgrave.

Hartman, Saidiya. 2007. *Lose Your Mother: A Journey along the Atlantic Slave Route*. New York: Farrar, Straus, and Giroux.

Hartman, Saidiya. 1997. *Scenes of Subjection: Terror, Slavery, and Self-Making in Nineteenth Century America*. New York: Oxford University Press

Harney, Stefano, and Fred Moten. 2013. *The Undercommons: Fugitive Planning*. Brooklyn, NY: Minor Compositions.

Heath, Brad. 2014. "Racial Gap in U.S. Arrest Rates: "'Staggering Disparity.'" *USA Today*, November 19. www.usatoday.com/story/news/nation/2014/11/18/ferguson-black-arrest -rates/19043207/.

Hesse, Barnor. 2011. "Marked Unmarked: Black Politics and the Western Political." *South Atlantic Quarterly* 110, no. 4: 974–84.

Hesse, Barnor. 2014a. "Escaping Liberty: Western Hegemony, Black Fugitivity." *Political Theory* 42, no. 3: 288–313.

Hesse, Barnor. 2014b. "Racism's Alterity: The Afterlife of Black Sociology." In *Racism and Sociology*, edited by Wulf D. Hund and Alana Lentin, 141–74. Zurich: Lit.

Hesse, Barnor, et al. 1992. *Beneath the Surface: Racial Harassment*. London: Avebury.

Hinton, Elizabeth. 2016. *From the War on Poverty to the War on Crime: The Making of Mass Incarceration in America*. Cambridge, MA: Harvard University Press.

Institute of Race Relations. 1987. *Policing against Black People*. London: Institute of Race Relations.

Iton, Richard. 2008. *In Search of the Black Fantastic: Politics and Popular Culture in the Post-Civil Rights Era*. Oxford, UK: Oxford University Press.

Jackson, George. 1971. *Blood in My Eye*. London: Penguin Books.

John, Gus, and Derek Humphrey. 1972. *Police Power and Black People*. London: Granada.

Keith, M. 1993. *Race, Riots, and Policing: Lore and Disorder in a Multi-racist Society*. London: Routledge.

Lowe, Lisa. 2015. *The Intimacies of Four Continents*. Durham, NC: Duke University Press.

Lowery, Wesley. 2016. *They Can't Kill Us All: Ferguson, Baltimore, and a New Era in America's Racial Justice System*. New York: Little, Brown, and Company.

Marable, Manning. 2007. *Race, Reform, and Rebellion: The Second Reconstruction and Beyond in Black America, 1945–2006*. 3rd ed. Jackson, MS: University Press of Mississippi.

Mbembe, Achilles. 2001. *On The Postcolony*. Berkeley: University of California Press.

Mills, Charles. 1997. *The Racial Contract*. Ithaca, NY: Cornell University Press.

Muhammad, Khalil Gibran. 2010. *The Condemnation of Blackness: Race, Crime, and the Making of Modern Urban America*. Cambridge, MA: Harvard University Press.

Nelson, Alondra. 2011. *Body and Soul: The Black Panther Party and the Fight against Medical Discrimination*. Minneapolis: University of Minnesota Press.

Newton, Huey P. 2002. "A Functional Definition of Politics." In *The Huey P. Newton Reader*, edited by David Hilliard and Donald Weise, 147–49. New York: Seven Stories.

Patel, Tina G., and David Tyrer. 2012. *Race, Crime and Resistance*. London: Sage.

Prokhovnik, Raia. 2008. *Sovereignty: History and Theory*. Exeter, UK: Imprint Academic.

Olson, Joel. 2004. *The Abolition of White Democracy*. Minneapolis: University of Minnesota Press.

Ranciere, Jacques. 1999. *Dis-Agreement: Politics and Philosophy*. Minneapolis: University of Minnesota Press.

Rankine, Claudia. 2014. *Citizen: An American Lyric*. Minneapolis: Graywolf.

Rellek, Nic. 2010. "MadConceptz: Denzel Washington Talks about an Early Film Role in 'The Nigga They Couldn't Kill.'" *Madconceptz* (blog), November 18. madconceptz.blogspot .com/2010/11/denzel-washington-talks-about-early.html.

Saxton, Alexander. 2003. *The Rise and Fall of the White Republic: Class Politics and Mass Culture in Nineteenth-Century America*. London: Verso.

Sharpe, Christina. 2016. *In the Wake: On Blackness and Being*. Durham, NC: Duke University Press.

Stoler, Ann Laura. 2002. *Carnal Knowledge and Imperial Power: Race and the Intimate in Colonial Rule*. Berkeley: University of California Press.

Taylor, Keeanga-Yamahtta, 2016. *From #BlackLivesMatter to Black Liberation*. Chicago: Haymarket.

Threadcarft, Shatema. 2016. *Intimate Justice: The Black Female Body and the Body Politic*. New York: Oxford University Press.

United States Department of Justice, Civil Rights Division. 2015. *The Ferguson Report: Department of Justice Investigation of the Ferguson Police Department*. New York: New Press.

Wagner, Bryan. 2009. Disturbing the Peace: Black Culture and the Police Power after Slavery. Cambridge, MA: Harvard University Press.

Wells, Ida B. 1995. "Lynch Law in America." In *Words of Fire: An Anthology of African-American Feminist Thought*, edited by Beverly Guy-Sheftall, 70–76. New York: New Press.

Wells, Ida B., and Jaqueline Jones Royster. 1997. *Southern Horrors and Other Writings: The Anti-Lynching Campaign of Ida B. Wells, 1892–1900*. Boston: Bedford.

Unrecognizable:
On Trans Recognition in 2017

Aren Aizura, Editor

Aren Aizura

Introduction

If the state, capitalism, and surveillance want us to be visible somebodies,
it might be a good time to be undercover nobodies.
—Reina Gossett, Commencement Address at Hampshire College, May 2016

The essays in this section confront urgent questions regarding trans-gender recognition in the current political moment, scheming against what we understand as the empty promises of visibility and legibility. Even as far-right conservative and authoritarian political forces are on the rise throughout the world, United States President Donald Trump has promised to roll back the "liberalism" of Barack Obama by repealing health care laws, building a wall along the Mexican border, and, as a postscript, rolling back LGBT recognition, including transgender health coverage and antidiscrimination laws. Since Trump was elected, the trans communities I inhabit in the United States have expressed fear and outrage at the possibility that the "transgender tipping point" might be about to tip back. Diana Tourjee (2016) wrote in November that "transgender Americans have experienced unprecedented support from the Obama administration." In the same article, Mara Keisling, from the National Center for Trans Equality, is quoted citing one hundred fifty policy changes that helped transgender people during the Obama administration, from including gender identity in workplace and on-campus discrimination laws to outlawing exclusions of transgender-related health care. These are all set to be rolled back during the Trump presidency.

Assuming that a Republican congress will repeal the Affordable Care Act (ACA), the federal directives recognizing gender identity in equal oppor-

The South Atlantic Quarterly 116:3, July 2017
DOI 10.1215/00382876-3961721 © 2017 Duke University Press

tunity legislation, and likely coverage of trans-related health care, will disappear along with coverage of preexisting conditions and Medicaid. In transgender identity, evangelicals sense an effective wedge issue that helps them further criminalize abortion and attempt to restore the primacy of privatized, heteronormative social relations. Since 2012, Republicans have attempted to pass laws denying gender-nonconforming people access to restrooms and public accommodations, invoking the specter of gender-nonconforming people, particularly trans women, as sexual predators in an effort to restore heteronormativity to public space. Some of these bills have been successful: North Carolina's "House Bill 2" requires one to use the restroom corresponding to the gender on one's birth certificate. Some of the laws propose fines or jail terms for what under these requirements would be illicit use of public restrooms (Ford 2015). Others legislate bounty payments for students who "discover" transgender people in campus bathrooms, effectively rewarding transphobic surveillance of public facilities (Eveld 2016). Trans activists have joked that perhaps they can support themselves financially by informing authorities about their own restroom use.

These concerns are not insignificant. But some within trans politics and theory have always questioned the tipping-point analogy and, with it, the logic of transgender recognition itself. To accept the recent historical moment under President Obama, or under Tony Blair at the time the UK Gender Recognition Act was passed, as one of "recognition" means to accept the neoliberal imperialist project within which those laws were passed. As the writers in this section make clear, recognition may have arrived, but justice for transgender people has not yet begun. More accessible health care under the ACA did mean that hormones were covered under Medicaid, eventually; but the ACA itself never promised free health care for all. Special new jails to house transgender prisoners do not end incarceration. Transgender inclusion in the military literally deploys trans and gender-nonconforming people in the service of "counterterrorist" colonial wars in Israel, Iraq, Afghanistan, Syria, Yemen, Nigeria, Somalia, and a variety of other locations. Meanwhile in the realm of representation, imperialist liberals entrench Islamophobia by arguing that because "Islam" is homophobic and transphobic, protecting queer and trans populations means expanding the militarized imperial project of spreading neoliberal economic policies, democracy, and freedom to the "rest of the world" (Puar 2007; Haritaworn, Tauqir, and Erdem 2008: 10). In some instances, trans visibility also means becoming scapegoated for the ascendance of the Right. In an article lambasting the "identity dramas" of calls for racial and gender justice during the 2016 election campaign,

Mark Lilla (2016) called out the new visibility of choosing gender pronouns as part of a "moral panic about racial, gender and sexual identity" that Democrats pandered to, along with campaigning targeted at blacks, Latinx, and women. For Lilla, the visibility of transness as an election issue alienated white working-class and religious voters who considered gender diversity ridiculous; this, rather than white supremacy, provoked the surprise "whitelash" that elected Trump.

To question recognition does not only mean interrogating its broader political context. It also means considering how the affective invocation of visibility plays into neoliberal scarcity politics. In a speech on trans justice in 2016, Reina Gossett likened life under capitalism to the distinction between being "somebody" and being "nobody." Quoting Denise Ferreira da Silva (2016), Gossett asks "Do we want to be somebody under the state or nobody against it?" (a quotation that also appears as an epigraph to Eric Stanley's essay in this section). In the printed version of this speech, Gossett, along with Grace Dunham and Constantina Zavitzanos (2016), writes about the affective state of being seen, being "hot shit"—being somebody: "[A]s somebody I am enough of a body, respected enough or known enough, to be worthy of giving this speech to you all. Maybe that's about fame, maybe that's about clout, maybe that's about respect. Whatever it is, I've spent enough of my life feeling like a nobody to feel how different it is to be called upon as a somebody."

While Gossett refers to her own experience here, her description encapsulates something like what the tipping point *felt* like: suddenly transgender people were there. We were everywhere. We were hot shit. But precisely *because* capitalism loves differentiation, Gossett Dunham, and Zavitzanos (2016) warn against investing too much in being somebodies. Individual fame, she writes, is bound up in the "commodification and extraction of . . . life and affect and aesthetics and other labor." Value extraction occurs at this juncture. For example, trans women-of-color activists get invited to give talks at fancy private colleges and nonprofits but cannot find permanent jobs to pay the rent. Transgender *YouTube* stars engage in commodity activism by appearing in videos sponsored by major skin care brands (Reinke 2016: 89) but remain financially dependent on haphazard contributions to crowdfunding sites like Kickstarter and Patreon. Capital also thrives on the differentiation resulting from transgender's status as a "new" civil rights movement competing with other marginalized populations for a seat at the table and thus separate from them by definition. Meanwhile, the *transitivity* and mobility of trans itself becomes a popular way to illustrate neoliberal social mobility and flexibility (Aizura 2011; Puar 2015).

So much for being somebodies.

The title of this section, "Unrecognizable," is intended to highlight a conviction shared by these essays that even if recognition is inevitable, we may not always want to be identified. In addition, the prefigural forms that trans politics takes here may not be recognizable *as politics* to liberalism, capitalism, feminism, or queer movements—not even, at times, to us. These essays invent new terms to describe the impossibility and violence of recognition and speculatively suggest an entirely different relation to visibility. In relation to the backlash, too, they ask: What are the stakes of familiarity when familiarity breeds contempt?

These essays elaborate in different ways on a familiar theme: "transgender politics" may be unrecognizable when it invests not in an identity category but in disrupting the litany of injustices that comprise twenty-first-century capitalism. If race, gender, and sexuality determine the norms of intimate and public social relations, those of democracy, nation, prison, property, labor, and (settler) colonialism, a trans politics aimed at disrupting those institutions may not read as politics at all. But as subjects within all of these institutions, gender-nonconforming people, and especially gender-nonconforming people of color, are nobodies. Being a somebody means visibility: becoming a population, becoming a demographic, becoming (part of) a class, becoming clockable. In all of these contexts, it means having to arm yourself with your brokenness. Even as revolutionary subjects of labor in the most Marxian contexts, which are more often than not absurdly heteronormative, gender-nonconforming subjects are still pretty useless somebodies. Aspiring to nobodiness, on the other hand, means being with others who are marked as nobody too, finding communality and maybe care: "There is pleasure in nobodiness. There is love, care, and laughter there. There is art, and study. There is life" (Gossett, Dunham, and Zavitzanos 2016). Rather than looking to the celebrity or micro-celebrity culture of trans politics, theory, or art, we look to the people who we have not yet met and whose liberation is implicated in our own: "I can't wait to shake the hand of the person whose name I don't know who's in solitary in the prison 50 miles from my house" (Lazare 2017). Through this logic, we will know each other in our unrecognizability.

Being unrecognizable takes multiple forms and goes by many names. It means being nobodies for Gossett, imperceptibility for Deleuzians (Crawford 2008: 140), and opacity for Stanley. It means radical transfeminism for Raha; the coalitional counter-praxis forged by a resistance to the birth certificate's signification in feminist, queer, and trans communities, and communities of color for Armstrong; and fugitivity for those drawing from a black feminist or black radical tradition (Gumbs 2016; Bey 2016). This critique of recognition holds resonance for the moment of trans liberalism, for an analysis of the tipping point. But it also resonates as the moment of liberalism in power wanes—especially as an "LGBT-friendly" centrism just slightly to the left of Trump, Vladimir Putin, and Theresa May becomes the standard by which mainstream politics frames its rejoinders to authoritarian populism (Lazare 2017). More than anything, this teaches us that we cannot do trans politics without an analysis of political economy, without an analysis of the history of racialization and the violence of liberalism, as well as of hetero- and gender normativity. Trans politics in its most trenchant form wants abolition, an end to wealth, full communism, free water, food, air, and health care, reparations, and decolonization (literally, not figuratively). We cannot achieve any of these things without reimagining the forms of collectivity, feeling, and being-with that animate our revolt. We will not always be able to predict when we will need to be marked or when we will feel the pleasure of unmarking. But we can try to attune to the pulse of our collective need, keep the beat, and find the flow.

References

Aizura, Aren. 2011. "The Persistence of Transsexual Travel Narratives." In *Transgender Migrations: The Bodies, Borders, and Politics of Transition*, edited by Trystan Cotton, 139–56. New York: Routledge.

Bey, Marquis. 2016. "The Shape of Angels' Teeth: Toward a Blacktransfeminist Thought through the Mattering of Black(Trans)Lives." *Departures in Critical Qualitative Research* 5, no. 3: 33–54.

Crawford, Lucas. 2008. "Transgender without Organs: Mobilizing a Geo-Affective Theory of Gender Modification." *WSQ: Women Studies Quarterly* 36, no. 3–4: 127–43.

Eveld, Edward M. 2016. "Transgender Restroom Bill in Kansas Alarms LGBT Student Advocates." *Kansas City Star*, April 13. www.kansascity.com/news/politics-government/article71716992.html.

Ferreira da Silva, Denise. 2016. "Introduction: Refuse Power's Grasp." *Arika.org.uk*, December 2. http://arika.org.uk/events/episode-8-refuse-powers-grasp/introduction.

Ford, Zach. 2015. "Indiana Lawmaker Introduces 'Pay To Pee' Bill For Transgender People." *ThinkProgress*, December 15. thinkprogress.org/indiana-lawmaker-introduces-pay-to-pee-bill-for-transgender-people-1920bf6cfb9e#.xjfnm3uh5.

Gossett, Reina, Grace Dunham, and Constantina Zavitzanos. 2016. "Commencement Address at Hampshire College." *Reinagosset.com*, May 17. www.reinagossett.com/commencement-address-hampshire-college/.

Gumbs, Alexis Pauline. 2016. *Spill: Scenes from Black Feminist Fugitivity*. Durham, NC: Duke University Press.

Haritaworn, Jin, Tamsila Tauqir, and Esra Erdem. 2008. "Gay Imperialism: Gender and Sexuality Discourse in the 'War on Terror.'" In *Out of Place: Interrogating Silences in Queer Raciality*, edited by Adi Kuntsman and Esperanza Miyake, 9–34. London: Raw Nerve.

Lazare, Sarah. 2017. "Now Is the Time for 'Nobodies': Dean Spade on Mutual Aid and Resistance in the Trump Era." *Alternet,* January 9. www.alternet.org/activism/now-time-nobodies-dean-spade-mutual-aid-and-resistance-trump-era.

Lilla, Mark. 2016. "The End of Identity Liberalism." *New York Times,* November 18. www.nytimes.com/2016/11/20/opinion/sunday/the-end-of-identity-liberalism.html.

Puar, Jasbir. 2007. *Terrorist Assemblages: Homonationalism in Queer Times.* Durham, NC: Duke University Press.

Puar, Jasbir. 2015. "Bodies with New Organs: Becoming Trans, Becoming Disabled." *Social Text* 124, 33, no. 3: 45–73.

Reinke, Rachel. 2016. "Getting to Be Seen: Visibility as Erasure in Media Economies of Transgender Youth." PhD diss., Arizona State University.

Tourjee, Diana. 2016. "The Unclear Future of Trans Rights under Trump." *Broadly,* November 9. broadly.vice.com/en_us/article/the-unclear-future-of-trans-rights-under-trump.

Eric A. Stanley

Anti-Trans Optics: Recognition, Opacity, and the Image of Force

If the state is ready to kill to defend itself from the black, sexual,
trans body brought before it, do we want to be somebody before the state,
or no-body against it?
—Denise Ferreira da Silva, "Refuse Powers' Grasp"

With the height of trans visibility has also been the height of trans violence
and trans murders.
—CeCe McDonald

"*He-she*, come here!"

Defiantly looking away with her arms and legs crossed, Duanna
Johnson refuses the hail of Bridges McRae, an officer with the Memphis
Police Department.

"*Faggot*, I'm talking to you!" McRae's demand grows with angered
force against Johnson's resistance.

Johnson, a black transgender woman, had been arrested earlier that
evening under the suspicion of prostitution, a charge often levied against
trans women of color who dare to exist in public. On that February night in
2008, in the Shelby County jail's intake area, she remained seated in silent
protest, refusing to become the subject, which is to say the object, of the anti-
trans, anti-queer, and anti-black utterances of Officer McRae.[1]

Framed within the frame, a closed-circuit television (CCTV) captured
the event. The high-angle wide shot opens with Johnson sitting in a chair a
few feet behind McRae. The silent image shows McRae standing with his

The South Atlantic Quarterly 116:3, July 2017
DOI 10.1215/00382876-3961732 © 2017 Duke University Press

uniformed back toward Johnson as he fills out paperwork at the booking window. The low resolution pixelates the unfolding image as the continuous long shot mediates the frame. More impressionistic than high definition, the image surveils as it conceals. Two other uniformed officers casually talk in the background, while a third waits in line behind them. The camera captures through its still gaze a *tableau vivant*: the everydayness of administrative violence.

Enraged by Johnson's audacity, McRae turns away from the window and walks a few steps over to where she remains seated. He reaches to snatch her face or possibly her neck, sending her into a fast lean backward in an attempt to escape his grasp. The commotion breaks the still of the room, and the person sitting behind Johnson gets out of their seat; it also catches the attention of the other officers. McRae retreats a few inches and readies himself for the real attack. He slips handcuffs around his leather-gloved right hand, cocks his arm back, using physics and the force of history to ensure the most brutal swing possible. A crowd of officers move in closer to guarantee an unobstructed view. James Swain, a fellow officer, enters the frame and circles around behind Johnson. He then pins her shoulders to the chair so she cannot use them to shield herself from McRae's blows.

After a few more strikes, Johnson's skin gives way and a stream of blood runs down her face. Fearing her suspended death is about to materialize, Johnson springs to her feet and starts swinging her arms like a windmill in self-defense. Seconds later, she returns to her seat as McRae again punches her. Tired from the attack, or perhaps bored, McRae reaches for the pepper spray holstered to his belt and sprays Johnson's eyes, nose, and mouth. The pain causes her body to collapse as McRae forces his weighted knee into her spine, grinding her further into the tile floor as he cuffs her hands behind her back, marking his victory.

Brutalized, bleeding from head wounds, and pepper sprayed, Johnson's tortured and bound body flails in contempt. In a gust of adrenal agony, Johnson works her way back into a chair, unable to escape the toxicity of her own flesh. She again stands and paces pack and forth with her hands cuffed behind her back, still unable to clear the chemicals and blood from her eyes, nose, and mouth.

The tape ends as an officer with medical supplies examines McRae in the foreground of the frame while a nurse enters and walks past Johnson to also attend to him. Four officers and the nurse casually talk with McRae, possibly replaying the drama in celebration. Johnson, now in the background, again sits in the row of chairs, just a few seats over from where the beating began. Rhythmically rocking back and forth, she remains shackled, soaked in weaponized chemicals, with no medical attention, inhabiting the slow death of carceral life.[2]

After the initial beating, Johnson appeared on local news stations to publicize the abuse she was subjected to and disseminate the CCTV recording. While Johnson's stated wish for the public to witness her beating might seem to remedy the ethical impasse of viewing the tape, we remain sutured to the impure practice of looking. In other words, both seeing and not seeing the video bind us through presence and absence in the scene of raw violence. How, then, might we account for, that is to say, how might we be indebted to Johnson as we consume her image? Left unseen, the Johnson video might help us not know our own complicity in the violence she was forced to endure. Yet I choose to narrate it because staying in the space of the visceral is perhaps the only place one can inhabit with the disavowal of the ethical itself.

The image, of course, does not begin or end with the tape. Taking the stand in his own defense, Officer McRae claimed the beating was in self-defense and necessary to restrain Johnson because she was "completely out of control" and that her movements made him "startled, scared, and afraid" (Buser 2010). The self-defense strategy McRae's attorney constructed was built on Johnson's *inappropriate* physicality as a tall, black trans woman. During the trial, both McRae and his defense attorney Frank Trapp exclusively referred to Johnson as "he" and by her legal name, which was not Duanna Johnson. When asked about this by the federal prosecutor, McRae responded, "It's not important. I was just referring to him as he" (Buser 2010).

Even with the incriminating testimony of a fellow officer and the surveillance tape, on the last day of the trial, the jury reported that it could not reach a verdict. US District Court Judge Anderson then gave the jurors an Allen charge, ordering them back into deliberation over the weekend. When the jury appeared the following Monday, they reported that they were still deadlocked. Thus, the judge officially called a mistrial.

Wanting to avoid another trial, McRae eventually pleaded guilty in August 2010. His plea deal was for the charges stemming from the beating of Johnson and for tax evasion. On his tax form on file with the Memphis Police Department, he had claimed ninety-nine dependents, which meant that he never paid income tax while he was employed as a police officer. The sentence for both the beating and the tax evasion was two years in a minimum-security federal work camp, two years of probation, and a fine of $200.

Testimony from Johnson herself might have helped stall the frames that pictured her as a force against which McRae needed to defend himself. Or perhaps the sentimentality produced by a victim's words would have, at least momentarily, suspended the anti-blackness of the visual and the gender normativity of its syntax. Yet tragically, Johnson was shot dead on November 9, 2008, just five months after the beating. Not far from the shores of the Mississippi, in North Memphis, her body was found on the otherwise deserted Hollywood Avenue. According to initial reports she was shot "execution style" in the head at close range and was left to bleed out on the cold pavement (Mogul, Ritchie, and Whitlock 2011: 142).

Images of Time

Johnson is gone, but the tape remains. How might we read, or radically misread, the visual grammar of the tape to understand both the kinds of force it represents and to work against its seeming inevitability? The horrific murder of Johnson might also be understood as the tape's extradiegetic final scene, the unfolding of a narrative structure that is not simply *racist* and *transphobic*, which are terms too adjacent to name the structuring work these forms of violence index.

Tracing the history of the cinematic, as many have argued, is also a way of charting the instantiation of globalized white supremacy. To be clear, while we must attend to the racist or otherwise phobic depictions that have compromised public visual culture from lynching photography and D. W. Griffith's 1915 *The Birth of the Nation* to contemporary times, if we end there we remain in a discursive loop where we continue to struggle within a regime that will never offer relief. After all, racist content would have little power if its form were not structured similarly. Here, then, reading with the tape of Johnson's beating, we can see the ways optics, as that which both includes and exceeds narrative, produces Johnson as the "no-body" da Silva asked us to think.[3]

Franz Fanon's often-cited passage from 1952 on his experience of watching a film in a Paris theater sketches the multiple spaces of seeing and being seen that constitute the visual as a racialized practice. Fanon states (1967: 140) "I cannot go to a film without seeing myself. I wait for me. In the interval, just before the film starts, I wait for me. The people in the theater are watching me, examining me, waiting for me." Fanon suggests that the anticipation of blackness in the viewing apparatus of the cinema, which I would extend to viewing beyond the theater as well, is imbued with a form of anti-blackness that is not only seen but also otherwise sensed. Perhaps the most generative aspect of this analysis is that even before the film begins, the racialized gaze is there, anticipating him, while he also awaits its arrival. Fanon's scheme both expands the "time" of the film, meaning it does not begin or end with the rolling of images, and moves us away from assuming that the most insipid forms of colonial racism, here anti-blackness, appear through image alone (Keeling 2003; Marriott 2007).

Expanding the time of the image and the image of time allows us to read the murder of Duanna Johnson as the narrative conclusion of the beating tape. Further, while Fanon was writing specifically about the cinematic, his scheme allows us to build a similar analysis of our psychic bonds with and through surveillance as genre in the contemporary moment. The CCTV footage of Johnson functions much like what Gilles Deleuze (1989: 101), after Henri Bergson, called a "time-image." For Deleuze, a time-image is the collapsing of past, present, and future that "makes time frightening and inexplicable" (101). While Deleuze was talking about simultaneity in narrative cinema, the time-image here might help us understand the specific genre of the tape where past and future are remade through the present. Or, in other words, the time-image of the tape reminds us that, perhaps for Johnson, there is no moment other than the time of violence.

Here, Fanon's insistence that the time of the image does not align with the opening scene of the film and Deleuze's time-image illustrate the brutal semiotics of violence that await, in the interval, both the structure of the visual and the structure of life outside the theater for trans women of color. Given that representation produces and does not simply echo what is assumed to reside in the real, what, then, might representation and recognition offer for a trans politics that resides on the side of flourishing?

Clocking

By way of obscuring the question of reparation and redistribution, representation has been produced as the primary site of struggle over "diversity" for mainstream politics (including mainstream LGBT politics) in the United States. The last decade has witnessed a vast proliferation of trans representations that are offered as remedy to the relentless economic, psychic, affective, and physical violence many trans people, and in particular trans women of color, endure. These expanding representations are also used to buttress an argument supporting the unfolding *progress* of dominant culture. Yet, if we return to CeCe McDonald's words that open this essay, we know that with this increased representation comes heightened, or at least sustained, instances of violence. While 2014 was named the "Trans Tipping Point" by Time magazine, this year, 2016, has counted the highest number of trans women of color being violently murdered in the United States. Yet, following the Johnson tape, if we are to understand the visual itself as technologies of anti-black and anti-trans optics, then how might we continue the important project of representation in a visual regime hostile to black trans life?

Rather than an opening toward recognition, a position where one can make a claim instead of being exclusively claimed, representation for Johnson is the prefiguration of her undoing. Her being "clocked" as trans led to her initial arrest, subsequent beating, and, even perhaps, her murder. Being clocked, or being seen as trans, enacts the double bind of recognition: being seen by the other brings you into the world, but more often than not it is also that which might bring you out of it. Through representation—both the CCTV video and descriptions of Johnson in court—the defense was able to produce what Judith Butler (1993) and others have called a reversal of defense, where the party harmed is, through the magic of the law, transformed into the assumed aggressor. Johnson, and not the state, is made to hold the burden of proof.

Tracing a genealogy of the racial and gendered parameters of recognition from G. W. F. Hegel and Fanon to da Silva and McDonald and beyond, how might we imagine the project of recognition as both nondialectical and nondevelopmental? The brutal scene of Johnson's beating, replayed as the composed testimony of the quiet court, reminds us that recognition is not a smooth space of inevitability, even in struggle. Johnson's trans identity forces us against a substitutive logic, to once again face the ways race and gender, as lines of recognition, symbols, and embodied parameters, ask for more.

While Fanon rightly turns our attention to the limits of recognition in the colonial scene, he also maintains the teleology of subjectivity by holding on to the dialectics of structure, even for those deemed nonsubjects. Or, if for him revolutionary violence offers a way through the violence of anti-black coloniality, how might we push further on Fanon for those who must remain, as da Silva might suggest, "no-bodies against the state"?

From Optics to Opacity

Johnson's attack and its cinematic afterlife capture the structures of recognition and misrecognition, representation and disappearance that constitute the work of gender and race in and as the fields of the visual. While writing from a place of gender self-determination that works toward gender as an opening, what is left of our various analytics of recognition? Or, how might we return to the beating tape: not simply to offer yet another way to imagine what we already know—that race, gender, and violence are tightly bound—but to ask how this bind might be undone?[4]

Furthermore, what tactics of production and sabotage might bring about visual cultures that detonate the never-ending list of anti-trans violence? This question specifically addresses those trapped in the interval of seeing and being seen. We must pose it without a fantasy of closure. To put it another way, at the center of the problem of recognition lies this: how can we be seen without being known and how can we be known without being hunted?[5]

Indeed, being a "no-body against the state," a position some are already forced to live, stands against the sovereign promise of positive representation. Read not as absolute abjection but as a tactic of interdiction and direct action, being a "no-body" might force the visual order of things to the point of collapse. On the issue of recognition and radical singularity, Édouard Glissant (1997: 190) has stated, "from the perspective of Western thought, we discover that its basis is this requirement for transparency. In order to understand and thus accept you, I have to measure your solidity with the ideal scale providing me with grounds to make comparisons and, perhaps, judgments. I have to reduce." This reduction, which Fanon might call being overdetermined, is, as we know, unequally distributed and mandated. Glissant offers a totality of relation in opacity, the radical work of nontransparency that allows for non-dialectic difference—the collectivization of radical singularity.

Glissant continues, "Agree not merely to the right of difference but, carrying this further, agree also to the right of opacity that is not enclosure within an impenetrable autarchy but subsistence within an irreducible singularity" (190). We might read the current order of popular trans representation to be a variation of agreeing to the "right of difference," as transparency is the precondition of visibility politics.

Opacity is here useful not necessarily as a practice of "going stealth," residing below or beside the regimes of being seen but not known, although it might be. For Glissant (1997: 193), it is a form of solidarity without being grasped. Here, I am suggesting that it might be one form a radical trans politics might take. Opacity with representation: an irreconcilable tension that opens to something other than the pragmatism of the transparent and its visual economies of violence.[6]

There is no return and no triumphant narrative to be gleaned here, either from the brutal attack on Johnson or her subsequent death. There are, of course, countless instances of trans/queer people organizing, thriving, and resisting, even in the midst of ruthless encounters. Furthermore, anti-trans and anti-black optics of the visual must be confronted, by expanding and dangerous practices that open the frame while also doing away with its necessity. And yet there is the inescapable fact that the archive of harm, dismemberment, state-sanctioned torture, and death is still unfolding. This unfolding, which we might call modernity, continues to claim those who exist against it, banishing the possibility of another history, but perhaps not banishing the image of something yet to come.

Notes

This piece is dedicated to Duanna Johnson, and all those who struggle against police violence. I would also like to thank Angela Davis, Donna Haraway, Toshio Meronek, and C. Riley Snorton for conversations that helped form this piece. Any mistakes are my own.

1   The video is viewable on *YouTube* at youtube.com/watch?v=-IAPTk69XP0.
2   Further commentary on the beating of Johnson can be found in Richardson 2013: 163–66.
3   With the proliferation of personal technologies (camcorders, camera phones) a genre of the visual has emerged that both references the tropes of cinema and creates new viewing sensibilities. Perhaps inaugurated by the release and reproduction of the 1992 beating video of Rodney King, now every few days a new video surfaces visualizing the multiple forms of harm the police, or their ambassadors, perform against black people. See Gooding-Williams 1993 (especially Ruth Wilson Gilmore's chapter "Terror Austerity Race Gender Excess Theater") and Sharpe 2012. On the history of surveillance and black life, see Browne 2015 and Fleetwood 2011.
4   I am here thinking about the relationship between image, language, and meaning in Stuart Hall's work, particularly *Representation* (1997).
5   For some examples see the trailer for Reina Gossett and Sasha Wortzel's forthcoming film, *Happy Birthday, Marsha!* at www.happybirthdaymarsha.com/. Also see Chris Vargas's (2016) project in MOTHA (Museum of Transgender Hirstory and Art) www.sfmotha .org/. Both projects, in different ways, ask what forms a trans aesthetic might take.
6   While I am compelled by Zach Blas's (2013) theorization of "queer opacity" I am here thinking of opacity as prefigurative practice.

References

Blas, Zach. 2013. "Escaping the Face: Biometric Facial Recognition and the Facial Weaponization Suite." *NMC Media-N*, CAA Conference Edition, July 10. median.newmediacaucus .org/caa-conference-edition-2013/escaping-the-face-biometric-facial-recognition-and -the-facial-weaponization-suite/.

Browne, Simone. 2015. *Dark Matters: On the Surveillance of Blackness*. Durham, NC: Duke University Press.

Buser, Lawrence. 2010. "Memphis Police Officer on Trial Says Transgender Prisoner Was Aggressor." Memphis Commercial Appeal, April 13. https://groups.google.com/forum /#!topic/transgender-news/XrjoF-dqMnQ (accessed April 2, 2012).

Butler, Judith. 1993. "Endangered/Endangering: Schematic Racism and White Paranoia." In *Reading Rodney King/Reading Urban Uprising*, edited by Robert Gooding-Williams, 15–17. London, New York: Routledge.

Deleuze, Gilles. 1989. *Cinema 2: The Time Image*. Minneapolis: University of Minnesota Press.

Fanon, Frantz. 1967. *Black Skin, White Masks*. New York: Grove Press.

Fleetwood, Nicole R. 2011. *Troubling Vision: Performance, Visuality, and Blackness*. Chicago: University of Chicago Press.

Glissant, Édouard. 1997. *Poetics of Relation*. Ann Arbor: University of Michigan Press.

Gooding-Williams, Robert, ed. 1993. *Reading Rodney King/Reading Urban Uprising*. New York: Routledge.

Gossett, Reina, and Sasha Wortzel. Forthcoming. *Happy Birthday, Marsha!* Star People Films. www.happybirthdaymarsha.com/.

Hall, Stuart. 1997. *Representation: Cultural Representations and Signifying Practices*. London: Sage in Association with the Open University.

Keeling, Kara. 2003. "'In the Interval': Frantz Fanon and the 'Problems' of Visual Representation." *Qui Parle* 13, no. 2: 91–117.

Marriott, David. 2007. *Haunted Life: Visual Culture and Black Modernity*. New Brunswick, NJ: Rutgers University Press.

Mogul, Joey L., Andrea J. Ritchie, and Kay Whitlock. 2011. *Queer (In)Justice: The Criminalization of LGBT People in the United States*. Boston: Beacon Press.

Richardson, Matt. 2013. *The Queer Limit of Black Memory: Black Lesbian Literature and Irresolution*. Columbus: Ohio State University Press.

Sharpe, Christina. 2012. "Blackness, Sexuality, and Entertainment." *American Literary History* 24, no. 4: 1–15.

Vargas, Chris E. 2016. *Trans Hirstory in 99 Objects*, at the Henry Art Gallery, August 13, 2016–June 4, 2017. MOTHA: Museum of Trans Hirstory and Art. www.sfmotha.org/.

Amanda Armstrong

Certificates of Live Birth and Dead Names: On the Subject of Recent Anti-Trans Legislation

During the spring of 2016—a season overshadowed by North Carolina's anti-trans House Bill 2 (HB2)—I received a security alert from the University of Michigan Police Department containing the following account of an assault: "A student reported that while she was in a women's restroom, a male subject entered the restroom and forcibly hugged her before she could flee. An unauthorized, handmade 'out of order' sign was found posted to the restroom door."

Reading the e-mail threw me. I was struck thinking about how terrifying the assault must have been for the person who faced that man with his outstretched arms. I ran loops in my head, imagining how I might have responded, wondering whether I would have been able to flee when faced with the shock of the event. And having to pee every hour or so did not help. My repeated trips to the women's room that afternoon provoked feelings of nausea and more intense nervousness than usual. In addition to fearing a repetition of the earlier assault, I was concerned that there might be police keeping an eye on the bathroom, and that an officer might decide to follow me through the door. What if a cop clocked me, read me as a trans woman, that is, as "really" a man, which is to say, as a potential perpetrator of the assault I feared?

To untangle this experience, wherein my fearful projection doubled up and turned in on itself, I want to venture a reading of the condition of trans life at the moment of our ambiguous social recognition. *Recognition* is a two-sided term here. On one hand, emerging from a genealogy of German idealist philosophy, it speaks to a condition of selfhood realized in and through

The South Atlantic Quarterly 116:3, July 2017
DOI 10.1215/00382876-3961743 © 2017 Duke University Press

intersubjective encounters (Hegel 1977; Honneth 1996; Fraser 2000). Insofar as the other takes me to be an agent, I appear as such, including to myself. And to the extent that state institutions encode my status as a rights-bearing subject, my social recognition, realized in passing during intersubjective encounters, is more stably secured.

When we are talking about trans subjecthood, however, the term takes on another sense—namely, recognition as reading, clocking: the moment when a person is recognized *as trans*. This instant of recognition need not be damaging. There is a kind of knowing, often affirming, trans mutual recognition. In such a positive encounter we are genuinely *seen* by another, whom we also see, and who sees our seeing. And then there is the fact that not all trans people's intersubjective relations are structured by the interplay between passing and being clocked. For many of us though, the potentiality and/or actuality of such recognition-qua-reading organizes our social interactions, and generally cannot be dissociated from the threat of harm. Where trans life is treated as disposable, to be read *as trans* puts one in the position of the potentially abject. And insofar as the one who reads is a cop patrolling the threshold of a restroom, this scene of threat is staged in the name of the law.

A number of states in addition to North Carolina acted to increase police surveillance of gendered restrooms during the spring of 2016. Several anti-trans bathroom bills introduced around the same time as HB2 stipulated that it was unlawful to use a gendered restroom that did not correspond with the sex listed on one's birth certificate. Such laws authorize the police to read the genders of those entering public restrooms and to pursue as criminals those they suspect of living gender in ways that exceed the trajectories anticipated by their birth certificates.

Of course, police harassment of trans and queer people in and around public restrooms is nothing new. Whether on the piers of Manhattan or in Detroit's Rouge Park, Black and Latinx trans and queer people in particular have long faced violence from cops, who have routinely entered bathrooms to arrest or assault those using the facilities (Mogul, Ritchie, and Whitlock 2011: 45–68). While laws like HB2 thus do not call police harassment newly into being, they nevertheless promise to make such harassment more widespread, while also making apparent some of the cultural logics of transmisogyny.

Without exception, recent bathroom bills have been promoted in the name of nontrans women's safety. KeepNCSafe.com, an anti-trans advocacy organization, uses the slogan: "Protect women's bathrooms, showers, and locker rooms." And in justifying North Carolina's *Public Facilities Privacy and Security Act*, Governor Pat McCrory echoed this slogan, saying the Charlotte antidiscrimination bill "defies common sense and basic community norms by allowing, for example, a man to use a woman's bathroom, shower, or locker room" (McCrory 2016). The specter invoked in these talking points is that of the transfeminine predator: the male-assigned person who would exploit nondiscrimination protections to enter women's spaces and harm those within. The mythic figure of the transfeminine predator is an effect of the imaginative fecundity and barrenness of the dominant culture: this culture churns out fantastical narratives that dramatize our propensity for masculine violence while simultaneously being unable or unwilling to imagine us as women, despite our avowed identities and vulnerability to misogynistic injury. The force of this (un)imaginative complex makes trans women's presence in women's restrooms appear as a threat to, and a violation of the privacy of, those authorized to use the facilities.

That advocates of anti-trans bathroom bills have construed the birth certificate as the keeper of authentic gender offers a clue to the dominant culture's imaginative barrenness, and more generally to the organizing logics of anti-trans violence. Through its name, the birth certificate calls to mind the subject's earliest days. When a birth certificate is mentioned, a baby is conjured in the imagination. As it features in debates on trans people's access to public facilities then, the birth certificate frames trans life in terms of an opposition of infancy and adulthood, before and after, origin and telos. And while origin and telos can each lay claim to a given phenomenon's essence, our Platonic inheritances give an edge in this regard to the former. Jay Prosser (1998: 61–134) shows how trans autobiographies have often picked up on the Platonic association of origin and essence, insisting that the author/protagonist's original and true gender identity was lost at the moment of their birth, only to be regained through transition. And when we insist that we have "always known ourselves to be" the gender into which we transition, we are engaged in an effort to legitimize ontologically this gender identity through a story of origins. We can perhaps read these tactics of self-authorization as defensive measures taken against a culture that tends to perceive in trans people the shadow of our younger selves, the signs of our birth-assigned genders, and the echoes of our dead names, and to take these traces of our past selves as evidence of our essential, inner-gendered state of being.

As Carolyn Steedman (1995: 1–20) demonstrates, emergent nineteenth-century notions of subjective interiority presumed a remembered childhood. The adult individual's efforts to recall episodes from her distant past and to articulate continuities between earlier and later selves materialized her psychic essence. The adult's relation to the child she once was promised to secure her subjective interiority. Often when we are read *as trans*, such an interpretive project is taken from and turned against us. The one who reads presumes both to see our past in our present and, perhaps, to reconcile the apparent discontinuity: at times, they undertake to show us who they take us *really* to be. They may know nothing about our childhood, but in seeing us as trans, they assume that they not only know but in some sense also possess the stories of our lives. An imaginative staging of this association between clocking and seeing a trans person's earlier self appears in "Alone Together" (Mitroff, Florido, and Sugar 2015), an episode in season one of the animated *Steven Universe* series. In this episode, the child characters Steven and Connie fuse into Stevonnie, who appears as a teenage multiracial transfeminine character, too big for her still kid-sized outfit. After a teenage boy aggressively sexualizes Stevonnie at a dance party, Stevonnie ultimately splits back into the two children. This episode's simultaneous play across various identity categories, structured by the fictional premises of the show, can be read allegorically as a depiction of the dangers and dynamics of being read as a trans woman. When the clock strikes, the young boy and girl are thrown, disoriented, out of the body within which they had only recently been housed.

When we are read *as trans*, our inner life, exemplified by our earlier selves, is externalized. Being read is one of the ways that trans people, particularly those who are multiply oppressed, are socially denied interiority and forms of reserve, privacy, and respect enjoyed by nontrans people. Such social denial is also accomplished to the extent to which we are barred from safe and undisturbed access to restrooms and other public facilities. Restrooms are ideally backstage sites, to use a category from Erving Goffman's (1990: 75, 98) sociology of interaction.[1] We use them to void bile, adjust our clothes, and do our makeup in peace. But except perhaps in all-gender bathrooms, trans people generally do not enjoy such a relaxed experience of the backstage. If anything, as we enter a gendered restroom the air becomes thicker with potential hostility. For trans people, the relationship between backstage and front stage is reversed, or simply does not obtain.

And yet, when I read that security alert from the University of Michigan police, I was shaken. As hostile as women's restrooms can feel, imagining that particular man entering the bathroom down the hall and approaching my body involved imagining an intensity of threat that I do not typically experience while using the restroom. Despite everything, something of the backstage effect still obtains for me in using women's restrooms. Perhaps this is why I find debates over trans women's use of gendered restrooms so upsetting: I can imagine the fear that these debates treat as a natural response to my body. The debates compel me to imagine myself appearing as a threatening presence through the eyes of another. But there is no way to think along these lines that does not call up painful experiences of the threats that have often followed my being clocked. I cannot but recoil at the violence of this self-denying vision.

This interior splitting can be refigured as a critical observation: when we are clocked—and the transphobes would like to make us into a broken clock, locked to our birth certificates, perpetually telling the same out-of-date time—not only is our interior subjectivity potentially taken from and turned against us, but we can also be made to appear as a threat to the privacy, interiority, and bodily integrity of the other. We bear, in both senses of the word, the violation of selfhood: we at once suffer and appear likely to transmit the violation. We appear to threaten the violation of selfhood not only because traces of masculinity are read off our bodies, but perhaps also in that we are read as subjects without reserve. As subjects without the "backstage" we provoke in the other anxious imaginings of a life lived without reserve, privacy, or other forms of self-protection. When we see ourselves being seen in such a phobic way, we often spin out our own anxious imaginings, whether of potential physical harm, arrest, or public shaming. Does the one who reads also see this fear in us? Is she also troubled by a doubled self-perception of vulnerability and (imputed) potential to harm?

There is something of a bad infinity[2] in this interplay of (mis)recognition and anticipated harm—a bad infinity that structures not only punctual encounters in the restroom but also sprawling debates in contemporary feminism. Such debates tend to polarize around the question of relative vulnerability. Trans exclusionary feminists call upon the full force of the myth of the transfeminine predator, presume uncomplicated socializations into gendered roles, and highlight forms of misogynistic violence directed by men against the bodies of nontrans women. They do so in an attempt to bar trans women from autonomous feminist organizing spaces. In response, trans advocates contest the myth of the transfeminine predator, offer alternative accounts of socialization, and emphasize the forms of misogynistic and transphobic violence faced by trans women. We do so to insist that a feminism walled off against trans women betrays its principles.[3] While I am clear about which side of this debate I inhabit, increasingly I have come to experience the debate itself as politically deadening. The debate encourages its participants to define their feminist politics in terms of how they approach questions of inclusion/exclusion vis-à-vis the category of woman, rather than in terms of how their practical activities help build alliances across difference, clarify shared interests in undoing gender oppression, or forge struggles for large-scale social transformation. Even as we counter trans exclusionary feminisms, can we also think beyond the polemical terms associated with these debates? Effective political practice and meaningful ethical life require efforts both to step outside the terms of these polemics and to unwind the recursive spirals of (mis)recognition and anticipated harm sketched above. In what follows, I want to suggest a few approaches to this sidestepping.

One possibility would be to reframe the interplay of (mis)recognition and anticipated harm in a way that allows this dynamic to become less a downward spiral, in which two bodies falling through space polarize into protective postures, and more an occasion for new forms of critical reflexivity. This is not simply a matter of reiterating the ethical commonplace that we all are capable of doing harm, true in the limited sense as this may be. Social existence divides bodies into those authorized to rape and those taken to be rapeable, bodies authorized to kill and those taken to be killable, bodies authorized to jail and those taken to be jailable. A bland ethical universalism would paper over such fissures. But what about relations between bodies navigating differently precarious relations to social recognition, or between those differently exposed to gendered and racialized violence? As we engage in what Judith Butler (2004: 33) has referred to as an "insurrection at the level of ontology"—as we struggle to alter the bases of realness by undoing the association of origin and essence, and by challenging the (un)imaginative complex that treats trans women as not ever, not yet, not really women— is there not also a way to think our capacity to harm other socially unrecognized bodies (including the bodies of other trans people) in terms that are not socially derealizing? How can we entertain our capacity to enact harm without echoing the dominant culture's presumption that surely there is a violent young man lurking inside us somewhere? Or, along other lines, how can we hold the critical awareness that white, nontrans women's recognized vulnerability has historically been weaponized, especially in the service of white supremacy (Bernstein 2010: 45–72), while refusing to downplay the pervasiveness, normalized quality, and harmful effects of misogyny? While there are surely some real tensions between different strains of trans, feminist, queer, and/or antiracist politics, a quotidian dialectics in which we experiment with holding such counterposed thoughts together might open onto alternative political problems, more generative conversations, and previously under-realized points of shared experience or interest.

Aiming to think together trans people's vulnerability and potential to enact harm opens as well onto the political questions of how our politics and identities might be caught up in emergent forms of normativity, state power, and capital accumulation. We can sharply reject Žižek's claim in an August 2016 essay that trans campaigns for bathroom access are necessarily wedded to a neoliberal project (Žižek 2016), while also critically interrogating potentials for incorporation or recuperation in contemporary trans politics.[4] One way to open this inquiry would be to consider how episodic the recent waves of socially general trans bathroom panic have been (cresting in the spring of 2016, evidently lulling in the aftermath of the massacre at the Pulse club in Orlando, and then being resuscitated by a national election in November). The apparently flagging quality of antitrans backlash politics suggests that the vision of the subject promoted by its advocates may be residual. Perhaps the model of the subject fixed in place by his or her birth certificate has no future. Perhaps trans subjectivities mediate a new dispensation of personhood that is more consonant with emergent demands of accumulation and state control.

I would be inclined to respond to this provocation in a two-sided way. It seems to me that the 2016 flurry of antitrans legislation gestures toward a new hegemonic dispensation of the subject just as much as the "protrans" coalition that emerged to challenge this legislation—a coalition that, admittedly, included multinational corporations and the US Department of Justice. With this new organization of the self, presumptions of privacy are jettisoned and gender mutability is assumed, but even so, forms of normativity and differential access to reserve are maintained. The trans subject thus becomes a vanishing mediator for a new model of the person: we simultaneously exemplify and open up possibilities for a new sort of subjectivity and become the bodies against which new abjectifying lines are drawn. Or, reframed slightly, this new order is characterized by a starker separation between socially recognized groups of trans people, on the one hand, and those enduring intensified forms of policing, exposure, and subordination on the other hand.[5] (In this vein, it is worth noting in relation to the opening anecdote that, even while the bathroom down the hall felt particularly hostile that day, there was nevertheless a backstage site to which I could retire—namely, my academic office.)

If we take seriously this latter scenario of increasing polarization between trans populations, a different view of the 2016 debate over antitrans bathroom bills comes into focus. This revised view would emphasize how the configuration of the debate offered occasions for relatively privileged trans people to align themselves with forms of social normativity and state power and to systematically forget the forms of state and vigilante violence endured particularly by black and Latinx queer and trans people.

For example, some of those who spoke out against HB2 pointed out that, far from keeping men out of women's restrooms, the law mandated that most trans men use women's facilities. Selfies of bearded, muscular white trans men circulated across social media, paired with captions such as: "@PatMcCroryNC It's now the law for me to share a restroom with your wife" and "Hey conservative fearmongers—pls explain to me again why you want me in the women's restrooms. . . ." Such posts called up the same anxieties as those mobilized by KeepNCSafe, attempting to undo the justification of the bathroom bills by revealing an internal contradiction in the paternalistic project of trans exclusion. As much as these posts effectively challenged the invisibilization of trans men in debates over bathroom bills, they also entered into a patriarchal discourse *among* men, *about* the management of women. The posts addressed themselves to governors and conservative activists, rhetorically asking what would best shield women from danger (or perhaps from illicit desire). The posts thus realized a masculinist medium of communication between state legislators, conservative activists, and relatively privileged trans men.

Others critical of the bathroom bills took the tack of comparing the fictional quality of trans predators with the reality of indiscreet Republican men. As a popular tweet had it: "Time to remind folks that there have been more US Senators arrested for sexual misconduct in bathrooms than trans people." While I can appreciate the importance of drawing attention to the fantastical fabrication of the "trans sexual predator" figure and its function as a transphobic myth, the literal claim of this post is almost surely untrue. Black and Latinx queer and trans people face particularly intensive police harassment in and around public bathrooms and are not infrequently detained under public indecency or antiprostitution statutes for acts ranging from having sex to carrying multiple condoms to merely being present in heavily policed spaces. And do we really want to imply that the arrest of former US Senator Larry Craig for tapping his foot in a men's bathroom to solicit anonymous sex was legitimate? This widely shared tweet thus exemplified what was a relatively common inattention within debates on the bathroom bills to the violence of policing, particularly the policing of queer and trans people of color. To the extent that debates turned exclusively on the question of interpersonal injury, and more particularly on the question of whether (presumptively white) transfeminine people were more plausibly victims or perpetrators of interpersonal violence, the debates screened from view the pervasiveness and long history of police violence against multiply oppressed trans and queer people, including in and around public restrooms.

An intervention along these lines was staged by Qasima Wideman (2016) in an *Advocate* commentary titled "Y'all White Queers Better Quiet Down in North Carolina." Wideman's commentary recounts sitting in legislative debates in which white cis women spoke about their fear of "men in dresses" while white trans women affiliated with national nonprofits "pointed to their own 'respectable' bodies, post-gender-affirming surgery and hormone therapy. These women bragged about how well they passed as cis and implored the North Carolina General Assembly to admit them into the cult of white womanhood and see their lives as worth protecting." Meanwhile, trans people of color were shut out of the legislative debates and were dragged away by the police when they tried to insist on their right to offer testimony. Wideman's intervention was posed against the white supremacist and gender-normative configurations of the debate itself, puncturing the exclusionary circle maintained by this debate's relatively privileged antagonists.

One way to think the necessity of passing beyond the exclusionary bounds of this sort of debate would be to consider the function of the birth certificate simultaneously in recent anti-immigrant and antiblack mobilizations *and* antitrans mobilizations. In addition to the bathroom bills, we have witnessed in the last few years an obsessive attention directed toward President Obama's purportedly forged birth certificate and, more recently, efforts in Texas to deny birth certificates to children of undocumented parents. Through these various initiatives, the birth certificate has become something of a talisman for the Right. Those committed to coalitional politics on the left should be able to see in the birth certificate's fungible utility for those on the right the outlines, in negative, of a counter-praxis. We can affirm unequivocally that trans, queer, feminist, and antiracist politics challenge the conservatism implicit in the elevation of the birth certificate to the defining document of the self. Our politics rest on affirmations that transformation is possible, that our fates are not sealed at birth, that borders, prison walls, and other regulatory barriers can be unmade, and that biology is not destiny.

Notes

1 For Hegel (1975: 137 §94), a situation can be referred to as a "bad infinity" when the relations between finite and infinite remain essentially static, giving rise to a kind of churning or looping motion, wherein "the finite rises again the same as ever, and is never got rid of and absorbed."

2 Goffman's account of social interaction is informed by the dramaturgical metaphors of front stage and backstage. For Goffman, backstage moments are those wherein we let our guard down and worry less about how we appear to others, but also wherein we rehearse and otherwise prepare for our front-stage performances. Concerning bathrooms, Goffman (1990: 75) writes:

the bathroom and bedroom, in all but lower-class homes, are places from which the downstairs audience can be excluded. Bodies that are cleansed, clothed, and made up in these rooms can be presented to friends in others. In the kitchen, of course, there is done to food what in the bathroom and bedroom is done to the human body. It is, in fact, the presence of these staging devices that distinguishes middle-class living from lower-class living. But in all classes in our society there is a tendency to make a division between the front and back parts of residential exteriors.

3   A particularly prominent iteration of this debate was touched off on June 6, 2015, with the publication of Elinor Burkett's "What Makes a Woman?" in the *New York Times*. Select responses by trans and intersex people include Ginelle 2015, Costello 2015, and Beyer 2015.

4   For a response to Žižek, see Gossett 2016.

5   This argument builds on interventions along these lines made by Jasbir Puar and Aren Aizura. As Puar (2015: 46) notes,

Aizura writes that this trans citizenship entails "fading into the population . . . but also the imperative to be 'proper' in the eyes of the state: to reproduce, to find proper employment; to reorient one's 'different' body into the flow of the nationalized aspiration for possessions, property [and] wealth." This trans(homo)nationalism is therefore capacitated, even driven by, not only the abjection of bodies unable to meet these proprietary racial and gendered mandates of bodily comportment but also the concomitant marking as debilitated of those abjected bodies. The debilitating and abjecting are cosubstancing processes.

References

Bernstein, Elizabeth. 2010. "Militarized Humanitarianism Meets Carceral Feminism: The Politics of Sex, Rights, and Freedom in Contemporary Antitrafficking Campaigns." *Signs* 36, no. 1: 45–72.

Beyer, Dana. 2015. "What Makes a Woman? A Trans Woman Responds to a Mid-20th Century Era Feminist." *Huffington Post*, June 6. huffingtonpost.com/dana-beyer/what-makes-a -woman-a-tran_b_7533324.html.

Burkett, Elinor. 2015. "What Makes a Woman?" *New York Times*, June 6, 2015. nytimes.com /2015/06/07/opinion/sunday/what-makes-a-woman.html?_r=0.

Butler, Judith. 2004. *Precarious Life: The Powers of Mourning and Violence*. New York: Verso.

Costello, Cary Gabriel. 2015. "TERFs of the Times." *Transfusion*, June 7. trans-fusion.blogspot .com/2015/06/terfs-of-times.html.

Fraser, Nancy. 2000. "Rethinking Recognition." *New Left Review* 3, May–June: 107–20.

Ginelle, Leela. 2015. "Trans Women Are Women. Why Do We Have to Keep Saying This?" *Bitch Media*, June 9. bitchmedia.org/post/trans-women-are-women-why-do-we-have -to-keep-saying-this.

Goffman, Erving. 1990. *The Presentation of Self in Everyday Life*. London: Penguin.

Gossett, Che. 2016. "Žižek's Gender Trouble." *Los Angeles Review of Books*, September 13. lareview ofbooks.org/article/zizeks-transgender-trouble/.

Hegel, G. W. F. 1975. *Logic: Part One of the Encyclopedia of Philosophical Sciences*. Translated by William Wallace. Oxford, UK: Oxford University Press.

Hegel, G. W. F. 1977. *The Phenomenology of Spirit*. Oxford, UK: Oxford University Press.

Honneth, Axel. 1996. *The Struggle for Recognition*. Cambridge, MA: MIT Press.

McCrory, Pat. 2016. "Governor McCrory Takes Action to Ensure Privacy in Bathrooms and Locker Rooms." *GovernorNC.gov*, Press release, March 23. archive.is/o5cyo.

Mitroff, Katie, Hilary Florido, and Rebecca Sugar. 2015. "Alone Together." *Steven Universe*, episode 37, season 1. Cartoon Network.

Mogul, Joey, Andrea Ritchie, and Kay Whitlock. 2011. *Queer (In)Justice: The Criminalization of LGBT People in the United States*. Boston: Beacon Press.

Prosser, Jay. 1998. *Second Skins: The Body Narratives of Transsexuality*. New York: Columbia University Press.

Puar, Jasbir. 2015. "Bodies with New Organs: Becoming Trans, Becoming Disabled." *Social Text* 33, no. 3: 45–73.

Steedman, Carolyn. 1995. *Strange Dislocations: Childhood and the Idea of Human Interiority, 1780–1930*. Cambridge, MA: Harvard University Press.

Wideman, Qasima. 2016. "Ya'll White Queers Better Quiet Down in North Carolina." *The Advocate*, April 6. advocate.com/commentary/2016/4/06/yall-white-queers-better-quiet-down-north-carolina.

Žižek, Slavoj. 2016. "The Sexual Is Political." *Philosophical Salon, Los Angeles Review of Books*, August 2. thephilosophicalsalon.com/the-sexual-is-political/.

Nat Raha

Transfeminine Brokenness, Radical Transfeminism

To name the states of our brokenness:

> depression, hurt, trauma, fatigue/exhaustion,
> overwork, sadness, loneliness, stress, mental
> and physical tension, isolation; anomie and
> boredom and discontent; unemployment,
> underemployment, low wages;
> to be disregarded as a sexual subject; surviving
> abuse and abusive relationships, incarceration,
> violence including sexual violence;
> anger, Madness, and the labels of "crazy,"
> "psychotic," "mentally ill";[1] the transphobic slurs
> that are too familiar;
> to be outcast, or the pariah, to be exiled;
> the disqualification of the transfeminine.

To speak of desire in its multiplicities: the survival and breathing and possibility of transfeminine desire amid and beyond our social and material conditions—of austerity, racism, xenophobia, transphobia and transmisogyny, ableism, whorephobia.[2] How can we connect these conditions that undergird the negative affects of transfeminine life to ground a politicized understanding of our brokenness?

To speak of our states of brokenness: states where bodies are jammed, depowered, isolated, the struggle to begin to speak of these states; states of anger, distress, and depression, each feeding into the next; the horizon of

The South Atlantic Quarterly 116:3, July 2017
DOI 10.1215/00382876-3961754   © 2017 Duke University Press

the day closing,[3] closed, the pull of inactivity, tending toward the rejection of sociality; a state in which we suspend care for our bodies or are isolated in caring for our bodies; the fact that the quick fixes in self-care offered by capital, commodity exchange, and consumption are largely unaffordable; the state in which concentration disintegrates in front of one's pleasures; to go to the workplace or Jobcentre Plus,[4] silent, alienated, reinforcing one's depression; the state of understanding the workplace as a ruse of the expression of one's self and gender;[5] the state in which one's humanity is disqualified due to the work one undertakes, disqualified as feminists or as women for selling sex as a means to money, the psychic fallout of such disqualifications; the state in which community and cohesion do not materialize into socially reproductive, sustainable care (beyond lovers and individual friends); a state in which discourses of sexuality and sexual reproduction elide the lived particularities of our bodies;[6] a state without a discourse to speak of abuse and its impact on trans and queer bodies and lives in our/their particulars; a state in which desire and need and love emerge only through the inauguration of worlds that do not yet exist. Such are these states of our brokenness.

Trans Liberalism at the Borders of Brexit

At this pivotal, historical moment of neoliberal structural adjustment following the 2008 financial crisis and the ascendency of far-right politics this decade, the position of transgender people is marked by extreme contradiction. There is little doubt that public discourse and consciousness of trans issues in the West is developing, in part through positive media representation and trans celebrities, hailed as "The Transgender Tipping Point" by *Time* magazine's May 2014 issue, which featured Laverne Cox on its cover. Along with this new visibility comes a fresh push for transgender legal rights, including the pursuit of widespread legal gender recognition, employment rights, rights for trans-related health care, and marriage rights. However, the stratification of livable trans and gender-nonconforming lives along the lines of race, class, gender, dis/ability, nationality, and migration status remains firmly and increasingly in place, as neoliberal governments disinvest in social security, ramp up racialized policing and the criminalization of certain—largely Muslim and black—migrant persons, and facilitate innovative methods in the upward redistribution of wealth while amplifying xenophobic rhetoric and policy. This moment of liberal transgender politics, which I have elsewhere described as "trans liberalism," harmonizes with global capitalist restructuring and reaffirms this stratification (Raha 2015).

Such capitalist restructuring takes forms known as austerity, structural adjustment, and the extraction of wealth from surplus populations including incarcerated people, alongside migrant persons and refugees.

Following the election of Donald Trump in the United States, the outcome of the United Kingdom's referendum to leave the European Union (aka Brexit), and the far-right populism that is captivating Europe, the politics of trans liberalism faces a potential backlash from the far right. While the particular local and national contexts of trans politics and consciousness of trans issues across these countries varies considerably, the project of trans legal enfranchisement through parliamentary democracy may be fractured through increased policing at the level of one's citizenship, as "immigration enforcement" is both rhetorically invoked and practically implicated across all spheres of public and private life. In the case of the United Kingdom, Brexit further undermines the means to economic survival for all who do not hold a UK passport working in the country—that is, the rights to remain in the country to work and live, which have already been undercut this decade for black and/or Muslim people. Alongside the refusal of the Conservative government led by Theresa May to guarantee job security for European Union workers is the spike in racist and xenophobic violence following the referendum, amid the naturalization and perpetration of xenophobia by newspapers. Although the British Conservative government can claim a progressive attitude on LGBT issues following the legalization of same-sex marriage in 2013,[7] and while fresh trans equality legislation may be put to members of parliament this decade, the government has made immigration enforcement a statutory duty of employers, universities, schools, and landlords, and the United Kingdom continues to attempt to deny the right of asylum to LGBTQ asylum seekers. Legislation including the Prevent Duty (part of the Counter-Terrorism and Security Act 2015) and the Immigration Act 2016—both architected by Theresa May as Home Secretary—make it a statutory requirement for employers to check passports, visas, and work permits of current, and in some cases prospective, employees (with the possibility of facing criminal charges if they do not comply); for universities to report student attendance to the government, at the risk of losing their power to sponsor visas for international students; and for teachers to refer students at "risk" of "radicalization" to the government. Moreover, landlords face criminal charges for leasing property to people who are in the United Kingdom "illegally," and the government has extended its "deport first, appeal later" scheme to all migrant persons in the United Kingdom (Lea 2016). This is part of the materialization of the border in the workplace, the border in the home, the border in the school, the border in the university, the border at the Jobcentre Plus, the border in the hospital, the border in the marriage registry, the border in the street.

We face a new era of identity checks that will disproportionately impact people of color and trans and gender-nonconforming people (of color), especially for people without documents or anything but a UK passport. Trans and gender-nonconforming people face particular challenges in finding work, including but by no means limited to issues with documentation, issues around discrimination (despite limited trans protections in employment and during the hiring process under the Equality Act 2010),[8] the psychic difficulties of working within cis-dominated workplaces, alongside the underfunding of the LGBTQ voluntary sector amid general conditions of downsized, disinvested, and precarious work, housing and public services, and the ongoing criminalization of sex work. Further checks of one's immigration status will only compound these intersecting issues and create additional mental distress. The pursuit of trans rights, and LGBTQ rights more generally, through the channels of parliamentary democracy entails pursuing rights while the means of accessing those rights become predicated on our status as UK passport holders with access to wealth. This is not to say that the rights we currently have—particularly the Equality Act 2010—must not be defended; we must however be hyper-aware of how they may be undermined through other means that may not be clearly demarcated as "transgender issues." The most visible instance may be the government's current plans to scrap the United Kingdom's Human Rights Act 1998, which codifies the European Convention on Human Rights. The next stage of the transformation of material conditions under austerity in the United Kingdom couples the dismantling of social support, the welfare state, and the privatization of the National Health Service to the introduction of the border into all aspects of life. On which side of the border trans activism places its support will be critical for the efficacy and power of this movement.

It is statistically and socially evident—wherever such statistics exist—that capitalist restructuring and austerity policies have a disproportionate impact on LGBTQ people and people of color (Mitchell et al. 2013; Runnymede Trust 2015). Manifestations of intermeshing forms of transphobia and transmisogyny, antiblackness, racism, xenophobia, whorephobia, femmephobia, and ableism, working in concert to create conditions of slow death, social death, and actual death for poor trans women and trans femmes/of color and/ or trans sex workers are inextricable from structural economic transformations and exacerbated by the fresh governance around immigration.[9] At

the extreme of this continuum of violence is the murder of trans women—
and trans women of color and trans sex workers in particular—across the
globe and the overrepresentation of trans and gender-nonconforming people
in the prison populations such as in the United States.[10] In suggesting that
these social and economic conditions create a situation of slow death for poor
trans women and trans femmes/of color and/or sex workers, I draw on Lauren Berlant's (2011: 95) formulation where "*slow death* refers to the physical
wearing out of a population in a way that points to its deterioration as a
defining condition of its experience and historical existence." Berlant argues
that this is part of "the phenomena of collective physical and psychic attenuation from the effects of global/national regimes of capitalist structural subordination and governmentality" (95). This formulation presents a conceptual bridge across the affects and experience of transfeminine
brokenness—the constellation of affective states named in the previous section—to our position as poor feminized bodies within neoliberal capitalist
societies, whose situations may never be alleviated through trans rights, hate
crime laws, etc. In suggesting that poor transfeminine people exist and live
within a situation of slow death, I do not intend to romanticize or fetishize
trans life in general, and transfeminine life in particular, in a manner that
dehumanizes these/our lives (which in the context of cultural representation, leaves audiences to take pity on our lives while we are stripped of
agency); nor do I intend to reinscribe the pathologization of trans life—especially disabled trans life. Rather, I intend to politicize our sense of feeling as
a part of social and material injustice that must be transformed; and to center this physical and psychic attenuation in a historicized understanding of
our experience.

The quantification of social and material challenges facing LGBTQ
people in general, and trans people in particular, often leaves little space to
conceptualize the affective and emotional experiences that cohere and dema-
terialize under these conditions and their political implications. Quantitative
or statistical analysis also circumvents questions of agency and the opportunity to conceptualize transfeminist life and struggle as enacted and supported through forms of collectivity—of practical support, knowledge sharing, or politicized world-making. This essay offers one account of the social
and material basis on which transfeminine life is fractured and presents the
affects of such fractures. I offer it with an awareness that the political and
material background of trans and queer liberalisms within contemporary
neoliberal capitalism ensures that certain groupings of poor, trans, and
queer people are class fodder as cheap, precarious labor for the reproduction

of capital—at best granted formal legal rights, but with a cost. We struggle to afford access to these rights in the same way that neoliberalism has us struggling to pay the rent,[11] and with our rights we encounter fresh forms of racialized, xenophobic policing from the street to spheres of public and private life. I offer this essay in hope of the trans and queer world-making project that builds a coalitional politics, mutual care and support, around the affectivities of transfeminine brokenness (a project ongoing in certain places), and in the knowledge that new forms of (potentially militant) femininities may grow through such projects.[12] This essay tarries with the negative to synthesize possibility and inform action, to politicize our conception of these feelings for radical praxis.

The politics I and others have named *radical transfeminism* emerges in this political context. Radical transfeminism is a collective political praxis and critique developing in the tenuously United Kingdom and Europe, centering transfeminine bodies that are or find themselves precariously employed, poor, overworked, and pathologized—bodies of color and various shades of white; migrant bodies; dis/abled bodies; and/or "working" bodies. Radical transfeminism is oriented around forms of care and support, and through working together, over and across material precarity.[13] The forms of radical transfeminism I am speaking of here include forms of cultural production—art can be a powerful means for affective solidarity—alongside moments of political protest and solidarity and forms of socially reproductive labor: the care work of cooking and feeding and housing, resting and rearing, cleaning and washing and dressing, the work of creating our performative genders, the loving and sexual pleasure, and the emotional support that maintains our trans and queer bodies and lives.[14] Radical transfeminism intends to turn the tides of trans and queer liberalism through ground-level action in the world: showing the limits of such reformist politics and understanding their situation in contemporary Europe's ascendant far-right politics and the refusal of its governments to register the humanity of people fleeing war and violence perpetrated by both Western states and ISIS in the Middle East and to provide a humanitarian response to the so-called refugee crisis. While we situate and conceptualize varied trans and queer struggles as part of this century's challenges through direct democracy, we are also aware that the assertion of our bodies as transfeminine bodies within such struggles is both necessary and draining. Political work can open us up to forms of damage, even when riot police are out of sight; and the precarity through which we organize does not necessarily entail the possibility of safer spaces.[15]

Separations of Transfeminine Bodies and Work

When the lack of air cuts the thought that does not refract through another body. . .

On the other side of the Western world I meet a poet. Our conversation tends toward a story either of us could have told, with different colleagues or collaborators, different geography, different queer and trans scenes, different bodies of different shifts through land and location. We drop off mailing lists and are absent from the spaces we have helped organize and create. The ideas and critiques we voice do not carry. The disqualification of our knowledge, of suggestions, of creating the time for our involvement, of our work within forms of queer and trans community and cultural spaces—as trans femmes or trans women, or constellating near these descriptions—are the same. We call this phenomenon textbook transmisogyny. But I also think of how Susan Stryker (2008: 154) connects the disavowal of our knowledge rooted in the understanding of transfeminine bodies as antinormative bodies to a "more fundamental and culturally pervasive disavowal of intrinsically diverse modes of bodily being as the lived ground of all knowing and of all knowledge production." Stryker (2008: 154) argues that consequently the knowledge of how antinormative bodies are materially affected, and how such material effects transform knowledge, are "delegitimated as merely subjective," which "circumscribes the radical potential of that knowledge [in] critique . . . as feminism, communities of color, and third world voices have long maintained." Between the designation of the experiences rooted in transfeminine bodies as "merely subjective" and the disavowal of transfeminine knowledge as a site of knowledge in its multiplicities, the potentiality of our thought—and one might add our work—are circumscribed.

To (at best) be bearers of civil rights and socially or micropolitically disqualified as bearers of knowledge is nothing new. It is nothing new for trans femmes as it is nothing new for people of color as it is nothing new for women as it is nothing new for migrants as it is nothing new for people with disabilities as it is nothing new for intersex people of various genders. The difference is when we are organizing with fellow queers, fellow trans people, fellow feminists, fellow disabled people; sometimes we hold up the moments when we all get the issue—one person points to it as us all getting the issue that maybe next time only two people in the room will get. But the structure is such that sometimes we are not even in the room (when there are no trans women at your party) or near the politics (when there are no trans women in your feminist community). The disavowal of the knowledge of trans women and trans femmes, as Stryker suggests, as well as the exclusion of our bodies and the disregarding of the work we undertake, materially and psychically affects those denied and granted access to these rooms. This is the separation of our bodies and work and lives from queer, feminist, and trans world-making projects, which is itself a basic fracturing of such worlds, and the erasure of the poor trans femmes (often of color) who have inaugurated them—of the names known and now held up: Sylvia Rivera, Marsha P. Johnson, Miss Major. Sometimes we witness the really beautiful spectacle of queer/feminist/of color community holding up its sisters and siblings, only to be reminded again of our deviance through exclusion. The psychic and emotional impact of this is sometimes too hard to bear, let alone to begin speaking of. Sometimes we are either broken or not too broken such that we can speak to each other (as trans siblings, or queer sisters, among ourselves or to build solidarity across these lines) and build the moment of recognition that something historically specific kept us absent from whatever room it is or was, this or that month. Sometimes this knowledge cascades into and through our interiors, into accumulating collective, communal bodies. Sometimes the conversation does not even begin to cohere this way. Sometimes it does not materialize.

Capital Devaluations

I want to connect the epistemological disqualification of the transfeminine body as an antinormative body (in the sense articulated by Stryker) to the material precarity of antinormative bodies in general. The disqualification operating through vectors of transmisogyny, on a micropolitical level, is intimately connected to the devaluation of poor, feminized bodies under capitalism. This devaluation takes place both in regard to one's social position and one's relation to wages. The devaluation of poor, feminized bodies under capitalism is the basis of our brokenness as transfeminine bodies. It is compounded through a racialized and gendered division of labor where poor, feminized bodies and/or of color—often from or in the global South—sustain the lives, spaces, and desires inhabited by (predominately, but not exclusively, white) privileged, bourgeois bodies in or from the global North.[16] That our transfeminine bodies are barely deemed worthy of affective support either within capitalist society or within anticapitalist queer, feminist, and trans community organizing dovetails our devaluation through this racialized and gendered division of labor. Furthermore, the knowledge that might emerge through such affective struggles as considered above, be they individual or collective, is only valued when it is posited in certain, limited forms of narrative (*the* trans narrative) or is contained within narratives of recognition. In the context of trans and gender-nonconforming people generally inhabiting the lower echelons of wage distributions (recalling our unemployment, underemployment, overwork, boredom, and isolation), our position within a racialized and gendered division of labor further circumscribes the radical potential of our knowledge as rooted in antinormative bodies. The dull white-collar, service-sector, and/or manual work we undertake may entail dissonance, isolation, and distress through its reifying qualities,[17] while work such as sex work faces risks of criminalization and the affects of stigmatization. The distress and precarity surrounding work in both formal and informal economies reasserts a situation of slow death even as criminalization may lead to incarceration and deportation while negating one's agency, as, for instance, Toni Mac (2016) argues in the case of multi-agency immigration raids in London that criminalize migrant workers, including sex workers, while evacuating their agency before the law. Our labor within all such work faces the possibility of the same epistemological disqualification alongside its material devaluation. However, between precarity, reification, and the increasing presence of the border, methods of undercommoning (Harney and Moten 2013) might sustain us through difficult emotions, bring moments of affirmation, and steal a few hours back for our living.

If the politics of trans and queer liberalisms is based on reform of and assimilation into the structures of neoliberal capitalist society,[18] what form of transfeminist politics must be articulated, and through what kind of praxis, in order to turn the tide against such disqualifications and their historical impact? This is also a question of how poor, transfeminine bodies and the bodies of work we are responsible for have influenced queer, feminist, socialist, antiracist, decolonial movements of past and present, bodies and work that, next to trans bodies in general, have been and often continue to be rendered invisible in the histories of these movements. As Che Gossett, Reina Gossett, and A. J. Lewis (2012) remind us, the work of LGBTQ politics has always entailed work against police violence and trans genealogies of Black feminism show that Black feminism has always been trans.

Labor against Genders

The poet Anne Boyer likes my tweet about the temptation to write this essay entirely on public transport as a (creative/necessary) constraint. The fabric of queer and trans social reproduction surrounds the space between this writing. The poet (not Anne, but yours truly) must leave her house to write, as her desk is currently occupied by her second job. The fabrics of social reproduction—of domestic space and the forms of queer feminist sociality—are the garments in which the trans femme is dissatisfied, undersupported, unable to clasp and contain the negativity of her emotions. The waged and caring labors she undertakes leave too little time for dressing to express that carefully constructed self associated with stereotypical narratives of transition.

Sometimes the work she undertakes undermines her gender. She finds herself undertaking men's work or feminized office work in which trans does not signify. Some days she is a Communist spy writing academic papers on stolen time, smiling at customers as she greets them, serving them lunch. The precarity of her waged work dovetails with the precarity of her gender expression.

Her lovers may be the arms of healing, unsure how best to hold her, arms of few arms. Her chosen lovers or johns may fetishize or abuse her. She will capture intimate moments among those she can trust as a sister or sibling, to unravel toxicities, toxic masculinities, the odors of transmisogyny and sexism. These moments of violence graze deeply, the concert of romantic ideology, the trans women as scapegoat (Serano 2007), scarce life under capital. It is here where every tone of voice transgressing a felt gender, or supposed gender, may be used against us—where the gender norms cohering around the color of our flesh and the char of the garments, where our love or our breathing, may end.

Cultivating Transfeminist Worlds

October 2016: In Glasgow, we hear Reina.[19] In a discussion titled "life in flight from every prison"—part of the Refuse Powers' Grasp arts and politics festival organized by Arika (2016), where we hear Reina Gossett, Miss Major, Che Gossett, Dean Spade, Eric Stanley, Kai Lumumba Barrow, Joshua Allen, Sondra Perry, Juliana Huxtable, members of We Will Rise, Mujeres Creando, SCOT-PEP, and the English Collective of Prostitutes, among others—Reina speaks of five aspects of oppression. She identifies isolation as one of these aspects, which resonates with the hearts and lungs of the trans women and trans femmes in the room—at least, those friends I compare notes with after the discussion. Allen ties this to scarcity, its condition in the contemporary United States, how black trans excellence (#blacktransexcellence) can thrive despite the systems working against such life (these systems prevented trans prison abolitionist CeCe McDonald from getting her passport in time to be in this particular room). Reina suggests that there is no healing sometimes, that recovery from certain wounds is neither possible nor necessarily desirable. We hear that we need to be wary of the appropriation and individualization of self-care. We know there is no self-care without the production of self and care and that we cannot live without our lives. We later hear from Spade, who points again to isolation and ties it to our social deskilling, sometimes through too much living online. With Reina chairing this discussion, the question becomes what forms of mutual engagement break isolation and cultivate care. The isolation in question is explicitly that of incarceration in jail, but it is also implicitly the isolation within (and from) communities, with an undercurrent of the atomization of capitalist life once described by Marxists (Debord 1970).

Mijke van der Drift and I discuss over the next few days (and over days that are yet to follow) how the cultivation of care enacted in the spaces we inhabit this particular weekend visibly resonate through various trans (of color) and feminine bodies. When conversations turn difficult, we sense moments of disagreement and frustration in the bodies of friends current and new; these bodies remove themselves momentarily, physically from the space or psychologically into an interior, to be brought back into and supported through discourse in the measured, calculated manners of critical speech. These feel like new bases for articulations of mutual support, of abolitionist work within the everyday, here an everyday of public, activist speech, as Reina says, of prefiguring the world we want to live in.

If at times healing may neither be possible nor desirable, we instead work at the cultivation of care and mutual support that inaugurates a more livable world and calls for the transformation of the material conditions that fracture and break us, conditions structured against the sustenance of poor, transfeminine people/of color and of poor, feminized people/of color more generally. Checking in, comparing notes, collectivizing lunch and dinner, bringing bodies back into conversations and spaces, keeping tabs on what kind of interactions might bridge fractures in social structure and what interactions might graze. We work ourselves out of the liberal myths of enfranchisement and the exceptionalization of struggles. Trans liberalism might alter our sense of enfranchisement in the West, but rights will reaffirm the sense of law by which certain bodies of certain genders, races, nationalities, abilities, and religions deserve the right to live in a world owned and managed by so few people, and it falls far short of establishing a sustainable basis of world-making through the coproduction of care, in which we might be centered alongside other marginalized people. We radically revise our individualized histories and experience into a collective understanding built through our particulars, to understand that our individual struggles, the embedding of sadness, the negative affects we turn inward toward our bodies, are about the absence of a sustainable immediate world within which we could really reside.

The dialectic of struggle against a world that breaks us and for the inauguration of a world of mutuality and support where we can begin to live and thrive is always in progress, pushing the work of transformation below the visibility of the surface of neoliberal capitalist society. It is in the moments of dailyness that feel im/possible that the coproduction and autonomous support of thought and feeling and work in and through our bodies pushes back against contemporary divisions of labor, epistemological disqualifications, precarious work, devalued wages, and the strain of passport controls; it is in these moments that social reproduction and solidarity delay slow death, psychic strain, and/or deportation. If we might be fractured through the accumulation of such negative conditions qua the contemporary accumulation of capital, we also know that the work, support, and histories that might transform them are buried and disqualified as ourselves—which need to be unearthed, teased out, and held up.

Notes

This essay is dedicated to Mijke van der Drift and Chryssy Hunter for starting the project of Radical Transfeminism. With love and solidarity to Jos Charles, Anne Boyer, Reina Gossett, Mendoza; Samuel Solomon for comments and for supporting this work; Jackqueline Frost and Jackie Wang for making such writing a possibility; Nisha Ramayya and L. Uziell for conversations in Glasgow; Sarah Golightley, Angela and Claude for the queer domestic spaces; and to Aren Aizura for editorial patience.

1   I capitalize the word *Madness* in the spirit of its reclamation by Mad activists, psychiatric consumers, and survivors and Mad Studies scholars. The labeling of transfeminine people as "crazy," due to supposedly erratic behavior and emotions, must necessarily be understood in the context of gendered norms that privilege certain forms of sanity. Given its length, this essay refrains from explicating this context. For a discussion connecting trans activism to Mad activism and Mad Studies in Canada, see Kirby (2014).

2   This combination intends to reflect the mutual reinforcement between these social and material conditions—racism, transphobia, and whorephobia need to be understood through an integrated, historicizing lens in order to understand the multiple forms of violence levied at trans women of color, including trans-women-of-color sex workers. For a nuanced discussion of the issues around transfeminine stereotyping and these bodily intersections, see Aizura (2014).

3   I think of this horizon as in a dialectical relation with Muñoz's (2009: 1) formulation of queerness as a horizon of possibility.

4   Jobcentre Plus is the office for unemployment benefits in the United Kingdom and work-related disability benefits. The treatment of Jobcentre Plus users has been violently rationalized by Conservative-led governments since 2010. There have been a number of media controversies surrounding suicidal claimants. While there are currently no critical accounts of trans people's experiences of the Jobcentre Plus, accounts of how Employment and Support Allowance has been used as a means to force people with disabilities back into work are numerous.

5   In context of certain forms of gendered labor, the expression of one's gender may be part of the work. For a discussion of the relation of expression of gender to work, see Weeks 2011. For considerations of the relation of the self to wage labor, see Marx 1959 and Lukács 1971.

6   For a significant enactment and discussion of transfeminine sexual reproduction, see cárdenas 2016.

7   The problems of the "spousal veto" clause of the Marriage (Same Sex Couples) Act of 2013 in England and Wales—through which a partner can prevent their spouse from obtaining legal recognition of their chosen gender, once having changed their gender in the terms of the gender binary—have been raised at length within trans activist circles.

8   In the United Kingdom, discriminating against employees, or potential employees during the hiring process, based on the characteristic of their "gender reassignment" (broadly understood as anyone who is undergoing or has undergone a process of transition) is outlawed under the Equality Act 2010.

9   I have used the grammatical construction "poor trans women and trans femmes/of color and/or trans sex workers" to emphasize that each of these descriptions may intermesh with each other.

10   For a presentation of the issues facing trans and gender-nonconforming people in prison, see Stanley and Smith (2011). *Social death* is a term developed by Ruth Gilmore (2007).

11   There has yet to be a test case of trans discrimination in the workplace under the Equality Act 2010. Following their introduction in 2012, employment tribunal fees for discrimination cases now stand at £250 to make a claim and £950 to take the claim to a hearing (UK Government 2016). Furthermore, dramatic cuts to legal aid over the current decade have affected access to the law to the extent that criminal lawyers and barristers staged strikes against further cuts in 2014.

12   I have explored such politics as exemplified in the work of Street Transvestite Action Revolutionaries, historicizing their radical Third World and black liberation politics and collectivized care work as poor "street queens" of color who were sex workers. See Raha, 2017.

13   The formulation is offered in the argument made by sex workers that working together offers forms of protection among sex workers.

14   For a detailed conception of trans and queer social reproduction, see Raha 2017.

15   Regarding issues around resources for the production of safer spaces, the Radical Transfeminism conference in London deployed an "interactive" and "cooperative" politics of space that emphasized differences in experience of oppression and means to support understanding when one's views are challenged. See van der Drift, Hunter, and Raha 2015.

16   See Federici 2012, Farris 2015, and Aizura 2014.
17   The concept of reification is formulated in Lukaçs 1971 to describe the contemplative character of labor as transformed by Fordist modes of production. My intention here is to invoke the psychic impact of undertaking labor as a *"contemplative* activity."
18   The arguments regarding LGBTQ assimilation in the context of neoliberalism include Duggan 2003, Puar 2007, and Conrad 2014.
19   Those named in this section are the voices that build the discussions in this and the next paragraph of the essay.

References

Aizura, Aren Z. 2014. "Trans Feminine Value, Racialized Others and the Limits of Necro-politics." In *Queer Necropolitics*, edited by Jin Haritaworn, Adi Kuntsman, and Silvia Posocco, 129–47. New York: Routledge.
Arika. 2016. *Refuse Powers' Grasp Club–We Will Rise Fundraiser*. Featuring Juliana Huxtable, Elysia Crampton, and boychild. Tramway and the Art School, Glasgow, Scotland, October 21–23.
Berlant, Lauren. 2011. *Cruel Optimism*. Durham, NC: Duke University Press.
cárdinas, micha. 2016 "Pregnancy: Reproductive Futures in Trans of Color Feminism." *TSQ: Transgender Studies Quarterly* 3, nos. 1–2: 48–57.
Conrad, Ryan. 2014. *Against Equality: Queer Revolution, Not Mere Inclusion*. Edinburgh: AK Press.
Debord, Guy. 1970. *Society of the Spectacle*. Detroit: Red and Black.
Duggan, Lisa. 2003. *The Twilight of Equality: Neoliberalism, Cultural Politics, and the Attack on Democracy*. Boston: Beacon Press.
Farris, Sara R. 2015. "Social Reproduction, Surplus Populations, and the Role of Migrant Women." *Viewpoint Magazine*, no. 5. www.viewpointmag.com/2015/11/01/social-reproduction-and-surplus-populations.
Federici, Silvia. 2012. *Revolution at Point Zero: Housework, Reproduction, and Feminist Struggle*. Oakland: PM Press.
Gilmore, Ruth Wilson. 2007. *Golden Gulag: Prisons, Surplus, Crisis, and Opposition in Globalizing California*. Berkeley: University of California Press.
Gossett, Che, Reina Gossett, and A. J. Lewis. 2012. "Reclaiming Our Lineage: Organized Queer, Gender-Nonconforming, and Transgender Resistance to Police Violence." *Scholar and Feminist Online* 10, nos. 1–2. sfonline.barnard.edu/a-new-queer-agenda/reclaiming-our-lineage-organized-queer-gender-nonconforming-and-transgender-resistance-to-police-violence/0/.
Harney, Stefano, and Fred Moten. 2013. *The Undercommons: Fugitive Planning and Black Study*. Brooklyn, NY: Minor Compositions.
Kirby, Ambrose. 2014. "Trans Jeopardy/Trans Resistance: Shaindl Diamond Interviews Ambrose Kirby." In *Psychiatry Disrupted: Theorizing Resistance and Crafting the (R)evolution*, edited by Bonnie Burstow, Brenda A. LeFrançois, and Shaindl Diamond, 163–76. Montreal: McGill-Queen's University Press.
Lea, Sian. 2016. "The Immigration Act 2016 in Plain English." *Rights Info*, May 31. rightsinfo.org/immigration-act-2016-plain-english/.
Lukaçs, Georg. 1971. *History and Class Consciousness*. Cambridge, MA: MIT Press.

Mac, Toni. 2016. "Swoop and Rescue." *Versobooks.com* (blog), October 21. www.versobooks
.com/blogs/2895-swoop-and-rescue.

Marx, Karl. 1959. *Economic and Philosophic Manuscripts of 1844*. Moscow: Progress.

Mitchell, Martin, et al. 2013. "Implications of Austerity on LGBT People in Public Services."
London: NatCen Social Research. natcen.ac.uk/media/205545/unison-lgbt-austerity
-final-report.pdf.

Muñoz, José Esteban. 2009. *Cruising Utopia: The Then and There of Queer Futurity*. New
York: New York University Press.

Puar, Jasbir. 2007. *Terrorist Assemblages: Homonationalism in Queer Times*. Durham, NC:
Duke University Press.

Raha, Nat. 2017. "'Out of Jail and On the Streets Again': Street Transvestite Action Revolutionaries and the Praxis of Transfeminism of Color." Unpublished manuscript.

Raha, Nat. 2015. "The Limits of Trans Liberalism." *Versobooks.com* (blog), September 21.
www.versobooks.com/blogs/2245-the-limits-of-trans-liberalism-by-nat-raha.

Runnymede Trust. 2015. "The 2015 Budget Effects on Black and Minority Ethnic People."
London: Runnymede Trust. runnymedetrust.org/uploads/The%202015%20Budget
%20Effect%20on%20BME%20RunnymedeTrust%2027thJuly2015.pdf.

Serano, Julia. 2007. *Whipping Girl: A Transsexual Woman on Sexism and the Scapegoating of
Femininity*. Emeryville, CA: Seal.

Spade, Dean. *Normal Life: Administrative Violence, Critical Trans Politics, and the Limits of the
Law*. Brooklyn, NY: South End.

Stanley, Eric A., and Nat Smith. 2011. *Captive Genders: Trans Embodiment and the Prison
Industrial Complex*. Oakland: AK Press.

Stryker, Susan. 2008. "Transgender History, Homonormativity, and Disciplinarity." *Radical
History Review*, no. 100: 145–57.

UK Government. 2016. "Make a Claim to an Employment Tribunal." *Gov.UK*, October 25.
www.gov.uk/employment-tribunals/make-a-claim.

van der Drift, Mijke, Chryssy Hunter, and Nat Raha. 2015. "Politics of Space: For Use at the
LCCT – 26/27 June 2015." *Conference Stream on Radical Transfeminism* (Facebook page),
June 25. www.facebook.com/events/505965509556758/permalink/511009335719042/.

Weeks, Kathi. 2011. *The Problem with Work: Marxism, Feminism, Antiwork Politics, and Post-
work Imaginaries*. Durham, NC: Duke University Press.

Notes on Contributors

Aren Aizura is an assistant professor in Gender, Women, and Sexuality Studies at the University of Minnesota. His research interests include queer theory, transgender studies, transnationality and immigration, and political economy and labor. Aizura earned a PhD in cultural studies from the University of Melbourne. He is the coeditor of the *Transgender Studies Reader 2*, and his work has appeared in numerous journals and books, including *Queer Necropolitics* (2014) and *Trans Studies: Beyond Homo/Hetero Normativities* (2015). His next book, currently titled *Mobile Subjects: Travel, Transnationality and Transgender Lives*, will be published by Duke University Press.

Amanda Armstrong is a member of the Michigan Society of Fellows and an assistant professor in the Department of History at the University of Michigan. Her research focuses on histories of railway labor, race, and gender in the second British empire.

Barnor Hesse teaches in the Department of African American Studies at Northwestern University. His most recent publication is "Of Race: The Exorbitant Du Bois," which appeared in the journal *Small Axe* in 2016.

Juliet Hooker is a professor of political science at Brown University. She is a political theorist specializing in comparative political theory, black political thought, critical race theory, and multiculturalism. Recent publications include "Black Lives Matter and the Paradoxes of U.S. Black Politics: From Democratic Sacrifice to Democratic Repair," which appeared in the journal *Political Theory* in 2016, and *Theorizing Race in the Americas: Douglass, Sarmiento, Du Bois, and Vasconcelos* (2017).

Minkah Makalani is an associate professor of African and African Diaspora Studies at the University of Texas at Austin. He is the author of *In the Cause of Freedom: Radical Black Internationalism from Harlem to London, 1917–1939* (2011) and coeditor (with Davarian Baldwin) of *Escape from New York: The New Negro Renaissance beyond Harlem* (2013). His second book project, tentatively titled "Calypso Conquered the World: C. L. R. James and the Politically Unimaginable in Trinidad," explores James's return to Trinidad in 1958 and his thinking about democracy, the arts, freedom, and Africa in the postcolonial Caribbean.

John D. Márquez is an associate professor of African American studies and Latina/o/x studies at Northwestern University. He is the author of *Black-Brown Solidarity: Racial Politics in the New Gulf South* (2013) and *Genocidal*

Democracy: Neoliberalism, Mass Incarceration, and the Politics of Urban Gun Violence (forthcoming).

Nat Raha is a poet and trans/queer activist, living in Edinburgh, Scotland. Her poetry includes two collections, *countersonnets* (2013) and *Octet* (2010), and numerous pamphlets including "*£/€xtinctions*" (2017), "[of sirens/body and faultlines]" (2015), and "mute exterior intimate" (2013). She has performed and published her work internationally. Raha is a PhD candidate in Creative and Critical Writing at the University of Sussex, United Kingdom, and she is working on a thesis titled "Queer Capital: Marxism in Queer Theory and Post-1950 Poetics."

Junaid Rana is an associate professor of Asian American studies at the University of Illinois at Urbana-Champaign with appointments in the Department of Anthropology, the Center for South Asian and Middle Eastern Studies, and the Unit for Criticism and Interpretive Theory. He is the author of *Terrifying Muslims: Race and Labor in the South Asian Diaspora* (2011).

Eric A. Stanley is an assistant professor in the Department of Gender and Sexuality Studies at the University of California, Riverside, editor, with Nat Smith, of *Captive Genders: Trans Embodiment and the Prison Industrial Complex* (2015), and, with Chris E. Vargas, director of the films *Homotopia* (2006) and *Criminal Queers* (2013).

Debra Thompson is an assistant professor of African American Studies at Northwestern University. Her most recent book is *The Schematic State: Race, Transnationalism, and the Politics of the Census* (2016).

Shatema Threadcraft is an assistant professor of political science and a member of the graduate faculty of the Department of Women's and Gender Studies at Rutgers University. She is the author of *Intimate Justice: The Black Female Body and the Body Politic* (2016).

DOI 10.1215/00382876-3961783